THE WORLD IS OUR CLASS

CRITICAL PERSPECTIVES ON YOUTH

General Editors: Amy L. Best, Lorena Garcia, and Jessica K. Taft

The World Is Our Classroom

Extreme Parenting and the Rise of Worldschooling

Jennie Germann Molz

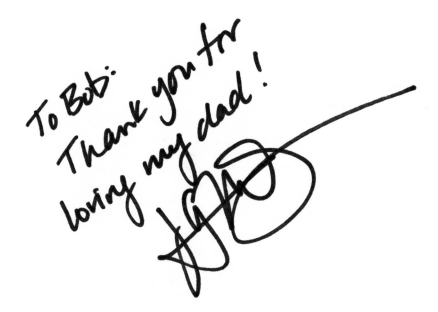

To Bob: Thank you for loving my dad!

NEW YORK UNIVERSITY PRESS

New York

NEW YORK UNIVERSITY PRESS
New York
www.nyupress.org

Library of Congress Cataloging-in-Publication Data
Names: Molz, Jennie Germann, 1969–   author.
Title: The world is our classroom : extreme parenting and the rise of worldschooling / Jennie Germann Molz.
Description: New York : New York University Press, [2021] |
Series: Critical perspectives on youth | Includes bibliographical references and index.
Identifiers: LCCN 2020016529 (print) | LCCN 2020016530 (ebook) |
ISBN 9781479891689 (cloth ; alk. paper) | ISBN 9781479834075 (paperback ; alk. paper) |
ISBN 9781479815128 (ebook) | ISBN 9781479810550 (ebook)
Subjects: LCSH: Students—Travel. | Education—Parent participation. |
Non-formal education. | International education. | Education and globalization.
Classification: LCC LC6681 .M65 2021 (print) | LCC LC6681 (ebook) | DDC 370.116—dc23
LC record available at https://lccn.loc.gov/2020016529
LC ebook record available at https://lccn.loc.gov/2020016530

New York University Press books are printed on acid-free paper, and their binding materials are chosen for strength and durability. We strive to use environmentally responsible suppliers and materials to the greatest extent possible in publishing our books.

Manufactured in the United States of America

10 9 8 7 6 5 4 3 2 1

Also available as an ebook

To my mom and dad, who first showed me the world
and taught me how to pack light

CONTENTS

PREFACE

I had been studying long-term backpackers for many years before I first ran across a family with school-aged children backpacking around the world together. It was 2009 and I was doing research for a book on travel and technology when I encountered Craig, a middle-class father from the Washington, DC area who was blogging about his year-long round-the-world journey with his wife, their eleven-year-old son, and their thirteen-year-old daughter. Up to that point, most of the travelers I had followed and interviewed in my research were in their twenties or thirties, young singles or couples who were taking time to see the world before settling down with a job, kids, and a mortgage.

The very phrase "settling down" captures a deeply held, but not necessarily accurate, assumption that family life takes place *in* place. Despite the vast amount of evidence to the contrary, we generally imagine modern families to be geographically anchored in homes, neighborhoods, and communities. There are exceptions, of course. Military families, diplomats and missionaries, corporate expat families and new age hippies, families whose survival requires seasonal or forced migration. But we tend to consider these movements as a sacrifice, an exception, or a temporary disruption to the otherwise stable nature of family life. Craig's family, and the many worldschooling families I met while conducting research for this book, throw those assumptions into question. Their journeys are not a last hurrah before settling into a geographically confined life with kids, school, and work. Nor are they a temporary vacation from everyday life. These families are living every part of their lives on the road.

When I met Craig, I knew immediately that I wanted to study families like his in greater depth. Since I was already immersed in another book project, I put the idea on hold, but these mobile families were never far from my mind. I returned to the idea in 2013, when I moved with my husband Martin and our son Elliot to Rovaniemi, Finland for six months. I was a Fulbright scholar at the University of Lapland, and we enrolled Elliot, who was eight years old at the time, in a local Waldorf school. I'd had some experience with alternative schooling as a child, but this was my first experience as a parent sending my child to anything but the local public school. It struck me that even in a place like Finland, where the public education system is literally the best in the world, some parents were seeking educational experiences for their children beyond the conventional classroom.

This time in Finland was also something of a test run. I had a notion of doing ethnographic fieldwork, ideally *as* one of these traveling families. I had a sabbatical scheduled two years later, which would give me enough time to design the research, start the online ethnography, and then dedicate several months to mobile fieldwork traveling the world as a family. Martin was on board immediately, but we wanted to gauge how Elliot fared in Finland before proposing the idea of long-term travel to him. Despite some early culture shock and challenges with the language barrier, he seemed to be thriving, so one afternoon I asked Elliot if he would be up for doing fieldwork with me on the road for a year. After I asked the question, he quietly got up from the table and came back with a piece of paper and a pen. "Let's start writing down all the places we want to go!" he said.

Elliot was ten years old when we launched our trip. He proved to be a stellar traveler and an invaluable research assistant. His enthusiasm and curiosity propelled our trip and my research in many ways. During the months that we were on the road, he was constantly on the lookout for other families with kids his age whom I could approach for an interview. And during those interviews, he played with the kids while I talked with their parents. Martin, for his part, was also an insightful research partner and would accompany me on interviews as well. Although he is not trained as a social scientist, he has a keen sociological imagination and a talent for asking just the right question or probing follow-up.

My decision to involve my family in my research was inspired by both logistical and epistemological aspects of the project. According to anthropologist Susan Frohlick, the myth of the solitary fieldworker setting off alone to collect knowledge in some remote place has had its day. Frohlick's decision to bring her spouse and two young children with her to conduct ethnographic research at a Mount Everest base camp pioneered a new imaginary of accompanied fieldwork. Ethnographers, mothers especially, are increasingly unwilling to bracket off, erase, or leave their own families behind when conducting and writing their research. And given the nature of my research topic, Martin's and Elliot's participation was not just incidental but absolutely crucial to the kinds of data I was able to collect and the insights I was able to elicit from our shared experience. This project owes an enormous debt to both of them.

Yet the project was shaped not just by the family members I brought with me, but also by those I left behind. Just as I started the research, my father began exhibiting symptoms that were originally thought to be the effect of Parkinson's disease but were later diagnosed as Progressive Supranuclear Palsy (PSP), a degenerative neurological condition that affects gross and fine motor skills. At the beginning of my sabbatical, we moved to New Mexico to be closer to my parents for a while before starting our trip. It was not lost on me that just as I was launching an ethnographic journey around the world to study mobile families' quest for the good life, my own father's quality of life was deteriorating in parallel to his diminishing ability to move or to move "correctly."

Early in the fieldwork, it was my father who drove Martin, Elliot, and me to the airport for the first leg of our trip. At that point, his symptoms were minor but worrying. His gait had become heavy and slow. At times, his body moved involuntarily; at other times, it refused to move at all no matter how hard he concentrated on putting one foot in front of the other. Not knowing how much longer my father would be able to travel prompted my parents to take a couple of trips—a vacation in Italy with my sister's family and a visit to Mexico with friends. But a few months later, my father was no longer able to drive, then no longer able to walk without the assistance of a cane and then a walker, and then no longer able to stand or walk at all.

Like the families in this study, my father always dreamed of traveling, and while we were never that rebel family that lived on the road, we traveled our fair share. We moved house nine times and lived in five different cities during my childhood, a biographical fact that usually leads people to assume my father was in the military. In fact, he was a Lutheran minister, a family counselor, and a crisis mediator, a career that required both a deep commitment to local communities and a significant amount of mobility. In his role as a crisis mediator, he traveled all over the country to help churches in turmoil and communities in grief. For example, he was sent to New York just days after the September 11, 2001 attacks to provide trauma counseling.

My mother was an educator, so summers were available for traveling. June, July, and August were given over to trips up north to visit relatives, road trips to the southwest to nourish our souls, mission trips Mexico to bring donations of clothing and shoes to an orphanage, and camping trips that fit our family's modest budget. Later, my parents' itineraries became more ambitious, in no small part because Martin and I moved (and moved and moved) all over the world. They would come visit us in every new place—Singapore, Italy, England, Finland—each of them carrying nothing more than a small carry-on suitcase.

As my father's physical mobility declined, his imagination began to fill in the gaps. He would dream aloud about traveling to Italy one more time, restoring an antique MG convertible for joyrides, hitching an Airstream to the van and driving cross-country. His wishes revealed just how deeply embedded the dream of mobility is in our visions of the good life. In the last chapter of his life, the world came to him. Unable to leave home much in his final months, he was blessed with a cosmopolitan network of friends and caregivers from different corners of the world who circulated in and out of the house, bringing with them the stories that animated my dad's imagination. He told me that it wasn't really the traveling that he craved, but the stories. I've dedicated this book to him and to my mother because it is a book of stories: stories about travel, about family, and about our collective future.

Introduction

Welcome to Worldschooling

We believe that the best teacher is experience and the best classroom is the world. We want our children to spend time in each of the major cultures of the world, to learn multiple languages and to become comfortable in their own skins and find their place as world citizens. We travel because we only have our children for a very little while and we want to make the best use possible of that time. We want to live each day to the fullest, together, doing the things that inspire each of us.
—Julia, blog post

Julia and Scott Porter are a white, middle-class couple in their forties. She is a former teacher from Canada who now works as a freelance travel writer and consultant. He is a database engineer from the United States. They are the parents of four children ranging in age from twenty-one to fifteen. Their eldest two are now "launched," as Julia puts it, but their younger two sons still live at home. What it means to be at home, however, is up for debate. For ten years, Julia and Scott raised their family on the road, educating their young children while cycling through Europe and North Africa, camping in Australia and New Zealand, and backpacking across Southeast Asia and Central America. Along the way, the kids read books, kept journals, climbed ruins, trekked and hiked and swam, sketched wildlife, learned new languages, and tried new foods.

Even before they had children, Scott and Julia had an inkling that traveling would be the best way to educate their kids and help them become global citizens. When Julia was a child, her parents took her and her brother out of school for a year to travel around Canada in a van, an experience she recalls as the most mind-opening year of her young life. Once she started her career as a classroom teacher, though, she says it took her "about five minutes in the public school system" to know that this was not what she wanted for her kids. As their children reached school age, Julia and Scott homeschooled them rather than enrolling them in public school, all the while saving money and planning to hit the road. When the children were eleven, nine, seven, and five, they packed their bags and bikes and headed off to Europe to start what they thought would be a one-year trip around the world. It turned into a decade-long journey.

A few months into their travels, the nest egg they had invested in the stock market evaporated in the wake of the 2008 financial crash. Julia and Scott briefly considered heading back to their full-time jobs in the United States, but they realized that they were actually spending less money living on the road than they had in their suburban lifestyle back home. The family had to "pivot," Julia recalls. Scott started taking on contract work that he could do online from anywhere in the world. Julia's blog, packed with helpful advice and candid accounts of the ups and downs of educating four children on the road, had become a popular hub for sharing information and inspiration with other families interested in pursuing a similar lifestyle. She was eventually able to parlay her success with the blog into freelance writing assignments and consulting work. By the time they celebrated the one-year anniversary of their family journey, Julia and Scott were making enough money from these online endeavors to keep traveling with their kids. And so they did.

They spent the next decade on the road, "living large with our kids," Julia writes, "four fabulous humans who'll live on into a future we'll never see." The family's travel story and their children's futures are still being written. A few years ago, when their eldest daughter turned eighteen, she headed off on her own backpacking adventure and then on to college. Her brother set sail soon after. The younger two boys, now both teenagers, are still traveling with their parents but are already charting the international paths they plan to follow when they are old enough to set out on their own. As their children begin to make their way into that unknown future, Julia remarks: "We can't think of a better gift to give them than the world as their classroom and a global vision of humanity."

* * *

This is a book about families like the Porters who press pause on their normal lives, or abandon them altogether, to travel the world with their young children. The Porters are at the forefront of an emerging phenomenon called *worldschooling*. Hailed as a "radical leap into hands-on learning," worldschooling is an alternative educational philosophy that embraces the world as a child's best classroom.[1] Worldschooling is similar to homeschooling, with the obvious caveat that it doesn't take place at home. Instead, a growing number of middle-class families are selling their houses, leaving their jobs, and taking their children out of conventional school settings to educate them while traveling the globe. Some worldschooling families travel on savings or during paid sabbaticals from their jobs, but many, like the Porters, fund their families' journeys by working remotely in online businesses and freelance careers.

While the families who worldschool are a diverse group, the Porters typify several key aspects of the worldschooling experience: the ability to earn an income online; access to online tools to support mobile learning; the social freedom to perform family life on the move; a growing dissatisfaction with institutional education and consumer society; and an abiding concern with preparing independent, resilient children ready for life and work in the global world of the twenty-first century. The Porters are also typical of the demographic makeup of the worldschoolers in my study, the vast majority of whom are white, relatively affluent professionals from countries in the Global North. Although the parents in my study might resist being categorized as affluent or middle class—after all, many of them forego salaried jobs and actively reject the trappings of a secure middle-class lifestyle—the fact is these families are endowed with considerable national, racial, cultural, technological, and financial advantages that enable them to move at will around the world. Throughout the book, I use the term Global North to signal the way nationality confers to these families a certain level of privileged mobility. Traveling with young children may not be an especially frictionless endeavor for these families, but the powerful passports they carry, coupled with their middle-class whiteness, ensure that they are, for the most part, welcome to move freely across international borders. As Jasbir Puar observes, "whiteness travels well," and this is certainly the case for the families in my study.[2]

At the same time, families like the Porters are vulnerable to the anxieties that preoccupy many middle-class parents today. Like their upper- and middle-class counterparts, worldschoolers are adamant about providing their children with an excellent education, but they have deep concerns about the educational reforms sweeping through their children's schools. They have also become disenchanted by the version of success society has sold them. They feel strapped by the demands of their corporate jobs, exhausted by long commutes, stretched thin by the hectic pace of life with overscheduled kids, and disillusioned by the empty promises of mass consumerism and suburban living. This is not the good life they had in mind. Nor is it the kind of life that will teach their children what they need to know to succeed in an uncertain future. This is what makes worldschooling such an appealing alternative. It offers an opportunity to escape the pressures of work and school and to spend precious time as a family while exploring and learning about the world together.

When I started my research, I was initially interested in exploring what it looked like to accomplish family life on the move. How do families navigate everyday undertakings such as schooling, work, or parenting on the road? As I began to piece together the narratives worldschoolers were posting online and recounting in interviews, however, I realized that the story they were telling was far more complicated. What they were recounting was not just a story about traveling as a family but about pursuing a mobile lifestyle as a strategy for coping with uncertainty.

In her book *Cut Adrift*, sociologist Marianne Cooper argues that we are now living in an "age of insecurity." She explains how five decades of neoliberal government policies and private sector labor relations have effectively shifted the economic burden of educating our children, caring for our families, saving for retirement, and securing our futures onto the shoulders of individuals. "If today's families want a safety net to catch them when they fall," she concludes, "they need to weave their own."[3] In her study of American families across the socioeconomic spectrum, Cooper describes the various economic and emotional strategies families use to "do security" in this age of risk and uncertainty. Depending on where they fall on the economic ladder, these families work to secure their futures by downsizing their expectations, holding onto jobs with meager benefits, or investing in their children's educations.

I discovered that the worldschooling families in my study, like the families Cooper interviewed, were also making significant lifestyle adjustments to cope with the rampant uncertainties of our time. What I found, however, was that the families in my study were not doing this by battening down the hatches, so to speak, but rather by uprooting and even abandoning their stable middle-class lifestyles. As this realization dawned on me, my question shifted. I was still interested in how they were accomplishing family life on the move, but now I also wondered how they came to conceive of an untethered lifestyle as the best way to weather this age of uncertainty. How did mobility become the key to living the good life in the midst of such insecurity?

Social life has never been as fixed in place as we might think, but over the past few decades, technological innovations, social transformations, and shifting economic arrangements have made it increasingly possible—and, in some cases, downright compulsory—to live our lives on the move. As I show in this book, worldschoolers see themselves as pioneers of a mobile life on the margins of society, often referring to their lifestyle choices as "risky" or as a "leap of faith." There is something to this claim, but rather than thinking of worldschooling as a marginal way of living, I argue that we should see it as symptomatic of a changing world. For worldschoolers, life on the move is a way of managing the burdens of uncertainty, risk, and responsibility that have been shifted away from governments or private sector employers and onto individuals.

The theoretical approach I take in this book is rooted in the mobilities paradigm, a sociology of the patterns of mobility and immobility that shape contemporary social life.[4] A central premise of the mobilities paradigm is that the whole world is on the move, or so it seems. According to sociologist John Urry, whose work catalyzed the "mobilities turn" in the social sciences, whether we are traveling or not, most of us, especially those of us in the rich nations of the Global North, are living lives crisscrossed by intersecting trajectories of people, images, ideas, objects, and risks.[5] This has significant implications for how we envision the settings in which our social lives play out and the texture of our everyday social relations.

As Urry and his co-author Anthony Elliott argue in their book, *Mobile Lives*, "in the face of a new global narrative of mobilities, the self-fashioning of lives is now recast and transformed."[6] My curiosity about how mobility recasts those aspects of social life we previously assumed to be fixed in place is reflected in the structure of the book. Each of the chapters in the book takes as its starting point one of the spheres of social life that worldschoolers mobilize in their search for the good life, beginning with school and education and then moving on to interrogate the mobile arrangements of work, parenting and family life, community, and citizenship. Worldschooling is not just a case of taking education on the road, however. Or work or parenting or citizenship, for that matter. It is a vivid illustration of how we dream and worry about our future well-being in a world in flux.[7] In this book, I reveal how worldschoolers leverage the opportunities and navigate the challenges of life on the move.

The claim I make is that worldschooling is not just an alternative approach to educating children, but a life strategy for responding to and coping with the profound uncertainties of contemporary society. This strategy plays out in two ways. On the one hand, worldschoolers are eager to live the good life today. As a mobile lifestyle, worldschooling is a way of embracing the unprecedented freedoms that individuals, especially those in the Global North, enjoy in the era of late modernity. For better or for worse, technological innovations, new online resources, and shifting arrangements of remote and freelance work have opened up completely new possibilities for where and how people live their lives. The uncertainties of modern life may be a source of anxiety for many, but for those with ample economic and cultural resources, like the families in my study, there is also something exhilarating about the chance to shrug off traditional scripts for living and follow one's dream to travel the world. Worldschoolers want to take advantage of these opportunities to savor a traveling lifestyle now, while their children are young and a world of experience awaits.

At the same time, the mobile lifestyle of worldschooling is oriented toward the future. When families reject conventional schools in favor of educating their children through travel, they do so with an eye toward preparing children for the uncertain world of tomorrow. In this sense, a mobile lifestyle becomes a source of new kinds of cultural capital that parents can accrue and convey to their children. The academic skills and emotional sensibilities they hope travel will impart—for example, knowledge of the world, a capacity for risk-taking and self-reliance, the ability to maintain friendships on the move, and the adaptable demeanor of global citizenship—are the very ones they imagine will help their children weather the rapidly changing social and economic landscape of a globalizing world.

What Is Worldschooling?

When the Porters first set off on their family's round-the-world journey in 2008, the term worldschooling did not yet exist. It first appeared later that year when Eli Gerzon, a twenty-five-year-old writer and traveler from Massachusetts, published a blog post announcing that he would be guiding a series of "worldschooling travel tours" in Mexico and Japan for teenagers. As Gerzon described it, he was offering a new approach to learning based on the idea that "the whole world is your school, instead of school being your whole world."[8]

Gerzon, who left formal schooling at the age of fifteen, was already a vocal advocate of alternative education movements, such as homeschooling and unschooling, but felt these terms failed to capture the kind of learning he experienced through travel. For Gerzon, homeschooling merely replicated a structured learning environment at home, with a parent instead of a teacher being in charge. Unschooling, a philosophy of free, natural learning introduced in the 1970s by John Holt, was closer to Gerzon's ideal of a less structured and more self-directed form of education, but he didn't like the fact that the name emphasized what the movement was not: *un*schooling. He wanted a more positive term for describing the lifelong process of actively experiencing and learning from the world around you. Hence, worldschooling.

The term did not catch on right away. For a long time, families continued to use a variety of expressions like roadschooling, travelschooling, wanderschooling, life-learning, or edventure to describe what they were doing. When I started conducting fieldwork for this project, the terminology was still unsettled. Some families had heard of worldschooling and were using the term to refer to themselves; others were still trying to figure out just where they fell in the spectrum of homeschooling, unschooling, and worldschooling, or whether any of these labels fit at all. Eventually, the terms worldschooling and worldschoolers began to circulate more widely, especially after appearing in a few newspaper articles about traveling families.[9]

Gerzon's original definition of worldschooling is relatively expansive, covering a wide range of learning practices. What worldschoolers have in common is less a set of defined educational practices than a shared philosophy that experiential learning is the best way to teach children about themselves and the world they live in. Worldschoolers might agree that travel is an ideal way to expose children to those lessons, but even families who are not traveling, and many who only wish they were, refer to themselves as worldschoolers. In fact, worldschoolers run the gamut from families whose children are enrolled in formal schooling to homeschoolers following structured curricula to radical unschoolers. They include stay-at-home families who refer to themselves as world-schoolers because they travel with their children during school breaks and summer holidays, as well as homeschoolers who take their children on extended field trips or engage them in experiential learning activities. Most of the families in my study are at the other extreme of the definition, having given up a home base altogether to travel the world, in some cases indefinitely, with their children.

Studying such a dispersed and mobile set of families presented considerable methodological hurdles. Finding these families, let alone figuring out how to meet up with and observe them on the move, was a daunting task, but one that was made much easier thanks to the Internet. I quickly discovered that many travelers were documenting their families' journeys on public blogs and convening in online forum discussions to share stories, encouragement, and advice with one another. For one component of the research, I conducted a virtual ethnography in these online spaces. For the other, I undertook physical fieldwork that involved traveling with and interviewing families in person. To do this, I became a worldschooling parent myself, traveling for seven months in 2014 with my son and husband. (For a full description of the mobile virtual ethnography on which the study is based, see appendix A.)

The analysis that follows is based on the stories I collected online and in person from more than fifty worldschooling families, including my own. (Detailed demographic information about the families in the study sample is provided in appendix B.) While the vast majority of families in my study share similar backgrounds in terms of race, class, and nationality, it would be an oversimplification to suggest that they all come to worldschooling from the same perspective or that they share a uniform set of ideals or experiences. Rather than develop a typology of worldschoolers, therefore, I paid attention to emerging themes, some of which are true for a large number of families but not all. For example, in chapter 1, I refer to a subset of worldschooling parents who subscribe to the educational philosophy of unschooling; in chapter 2, I focus primarily on parents and children who identify themselves as entrepreneurs; and in chapter 3, I call attention to those parents who adopt a free-range approach to parenting. This is not to suggest that all of the families in my study adhere to unschooling, entrepreneurial, or free-range parenting approaches to their journeys, and there is a good deal of variability even among the ones who do. Worldschoolers have much in common, which I highlight throughout the analysis, but neither the practice of worldschooling nor the families who pursue it can be reduced to a homogeneous profile.

This complexity makes it difficult to distill worldschooling into a single snapshot. Ask any worldschooler to describe a typical day in their family's traveling life and they will likely tell you there is no such thing. Every day is different, they might say. Part of the allure of worldschooling is the escape from routine and the freedom to experience whatever unique delights a particular destination has to offer. There are packing days and travel days and museum days and laundry days and beach days. Or they'll remind you that every family is different. Some are constantly on the move, trying to squeeze an ambitious worldschooling itinerary into a year off, while others are traveling slowly and indefinitely, staying in one place for months at a time before moving on to the next location. Some families are trying to maintain a schedule and a set curriculum, while others are in full unschooling mode. There are families who set aside a certain number of hours each morning for the kids to do schoolwork or meticulously plan educational outings to museums, libraries, and landmarks, while other families simply go wherever the day leads them. And every kid is different. A child might be game for any new adventure one day and then sullen, sick, or exhausted the next.

The portfolio of images, narratives, and vignettes that emerged during my fieldwork also reveals a multifaceted picture of what learning on the move looks like, or at least what parents hope it will look like. There are photos of children splayed in the grass sketching a fern into their journal, lugging a backpack through a crowded airport, working through math problems in a hostel courtyard, milking cows, exploring a night market, decked out in scuba gear, or reading a book while on a train. There are pictures of kids in front of the Colosseum, Angkor Wat, the Eiffel Tower, and Machu Picchu. There are stories of children visiting nature conservancies or doing volunteer work with local agencies, taking Muay Thai lessons or joining a writing class online, trying new foods, and learning to surf or meditate or pitch a tent. And, as is to be expected, there are stories of tears, stomachaches, and homesickness. It is nearly impossible to describe a day in the life of worldschooling that accurately reflects the wide range of educational activities and daily practices that families pursue on the road, but we can discern patterns of experiences, hopes, and worries these families share in common. My objective in this book is to attend to both the specific stories and these broader patterns to convey a deeper understanding of worldschooling.

While the term worldschooling is a neologism, the phenomenon it describes is far from new. Families have always traveled together. With or without the label of "worldschooling," parents all over the globe have, for millennia, been educating their children on the move and through hands-on experiences of the world around them. From immigrants and refugees to missionary, military, and diplomatic personnel, to corporate expats and cosmopolitan jet-setters, families from various political, social, and economic backgrounds have moved with their children in search of a better life. For example, in migration studies, we find poignant accounts of immigrant and refugee families doing family life in the context of involuntary movement as they seek a better future for their children. These are families who, despite their geographical mobility, may suffer from what anthropologist Ghassan Hage calls "stuckedness" due to their inability to exert agency over their movement.[10]

There is also a large literature of firsthand and scholarly accounts of "third culture kids" (TCKs) who grow up on the move and in between cultures following parents who are transferred to various military posts, diplomatic bases, missionary placements, or multinational corporate offices.[11] Their experiences of attending international schools, carving out a sense of belonging, making friends, or feeling untethered in the midst of movement parallel some of the emotional contours of worldschooling that I describe in the chapters that follow. And mobilities scholars have begun to pay more attention to family mobilities in other contexts as well, such as children's everyday mobilities, family tourism, or the way parents' commutes or business travel impact family life.[12]

Within western thought, worldschooling is also indebted to a long history of educational travel. The Greek historian Herodotus traveled the ancient world in search of knowledge. Enlightenment philosophers urged young adults to travel for their intellectual development. The sons and daughters of the British aristocracy often undertook a Grand Tour of Europe to put the finishing touches on their educations. And contemporary study-abroad programs promote travel as a source of worldly knowledge and self-development for young people. Worldschooling also owes much of its pedagogical ethos to the alternative education movements that emerged in the second half of the twentieth century. I describe these movements, namely free schooling, homeschooling, and unschooling, in more detail in chapter 1.

But the educational angle is just one piece of this puzzle. As I describe it throughout this book, worldschooling is a comprehensive lifestyle project in which parents' rejection of formal schooling converges with a host of other lifestyle choices related to work, parenting, community, and citizenship. In this sense, worldschooling overlaps quite extensively with the new mobile lifestyle trends that have gained momentum in recent decades. Thanks to a growing body of scholarship, we know quite a bit about the extreme mobilities of long-term backpackers,[13] the perpetual travel of diasporic tourists who repeatedly visit the same destination,[14] the experiences of lifestyle migrants, like the British retirees who seek milder climates and a slower pace of life in Spain, southern France, India or Thailand,[15] and the location-independent work patterns of digital nomads.[16] In previous generations these global nomads and lifestyle travelers likely would have been labeled "drifters," a term Erik Cohen introduced in the 1970s to describe long-term backpackers who had dropped out of society.[17] Today, however, these mobile lifestyles represent the kinds of lives and identities that are becoming more mainstream in the wake of globalization.[18]

In many ways, worldschooling is a logical extension of these historical precedents and a parallel to the more recent trends in lifestyle migration and digital nomadism. Yet, it also entails profoundly new ways of living, learning, parenting, and preparing children for the global lifestyles of the future. Although worldschooling can be traced to other forms of family mobility, its voluntary, independent, and relatively privileged nature distinguishes it from immigrant and refugee family mobilities. And although worldschoolers may share some common experiences with military, missionary, diplomatic, or expat families, they do not necessarily travel under the aegis of institutions like the church, the government, or the corporation. Although they share much in common with lifestyle migrants, digital nomads, and even study-abroad students, worldschoolers are not single twenty-somethings at the start of their careers, like many digital nomads, nor are they pensioners, like the older population often profiled in the literature on lifestyle migration. Instead, they are middle-aged parents with school-aged children, with all of the baggage about education, work, and family life that comes with this particular phase of life.

What worldschoolers do share in common with these other travel companions, however, is their quest for the good life through mobility. Ulrika Åkerlund and Linda Sandberg define lifestyle mobilities as practices individuals undertake "based on their freedom of choice [...] with or without any significant 'home base(s),' that are primarily driven by aspirations to increase 'quality of life' and that are primarily related to the individuals' lifestyle values."[19] What Åkerlund and Sandberg are talking about is neither temporary mobility nor permanent or forced migration, but rather the freedom to pursue ongoing physical mobility as an avenue to a better life.[20]

It is important to point out that visions of the good life are culturally specific and socially shaped. The qualities lifestyle migrants associate with the good life are not purely personal, but neither are they universal. In this case, as Åkerlund and Sandberg put it, these lifestyle movers are "driven by their desires to lead interesting, healthy, active, comfortable or fulfilling lives."[21] What's more, they are not seeking the good life in another place, but rather in the constant and ongoing movement between many places.[22] Indeed, this is what distinguishes lifestyle mobilities from other forms of tourism or migration; it is not about relocating to a different place, but rather about pursuing mobility as a way of life. Their definition refers to the growing number of lifestyle migrants, life-long travelers, and location-independent digital nomads who take their lives on the road, but it certainly fits worldschoolers, too, for whom an unconventional approach to education is just one among many lifestyle aspirations that propel families to travel. As I argue in this book, however, there is something strikingly new about the way worldschooling families navigate middle-class resources and anxieties by undertaking the project of parenting away from home and by imagining travel as a way of life for their families and young children.

This account of worldschooling also addresses a gap in the scholarship on inequality. While sociological and anthropological accounts of mobility and inequality often focus on the lives of the poor and vulnerable who are forced to move, they tend to neglect the voluntary lifestyle mobilities of affluent and privileged individuals.[23] As Marianne Cooper argues, we cannot understand emerging systems of stratification without understanding how these systems affect the lives of families across the class spectrum.[24] The analysis here focuses on middle-class families who voluntarily embrace mobility as a way of life. Throughout the book, I engage with several theoretical frameworks in order to move back and forth between the fine details of worldschoolers' lives and the larger social contexts in which they pursue mobility as a lifestyle strategy. In the next sections of this chapter, I offer an overview of these theoretical foundations, beginning with theories that map out the uncertain times of late modernity.

Uncertain Times

Sociologists have given this contemporary moment in which we are living many labels. They describe it as liquid modernity, reflexive modernity, late modernity, late capitalism, neoliberalism, the global era, the mobile era, the age of insecurity, and the risk society, to name a few.[25] If there is one theme that prevails in all of these theories, it is this: the central hallmark of modern life is uncertainty. This atmosphere of uncertainty stems from many sources. As the traditional guideposts for living recede and are replaced by an overwhelming proliferation of consumer choice, we find ourselves at loose ends about how to live and who to be. At the same time, the economic and social precarity wrought by neoliberal policies means we are constantly navigating changing conditions of work, diminishing access to social welfare programs, and new forms of selfhood. Meanwhile, complex global flows of people, objects, money, ideas, and media, ongoing geopolitical volatility, and increasing environmental hazards are making us hyper-aware of the new opportunities and the daily risks we face in a world in flux.

For sociologist Anthony Giddens, this sense of uncertainty is what distinguishes late-modern from pre-modern societies. In pre-modern times, people's lives were strictly governed by established customs, traditions, social roles, and class structures that essentially determined how their lives would unfold. With the dawn of modernity, however, established social hierarchies and traditional authorities began to lose their grip on people's lives. Industrialization created new kinds of jobs and mass production made a dizzying array of consumer goods available. Urbanization lured people away from traditional agricultural communities into the frenzied mix of city life. And new communications technologies allowed people to interact with diverse others beyond their local community. This meant that individuals had many more options for where to live, what kind of work to do, what to consume, and with whom to interact.

The result, according to Giddens, is that our identities and lives are no longer dictated by the circumstances of our birth but rather are reflexively created through the choices we make. And what we are really choosing, he argues, is a lifestyle. As tradition loses its hold over individual identity, lifestyle—a way of living that individuals fashion for themselves out of the "multiple choice" of consumer society—becomes increasingly vital to the reflexive project of self-constitution.[26] For Giddens, lifestyle also serves as something of an anchor amidst the uncertainties of everyday life. As he explains, "lifestyle involves a cluster of habits and orientations, and hence has a certain unity—important to a continuing sense of ontological security—that connects options in a more or less ordered pattern."[27] Faced with an otherwise fragmented existence, individuals increasingly relate to themselves and their lives as projects to be organized, crafted, and improved through reflexive techniques like lifestyle design.

Giddens's optimistic account of individual agency in late modernity has some notable limitations, however. The first problem, and one that will be obvious to anyone who actually lives in the world today, is that people do not have complete or equal freedom to reinvent themselves or shape their lives. The systemic constraints and the invisible privileges granted by race, class, gender, and nationality allow certain individuals to exercise more agency in their lifestyle projects than others. Another problem with Giddens's account of individual agency is that we have reached a point where we have no choice but to choose. Giddens writes that "we all not only follow lifestyles, but in an important sense are forced to do so."[28] Finally, traditional society may have been stultifying in many ways, but it also provided a concrete sense of identity and purpose. In the free-floating world of late modernity, as critics observe, we pay the price for the liberating weightlessness of identity in a loss of belonging, direction, and certainty.[29]

We also pay the price in the form of increased risk and responsibility. German sociologist Ulrich Beck introduced the term "risk society" to describe the new risks that industrial modernization created (such as pollution, oil spills, or nuclear disasters) but also our heightened consciousness of such risks, which now figure at the center of our public, political, and private lives.[30] In a climate of vulnerability and doubt, we are accountable for the outcomes of our many choices, which means that individuals become responsible for anticipating, preventing, mitigating, and coping with risk. Everything from making healthy choices to investing our savings wisely to deciding how to parent or educate our children is really about dealing with risk. As we will see throughout this book, worldschoolers organize their lifestyle projects around risk in complex ways. They are not only taking a calculated risk in their rejection of a "normal" lifestyle but also cultivating in their children the high tolerance for risk that they will need to thrive in an uncertain future.

Learning how to navigate the twin poles of risk and responsibility is vital to the reflexive project of self-making in contemporary society, not least of all in the shifting economic and social landscape of neoliberalism. For many critics, the current atmosphere of uncertainty and the precarious working and living conditions that are becoming prevalent are a result of neoliberal policies. Though neoliberalism has several connotations, generally speaking, it refers to a range of economic policies and government practices implemented over the past forty years to promote open markets, free trade, deregulation, and the privatization of social welfare programs.[31] Under such neoliberal policies, public services that were previously provided by the government are given over to private enterprise, a move justified by the claim that the free market can more efficiently and effectively see to society's needs. In such a neoliberal scenario, individuals are encouraged to think of themselves not as a collective body of citizens entitled to public benefits, but as consumers who deftly manage risk, make smart choices, and exercise personal responsibility. Scholars tell us that these structural uncertainties are felt especially intensely by today's young people, who face the stark realities of increasing unemployment rates, flexible but precarious working arrangements, and global competition for resources.[32] As the predictable security of state-provisioned social services and long-term employment recedes, people are set afloat in a sea of uncertainty.

While no one is entirely immune from uncertainty, where individuals and families are located on the social class ladder dictates, to a large degree, just how vulnerable they are to the vicissitudes of this shifting economic landscape. Writing about the US context, Marianne Cooper argues that individuals "live in vastly different *risk climates* that are shaped by how much they earn, how much they can save, the level of benefits they receive, and their likelihood of experiencing financial hardship."[33] While the wealthy families in Cooper's study used their considerable resources to build up a sense of security amidst insecure conditions, the worldschooling families I profile here take a somewhat different tack. They do not see the good life as one that is necessarily more secure, but rather one that is oriented toward uncertainty as an opportunity for autonomy, freedom, and self-actualization. What my research reveals, then, are the particular ways these relatively wealthy worldschooling families from the Global North leverage their economic, social, and cultural capital to embrace uncertainty as something positive and empowering for themselves and their children.

Throughout the book, I allude to the neoliberal modes of governance through which individuals are compelled to become self-governing, self-improving, and self-reliant subjects.[34] Neoliberal regimes encourage individuals to give entrepreneurial shape to their lives.[35] This means seeing themselves as savvy consumers, weighing choices in terms of costs and benefits, assuming responsibility for their own welfare, and making themselves competitive players in the global labor force. It also shapes the way individuals perceive and pursue the good life. As Sam Binkley explains in his book, *Happiness as Enterprise*, the neoliberal state's inducement to become "more self-reliant and enterprising, to depend less on government support, and to find their own way in a social world reinvented in the image of the market" extends as well to the pursuit of happiness and the "intentional project of personal well-being."[36]

As we will see in this book, worldschoolers do not look to the state to improve their quality of life in these uncertain times; the good life they pursue is one of their own making. Rather than participating in collective projects that might lead to a more secure society as a whole, worldschoolers take a go-it-alone approach. We see evidence of this in their decision to take their children's education into their own hands, and in their other life choices as well, such as becoming self-employed entrepreneurs, following their own individual styles of parenting, and finding communities that support their personal choices and pursuit of freedom. These families see themselves not as victims of a risk society or a precarious job market, but as the beneficiaries of a freer and more flexible world of work, play, and family life. They are mobilizing personal lifestyle strategies that make them the enterprising architects of their own lives.

One of the questions that arises as we consider family life in uncertain times is this: If we are living mobile lives in an age of insecurity, what does that mean for parents tasked with the responsibility of preparing children for the future? In this book, I also draw on literature from youth and parenting studies to understand how worldschoolers mobilize the practices of parenting and family life in light of these broader social changes.

Parenting Global Children

Despite the romantic image of family life unfolding around hearth and home, the reality is that modern families are increasingly on the move, whether physically or virtually. The white-collar jobs to which many middle-class workers aspire often require periodic relocation, intermittent international travel, or short-term overseas postings. Middle-class parents, in particular, are especially anxious to raise their children as global citizens who feel at home in this mobility. Worldschooling is just one of many different means by which family life can intersect with mobility, but it also reflects larger shifts in parenting culture among middle-class families that scholars have identified in recent decades. My analysis of these intersections is informed by three strands within this scholarship: family mobilities, intensive parenting, and the reproduction of social class.

Although the small field of family and children's mobilities has been described as a "road less travelled," mobilities scholars have become increasingly intrigued by the idea of family life as a mobile practice at various temporal and spatial scales.[37] For example, researchers have interrogated children's and families' mobility patterns in the small-scale movements of urban commuting,[38] in annual family holidays or trips to visit relatives,[39] and in large-scale mobilities like moving house or even moving abroad in order to be closer to good schools or employment opportunities.[40] In these cases, mobility is a register through which family relations are contested, performed, and sustained.

For the most part, however, these studies tend to describe family mobility as orbiting around a home base as parents and children commute to and from jobs or school, as parents travel away and back for business, or as families relocate to new home bases in other neighborhoods, cities, or countries. So far, very little research has examined the growing trend of middle-class families pursuing mobility as a lifestyle.[41] Perhaps the closest parallel to worldschoolers' global mobility can be found in the literature on international families and TCKs where scholars examine the lives of middle- and upper-class families who move abroad as missionaries, military personnel, diplomatic or non-governmental organization workers, or corporate employees. The social and emotional contours of mobile family life this scholarship sketches out resonate with many of the findings I discuss in the chapters that follow. For example, researchers find that TCKs who "grow up among worlds" develop expanded worldviews, a deep sense of empathy, and an ability to move seamlessly across cultures and languages, but at the same time, they must cope with a sense of unrootedness, unravel confused loyalties, and deal with chronic loss as they repeatedly say goodbye to friends.[42] In these cases, the family's international movement is usually prompted by a parent's career or other commitments, with the children's experiences and education posing a secondary concern that needs to be handled as part of the move. Indeed, scholars often frame family mobility as a disruption that needs to be managed, mitigated, or controlled.

With worldschooling, mobility is not a disruption; it is the whole point. For worldschooling parents, movement is an opportunity to cultivate the kinds of global identities and family bonding they desire. This brings me to the second theoretical framework from which my analysis draws, which pertains to the trend of intensive parenting in modern society. Although worldschoolers explicitly reject the philosophy of intensive parenting, this phenomenon is key to understanding their approach to raising global kids on the move.

If the children you know seem to be scheduled to the hilt, perpetually plugged in, and constantly coddled, chauffeured, managed, and surveilled in their daily lives, it is likely a result of the broad cultural turn toward intensive parenting. In her 1998 book, *The Cultural Contradictions of Motherhood*, Sharon Hays introduces the term "intensive mothering" to describe the emergence of a child-centered form of parenting that requires mothers especially to devote vast amounts of physical, emotional, and financial resources to raising their children.[43] As Hays described it, adopting this style of parenting meant that mothers prioritized their children's needs to the exclusion of their own personal or professional needs. What Hays described at the time as the unrealistic obligations of intensive mothering have since become normalized in the forms of helicopter parenting, paranoid parenting, and anxious parenting practiced by many upper- and middle-class families today, as I describe in more detail in chapter 3. In fact, the tenets of intensive mothering—acting as the primary caregiver, sacrificing one's own needs for those of the child, and paying constant attention to the child—have come to define what a "good mother" is among the wealthy classes in many parts of the world.

Even though at first blush worldschoolers seem vastly different from their stay-at-home counterparts, they share the same concerns as other affluent parents across the Global North. What does the future hold for our children? And how should we be educating, parenting, and preparing them to ensure they will thrive in that uncertain future? Implicit in these questions is both a sense of freedom and a sense of anxiety.

Modern parents, liberated from the dictates of tradition, enjoy an unprecedented amount of leeway in deciding how to raise their children. At the same time, however, they are responsible for making the right kind of parenting choices, especially when it comes to securing their children's futures.

Part of the reason intensive mothering has become so commonplace among middle- and upper-class families of the Global North relates to the myth of parental determinism. Sociologist Frank Furedi explains that, more so than ever before, parents today are blamed or credited for children's negative or positive outcomes. The burden of ensuring that children develop appropriately, safely, and well is placed almost entirely on parents' shoulders. The weight of this burden is compounded by the barrage of media stories that constantly report on the latest new dangers and by competing advice from the so-called experts about how to manage those threats. In this atmosphere of heightened fears, risk, and parental responsibility, parents tend to opt for intensive vigilance rather than giving children free rein. This helps explain why structured activities and adult-supervised playdates have become more popular, while the scope of children's autonomous play has been radically diminished.[44]

Parents' growing paranoia is not just about the immediate dangers that threaten their children. It is also about a kind of generalized anxiety about life in late modernity. This is what sociologist Margaret K. Nelson argues in her book, *Parenting Out of Control*. In her study of professional, middle-class parents, she finds that what drives parents' intensive involvement in their children's lives is a combination of social developments that have made the future—and children's future success—unsure. In an age of competitive college admissions, growing economic inequality, and shrinking options for upward mobility, parents feel compelled to micromanage their children's lives, not just through toddlerhood or the teenage years, but well into their twenties. Marianne Cooper found a similar theme among the wealthy families she interviewed, noting that many of the highly educated women in her study opted to stay at home after having children. Their time is devoted to scheduling their children's extracurricular activities, intervening with teachers and administrators, and guiding their teenage children through the competitive world of standardized tests and college admissions. These mothers "aren't home to bake cookies or make sure the house is clean," Cooper explains. "They are professional mothers who specialize in securing their children's futures."[45] Nelson and Cooper both arrive at the somewhat counterintuitive conclusion that the more financially well-off parents are, the more likely they are to worry about their children's educations and future prospects. In a neoliberal society that is light on social support in the form of childcare, child development programs, or higher education subsidies, and heavy on attributing children's outcomes to parents' actions, these kinds of intensive and concerted parenting techniques can be seen as a rational response to a competitive and uncertain social landscape.[46]

The third strand of literature that informs my analysis, then, examines the intersection between parenting, schooling, and the reproduction of social class. In her renowned book, *Unequal Childhoods*, sociologist Annette Lareau studied parenting styles across race, gender, and social class among a dozen families in the United States. Her analysis revealed important distinctions between the way middle-class parents and working-class or poor parents raised their children, with striking implications for children's future class status. In the poor and working-class families Lareau studied, parents taught their children to obey authority, including parents and teachers, but saw child development as a natural process that required little parental intervention. Children's free time was unstructured and they were allowed plenty of unsupervised free time.

Middle-class parents, on the other hand, adopted a style Lareau called "concerted cultivation." In line with Hays's concept of "intensive mothering," and the more recent parenting trends that sociologists like Nelson and Cooper describe, concerted cultivation is a child-centered and resource-intensive approach to parenting that sees children as projects to be developed. The middle-class parents in Lareau's study spent significant amounts of time, money, and energy fostering their children's capacities. They enrolled them in edifying extracurricular programs and taught them how to communicate and negotiate with authority figures in institutional settings like school. In particular, these middle-class parents were concerned with conferring cultural advantages and cultivating the skills children would need for future success. This meant getting their kids into the right extracurricular activities and prep schools so they would get into the right university and get the right kinds of jobs that would secure their place in the upper middle class. What looks like a series of personal choices about how to parent one's children, Lareau's study reveals, is in fact deeply embedded in existing structures of privilege.

This is the parenting environment in which we find worldschooling. Like the parents profiled in these studies, worldschoolers tend to be middle-class professionals from the Global North who are committed to cultivating their children's potential while protecting their well-being and ensuring their future success. They, too, are bombarded by media messages about the dangers children face and contradictory expert advice on parenting. They, too, are anxious about their children's welfare and about what the future holds in store for them. However, worldschoolers channel their anxiety in somewhat different directions, which I explore in more detail throughout the book.

For one thing, many worldschoolers feel overwhelmed by the expectation to constantly monitor and enrich their children. As I describe in later chapters, many worldschooling parents prefer a "free-range" approach to child-rearing, which they believe is more socially accepted in cultures outside of the United States. They are acutely concerned with cultivating their children's sense of independence, and they embrace opportunities posed through travel to push them out of their comfort zones. In parenting their children, worldschoolers often struggle to envision *a* path to success, seeing the future as unclear, but also full of possibilities. As I will show in this book, the way they prepare their children for this unpredictable but exciting future is by raising them to be global citizens who are adaptable, flexible, and ready for anything. Worldschooling is thus an investment parents hope will pay dividends by making their kids "future-proof."

At the same time, worldschooling parents hope a traveling lifestyle will rekindle a sense of family bonding, one they feel has been eroded by the long commutes, hours spent apart at work and school, and overloaded extracurricular schedules that dominated their lives at home. On the road, families are together all day, every day, which poses something of a paradox. While worldschoolers claim to reject the neurotically intensive form of parenting that has become commonplace, it would be hard to imagine a more intensive form of parenting than worldschooling. With at least one, and often two, parents dedicated full time to the child's educational, physical, and emotional needs, worldschooling is an extraordinarily resource-intensive form of parenting.[47] In this sense, we might think of worldschooling as concerted cultivation taken to a global extreme. It is a parenting approach that reflects the privileged position but also the deep anxieties of this new mobile class.

Reproducing Privilege in a World of Difference

As worldschoolers confront the uncertainties of life in late modernity, they do so in ways that express and perpetuate their privileged position in the world. In their quest to live the good life today and prepare their children for an unpredictable tomorrow, they rely heavily on the middle-class resources and sensibilities they bring with them, resources that often become even more valuable on the road. The families in my study, including my own, benefited from a number of advantages that facilitated their journeys, from the Global North passports they carried to their easy access to technology, hard currencies, and credit cards, to their fluency in English, their social media savvy, and their ability to frame travel as educational and portray their lifestyle choices as celebrations of freedom and personal autonomy. And that's before they even walked out of the door. In my analysis, I highlight the ways worldschoolers acknowledge and reflect on their own privilege, often in quite explicit and self-reflexive ways. But I also interrogate the implicit ways in which they reaffirm that privilege and convey certain social advantages to their children through their mobility.

To understand the intersection between privilege and mobility in the lives of worldschoolers, I draw on the field of mobilities studies where scholars have long been concerned with what sociologist Mimi Sheller calls "mobility justice."[48] Mobile lives are emblematic of the global inequalities that plague modern society. Within the mobilities literature, it is common knowledge that access to mobility varies on the basis of race, class, gender, age, or nationality and that the free and voluntary mobility of some people is premised on other people's constrained mobility or forced stasis.[49] A mobilities lens reveals the way this dialectic of mobility and immobility maps onto hierarchies of power, focusing our attention not just on who moves and who doesn't, but on the uneven conditions of mobility. Not everyone is on the road in the same way, nor is everyone welcome to stay home or make themselves at home in the world on equal terms.[50]

Worldschoolers are not alone in their mobile quest for the good life. They are joined on the road by lifestyle migrants, digital nomads, backpackers, tourists, international development workers, corporate expats, missionaries, study abroad students, voluntourists, and diplomats. These travelers share much in common with worldschoolers; they travel voluntarily, under relatively comfortable conditions, and often with the desire to live a better life or make the world a better place. But there are other, more vulnerable, groups of travelers on the road, ones for whom mobility is forced, constrained, or hazardous. These include migrants, refugees, asylum seekers, trafficked people, and laborers imported from the Global South to work in low-paid construction or caregiving jobs in the Global North. These people are certainly on the move, many of them also in the hopes of a better life, not because they want to move but because staying put has become untenable.

Consider, for example, the dire economic circumstances at home that compel many women from the Global South to leave their own children behind in order to work as caregivers for the children of wealthy professional couples in the Global North. Their care work makes it possible for the couple to travel for their own work, advance their careers, and secure their own family's privilege.[51] This scenario, repeated in different versions all over the world, illustrates how different conditions of being on the move or staying put reflect and reproduce privilege. It also shows how families are on the move together or geographically dispersed from one another under vastly different conditions.

Throughout the book, I bring attention to parallel scenarios in which worldschoolers benefit from the uneven mobilities and economic inequalities that exist on a global scale, thanks in large part to their Global North nationalities, their whiteness, and especially their middle-class status. In contrast to migrants, refugees, or asylum seekers, whose mobile experiences are rarely viewed as educational or whose children are not generally celebrated as budding global citizens, worldschoolers are able to frame their mobility in ways that confer value to their travels and transmit symbolic advantages to their children. The families I focus on in this book may not be among the ultra-wealthy jet-set elite, but they do occupy a relatively privileged position in this power spectrum of mobility.[52]

Nevertheless, as I mentioned earlier, I suspect that quite a few of the worldschoolers in my sample would object to being labeled as middle class, and for good reason. As we will see in chapter 2, many parents leave professional salaried jobs and deliberately divest themselves of the material trappings of middle-class life. When discussing budgets, the worldschoolers in my study indicate that they are spending on average USD\$1,000–\$3,000 per month, an income that would place most families below the poverty line in the United States, but one that allows them to live and travel quite comfortably in the poorer economies of the Global South. But income is not the only, or in this case most important, criterion for class status. For the purposes of my analysis, therefore, I draw on French sociologist Pierre Bourdieu's concept of cultural capital to understand how worldschoolers use mobility as a mechanism for expressing and reproducing their privilege.

Bourdieu argues that class hierarchies are sustained not just on the basis of economic wealth, but through symbolic resources, such as social or cultural capital.[53] Social capital refers to the number of people and the quality of relationships that make up one's social network, while cultural capital refers to intangible assets like one's education, styles of speaking and dressing, tastes and preferences, and a kind of cultural savoir faire that marks one's class status. As Bourdieu explains, those who possess high levels of cultural capital, such as artists or teachers, can move up the class ladder, even if they have relatively little economic capital to their name. What this means is that even though many worldschooling parents quit the jobs that landed them in a middle-class income bracket, they still carry with them large amounts of social and cultural capital that help them sustain a middle-class lifestyle on the move. And their search for the good life is very much shaped by middle-class aspirations and anxieties about securing their children's position of privilege in an unequal and uncertain world.

Worldschooling families display and accrue significant amounts of cultural capital through their travels by taking risks, experiencing other cultures, learning new languages, and becoming global citizens. In other words, through the lifestyle project of worldschooling, they are crafting a particular kind of self-identity, transforming themselves and their children into creative, entrepreneurial, adaptable, and global selves who are able to thrive in a changing and competitive world. Their mobile lifestyle is as much a declaration of membership within a stratified social class as it is an expression of personal identity.[54] What emerges in this book is a nuanced picture of how worldschooling parents seek to secure their children's privilege not in terms of material wealth, necessarily, but by circulating new kinds of social and cultural capital and by encouraging their children to become "mobile selves" who are prepared to handle—and even benefit from—future precarity.

Whether or not we are traveling the world with our families, we are all tasked with crafting a coherent and morally justifiable lifestyle, weighing trade-offs and sacrifices, and making smart decisions in light of an overwhelming menu of choices. This means that, while the practice of worldschooling may be new to many readers, the dramas that play out among these families on the move will likely ring a familiar bell. After all, these families are doing what many of us are doing: figuring out what it means to be a good person, to be a good parent, to be a good citizen, and to live a good life in these uncertain times.

Road Map for the Book

The stories I tell in the chapters that follow offer a detailed picture of the challenges of mobile education, the rise of remote work and digital nomadism, the trials and triumphs of parenting on the road, the mixed blessings of full-time family togetherness, the difficulties of finding community in the midst of mobility, and the responsibility parents feel to raise tomorrow's global citizens. In worldschooling we find a harbinger of the kind of lifestyle strategies that are becoming ever more prevalent in a society where individuals are encouraged to cope with increasing insecurity by exercising more choice and more control over their own lives.

Each of the five chapters that follow, and the interludes that punctuate them, addresses a specific set of strategies parents pursue to cope with current uncertainty and to cultivate the academic, entrepreneurial, social, and emotional skills they hope will prepare their children for success in an uncertain future. Chapter 1 focuses on education. I explore the anxieties and desires that motivate worldschoolers to take their children out of conventional schools to travel the world. I also describe how, once families start traveling, parents often shift toward a less structured and more child-directed form of "unschooling," which they perceive as a future-proof way of educating their children. Here, we begin to see how parents define the "good life" in terms of values like freedom, individualism, and personal choice. Embracing these particular values helps parents justify their decision to abandon the collective project of schooling for the more individualized benefits of learning through travel.

These values appear again in chapter 2, which focuses on the freelance, location-independent, and entrepreneurial work many worldschooling parents do. In this chapter, I describe those worldschoolers who launch their own online businesses to liberate themselves from office-bound jobs while earning income to fund their traveling lifestyles. This analysis reveals that the entrepreneurial logic worldschoolers apply toward their work infuses other aspects of their lives as well, leading them to think of their children's education, their family life, and their lifestyles as enterprises. It also animates their desire to foster children's entrepreneurial sensibilities as another way of hedging against future economic and labor uncertainty. Becoming an entrepreneur is one way these families convert uncertainty into opportunity, but I argue that what looks like an exercise in self-determination must be read against the backdrop of neoliberal ideologies that encourage individuals to relate to themselves, their families, and their lives through a market logic.

Chapter 3 addresses questions about parenting and family life on the move. The chapter begins with the concept of "extreme parenting" to orient a discussion of what it means to parent in a risk society. Through this notion, I compare worldschoolers' free-range approach to parenting to the forms of intensive or helicopter parenting that have become prevalent in contemporary society. I find that parents on both ends of this continuum are motivated by concerns for their children's future success, but that worldschoolers adopt a subtly different approach that prioritizes children's independence over their immediate safety. Worldschoolers upend conventional parenting culture by encouraging their children to embrace risk and become self-reliant. In this sense, worldschoolers' laissez-faire approach to parenting is actually part of a more intentional project to help children develop the kinds of skills that will serve them well in a precarious future.

The freedom of a mobile lifestyle comes with heavy emotional consequences, and in chapter 4, I interrogate how worldschoolers cope with feelings of loneliness, homesickness, and unrootedness on the road. This chapter focuses on the forms of online, temporary, and dispersed community worldschoolers seek for themselves and their children within the realm of mobility. Here, I detail how worldschoolers experiment with new forms of mobile togetherness and teach their children the social competencies they will need to make and sustain friendships and social networks in the mobile world of the future. Returning to themes from chapter 2, I also describe how some enterprising worldschoolers manage to commodify these mobile relationships and dispersed communities.

In these social arrangements, we see how worldschoolers navigate a desire for belonging alongside their desire for freedom, a tension that culminates in the aspiration to raise their children as global citizens. In chapter 5, I explore the way worldschooling parents define global citizenship in emotional terms, associating it with sensibilities like flexibility, adaptability, and comfort with difference. By focusing on the emotional dimension of global citizenship, I argue, worldschoolers hollow out the political obligations and collective agency of global citizenship, converting it instead into a more affective and personalized form of global selfhood. What becomes clear is that by teaching their kids how to "feel global," parents are preparing children to feel at home in a world of difference and equipping them with the emotional competencies they will need to flourish amidst constant change.

From the preview I have offered in this introductory chapter, we can already see how the tenets of a worldschooling lifestyle—freedom, risk-taking, an entrepreneurial and adventurous spirit, and a commitment to lifelong learning from the world around us—inform educational choices that prioritize child-centered learning, occupational choices that lean toward freelance and entrepreneurial work, parenting choices that hinge on free-range and future-oriented sensibilities, and citizenship choices that downplay political responsibilities in favor of feeling global. In the concluding chapter, I describe how these various aspects of social life—from education and work to parenting and family life, and from community to global citizenship—are framed as lifestyle choices that enable parents and their children to leverage precarity to live their best lives. Here, we see how the life lessons children learn when the world is their classroom transmit new kinds of value and new forms of cultural capital that children can carry with them into an uncertain future.

What we also see, however, is that worldschooling is ultimately a personal solution for living with the collective crisis of uncertainty. The individualized strategies worldschooling families use to cope—and even thrive—in this age of insecurity are more about guaranteeing their own children's advantages in a shifting world than they are about making that world a little more stable for everyone. In the epilogue, I propose the notion of a "good mobile life" as an alternative to a go-it-alone future that leaves individuals on their own to carve a livable life out of the shifting sands of uncertainty.

To some readers, the fact that I involved my own family in the project of worldschooling, and the way I write about worldschoolers' lofty aspirations for their children to become self-reliant, free-thinking, global kids, may be interpreted as an implicit endorsement of this practice. I want to be clear from the outset about where I stand. My goal in this book is neither to praise nor to disparage worldschooling or the families who pursue this lifestyle. The ethnographic account of worldschooling that follows is a partial, but I hope compelling, picture of why families become mobile, how they live their lives on the road, and the kinds of strategies they employ to set their children up for success against the broader backdrop of a rapidly changing world. In it, I try to provide a nuanced picture of the anxieties and hopes, the freedoms and constraints, and the class privileges that shape these journeys. As I see it, worldschoolers' critique of conventional schooling, rejection of "normal" life, and voluntary uprooting of their lives are sure signs of middle-class entitlement, but this lifestyle also offers a commentary on what it takes to live well in a neoliberal society that has made the world more uncertain for us all. At times, my analysis may make worldschooling sound like a dream come true—and for many of the individual families in my study it very much is—but it is a dream that comes at a steep cost to our collective well-being.

POOLSIDE

We could start seeing the change, even just in second grade, of her becoming . . . it's just that we could see that she was starting to lose some of her eagerness.
—Kim, interview

It is a hot but clear day in Ayutthaya, Thailand. I am sitting at the edge of our hostel's small pool with Kim Hoffmeyer and her husband Matt. As we talk, we watch our children cannonball into the water. Our conversation is punctuated by the kids' squeals as they climb out of the pool and then jump back in, over and over. The small table between our chairs is piled with towels, goggles, bottles of sunscreen, and snacks. I prop my recorder amidst the chaos and ask Kim and Matt to walk me through their decision to worldschool their daughter Dylan, age ten, and son Caleb, age eight.

The Hoffmeyers, who are white, like most of the couples I spoke with, were no strangers to traveling. Kim and Matt met in their early twenties while volunteering in Eastern Europe. They returned to the United States to get married and start their family, but they were impatient to hit the road again. When Dylan was two, they moved abroad again for work, this time to Malaysia. Caleb was born soon after. As the time approached for Dylan to start school, Kim and Matt considered enrolling her in a local preschool but decided to teach her at home instead. Although Kim was initially reluctant—"I would have never in a million years pegged myself as a homeschooler!"—she found a curriculum that worked well and ultimately enjoyed homeschooling.

After a few years abroad, the Hoffmeyers decided to move back to the United States. With Matt working full time on the couple's lifestyle blog and Kim committed to a new writing project, they decided to enroll Dylan and Caleb in a small private school. Although both Kim and Matt insist that they really loved the school, they admit that Dylan's educational experience was disappointing. "She was relearning stuff that she was taught just the year before in homeschooling," Matt says. "The teacher would present a subject, look at our daughter, and say, 'What do you know about this?' and she would rattle off a paragraph." "Random things," Kim interjects. "Like about the War of 1812!"

It wasn't just the pace of learning that concerned Kim and Matt, however. It was the realization that something about the conventional school setting seemed to be clouding Dylan's "natural personality" and extinguishing her spark of curiosity. "She would come home and talk about things that to me were just sort of dumb things, like Justin Bieber or who liked whom on the playground. [. . .] Just things that I felt like, I don't know if I want this to be the majority of her world," says Kim. "I wanted her to go back to caring about reading and playtime. So we decided to give homeschooling another shot."

Their son Caleb had given them another incentive to consider homeschooling. "The reason why we did homeschooling with Caleb is that he was diagnosed with a sensory processing disorder," Matt explains. Kim adds, "He doesn't sit still. He's not a 'normal' kid in that sense." Kim uses her fingers to insert air quotes around the word normal, indicating that she doesn't quite buy into the concept. "Very few five-year-olds do like to sit still," I respond. "Exactly," says Kim.

At the end of Caleb's first year in a pre-kindergarten class, the teachers recommended holding him back for another year before sending him to kindergarten. "What the teachers saw was he's not sitting still and he needs to learn how. He needs another year of classroom etiquette. Essentially teach him how to be institutional," Kim explains. "But what we saw," Matt interjects, "is that he was keeping up with his sister in mathematics. And we felt the teachers were putting the wrong emphasis on what my son needed to learn or how he needed to learn." After meeting with teachers and therapists, they decided homeschooling would be best for Caleb, too. "We just thought, we'll just have to give him lots of freedom to be himself," says Kim. "And now, he's reading chapter books end to end. We're so glad he wasn't put in a box, you know."

By then, the Hoffmeyers had started planning their family's year-long journey around the world. The dream had been in the works for a while, but with their blog providing some income and Kim's book manuscript submitted, they began preparing in earnest. They decided to spend one more year homeschooling and finalizing their travel plans before taking the kids on the road again. During that year, Kim acknowledges that she put a lot of pressure on herself to live up to the image of homeschooling she saw online and to keep up with the local homeschooling families in their area. Even though both Kim and Matt were working at home at the time, the planning and implementation of the children's curriculum fell largely on Kim's shoulders. And she took the responsibility very seriously. She set ambitious curricular goals and kept Dylan and Caleb on a rigid schedule to achieve those objectives, which sometimes led to the kids feeling frustrated and Kim feeling panicked. "Do you still feel that way?" I ask. "Sometimes," she says.

As we talk, she admits that she is slowly starting to let go of her idealized version of what homeschooling, and now worldschooling, should look like. Part of Kim's shift in attitude is due to some recent encouragement from another friend who has been worldschooling her children for a year. Kim recounts their conversation for me:

KH: I was looking at my homeschooling agenda for the year [on the road], and you know, what kind of curriculum, and I was thinking, "Oh my gosh, we are already so behind," and [my friend] was saying, "You know what? When I look back on my year [of traveling], we did not get much done traditionally. I had all these ideas for books we would read and where we would be in math," and she said, "Not much of it got done!" "But," she said, "at the end of the trip I could look back and see how much they learned."

JGM: And what *did* they learn?

KH: One of her sons who is Caleb's age, they were on a flight somewhere and they were working with money and conversions and exchange rates, and somehow he picked up fractions that way. He figured out what parts of a whole were and what it meant. And she was like, "I wasn't even trying! I thought we were just talking about money, and so it translated into something really practical for math." She was basically just encouraging me: They're learning stuff, you're just not aware of it yet.

I ask Kim if this less structured approach seems to be working with her kids. She thinks for a moment and then says, "It's still early on. We've only been traveling a month now, so we can't quite tell, but I can already see a difference in our kids like, oh, like life skills."

The kids are out of the pool now and are all huddled around a nearby koi pond. Dripping wet, they point and giggle as half a dozen white and orange fish swirl around the pond, some hiding behind rocks and others kissing the surface. As we walk over to wrap the children in towels, Kim says something I will hear again and again from the worldschooling parents I meet: "We're just doing it the way that makes sense for our family."

1

Spark and Fidget

Alternative Education for the Mobile Class

How do parents like Kim and Matt arrive at the decision to take their children out of conventional schools and educate them while traveling the world? It is hard to say whether worldschooling parents are motivated more by a desire to travel or by a growing discontent with their children's experiences at school. Usually, as in the Hoffmeyers' case, it is a combination of the two. The Hoffmeyers' story is unique in its details, but typical of the trajectory many families follow. For most families, the journey toward worldschooling is far from straightforward. It involves trial and error, fits and starts, slow realizations and sudden epiphanies.

Like the Hoffmeyers, many of the families in my study started by enrolling their children in traditional public or private schools, only to find themselves dissatisfied with the pace, structure, or behavioral norms classroom learning imposed. These concerns led parents to consider alternative educational approaches. Some moved their children to Montessori or Waldorf schools. Many opted for homeschooling. As it turned out, homeschooling came with an added benefit: flexibility. Parents who had traveled abroad when they were younger or who had long harbored dreams of world travel quickly realized that homeschooling did not necessarily mean staying at home. Consequently, homeschooling often became a gateway to worldschooling.

The next step, of course, was to actually get on the road with the kids. As Kim's experience illustrates, this step was more challenging than parents expected. Even the most conscientious parents found it difficult to align their vision of what schooling should be with the logistical realities of long-term family travel. Textbooks, worksheets, standardized learning outcomes, and curricular benchmarks do not travel all that well. While some families managed to follow a set curriculum on the road, a large number of the parents I talked to had become what one mother referred to as "accidental unschoolers." They found themselves abandoning the idea of doing school on the road and instead allowed travel itself to guide their children's learning.

By far the most frequent question worldschooling parents get from friends, co-workers, family members, and strangers on the Internet is this one: "What about the kids' schooling?" Simply being asked the question is evidence to some parents of just how ingrained compulsory schooling is in the cultural imaginary. The idea of *not* sending your kids to a traditional school is becoming more socially acceptable, especially with the increased popularity of homeschooling, but it is still a cultural anomaly. It is a social, and in some countries a legal, imperative that is rarely challenged. Some parents also interpret the question as an assumption that school is the place where learning happens. For people who have not encountered worldschooling, it can be hard to picture how day-to-day classroom activities translate to extended travel. They might see how kids can pick up art or culture or history by visiting different places, but what about math? What about science? What about socializing with other kids?

Worldschooling parents find these questions about schooling a bit dumbfounding, especially because they are steeped in quite the opposite belief: Traveling is not just an adequate substitute for a classroom-based education, but in fact a far superior way to teach children about the world. In response to the constant question about schooling, many of the parents in my study set aside space on their blogs and time in our interviews to detail what is wrong with conventional schooling and what is right with worldschooling. They provide long lists of the educational experiences their children have on the road. They engage thoughtfully with the writings of educational theorists like Charlotte Mason, Ivan Illich, John Taylor Gatto, and John Holt to justify the particular pedagogical path they have chosen for their kids. And they write candidly about their disillusionment with traditional classroom learning.

While parents had their own individual reasons for choosing to worldschool their children, and every family made this decision in the context of their own personal circumstances, there is a discernible pattern in the sentiments parents express about the limits of institutional education and the pedagogical promises of travel. This pattern coalesces around two terms that emerged again and again in parents' stories and that serve as the starting point for this chapter: spark and fidget. As I looked for the motivations behind families' decision to pursue a world-schooling lifestyle, I quickly picked up on parents' concerns that the modern education system was quashing children's creativity, suppressing their natural tendencies, and failing to prepare them for a complex future. But the decision to worldschool does not rest only on parents' dissatisfaction with institutional schooling. It is also motivated by the profound belief that travel itself is inherently educational.

In this chapter, I explore the relationship between the apprehensions parents express about conventional schooling and the hopes they pin on the educational power of travel. If parents perceive conventional schooling as an overly standardized and backward-looking bureaucratic institution, they see worldschooling, and the related philosophy of un-schooling, as the opposite: an individually tailored, natural, and creative way of teaching children about the complexity of the world around them. Neither of these perspectives is entirely new, however, and I start by situating parents' rationale against the larger historical backdrop of compulsory education and the legacies of school reform, alternative education movements, and educational travel. The historical benchmarks I highlight in this chapter are taken from the US context, but they parallel developments parents in my study describe in the United Kingdom, Australia, and South Africa as well.

From there, I describe how worldschoolers stumble into the practice of unschooling, a child-centered form of natural learning that happens to align nicely with the practical conditions of long-term travel. I conclude the chapter by arguing that even though worldschooling emerges out of a particular historical context, it represents something new in the way children's education is interwoven with a larger mobile lifestyle project. What becomes evident as parents justify their rejection of conventional schooling and embrace of worldschooling is that for them, education is no longer a taken-for-granted or even compulsory component of social life. Instead, they frame it as an individual choice, one that must be made in light of each family's aspirations to live a good life and to instill in their children the lessons that will serve them in the future. In this sense, I argue, the turn toward worldschooling is as much about shoring up the lifestyle aspirations of an emerging mobile class as it is about experimenting with alternative ways of learning on the move.

What's Wrong with School?
Modern Education and Its Discontents

Matt's and Kim's stories about Dylan losing her sense of eagerness and Caleb's inability to behave "normally" in school are vivid examples of the concerns parents express about conventional schooling, but these are by no means isolated incidents. On their blogs, worldschooling parents recount examples of how standardized tests had quashed their children's creativity, and in interviews they would sigh and say things like, "Well, he couldn't sit still." They complain that conventional education "pigeonholes" children into narrow definitions of intelligence, academic success, and appropriate behavior. And they worry that in institutional school settings, their children's "fidgeting" will be misread as a symptom of a learning disorder rather than encouraged as an embodied way of engaging with the world. On both counts, worldschoolers describe formal schooling as hopelessly stuck in a bygone era, drilling into students the industrial-era habits of conformity and deference rather than instilling the creative and risk-taking sensibilities children need to succeed in a fast-paced, diverse, and global world.

Sociologists have long observed that affluent parents, far more so than poor and working-class parents, tend to critique their children's schools, almost to the point of obsession.[1] As Marianne Cooper puts it, upper-income parents are "perpetually dissatisfied with school."[2] Well aware of the unpredictable global labor market their children will face and determined to give them every competitive advantage, these parents demand a "top-flight education" and they feel entitled, even obligated, to weigh in on everything from curriculum and testing to recess and classroom management.[3] Worldschoolers' concerns about schooling are thus not unique. Nor are they particularly new. In order to put worldschoolers' contemporary hopes and worries about their children's learning into context, it is necessary to review the longer history and larger debates that have surrounded the project of public education.

The story of modern public education in the United States begins with Horace Mann and the establishment of the Common Schools in the late nineteenth century. Mann, a prominent educational reformer and the first secretary of the Board of Education in Massachusetts, championed a consolidated, universal, and publicly funded educational system for all American children. Inspired by the Prussian model of state-controlled and -standardized education that was taking hold in Europe at the time, he believed that free public education could bring stability to a society still reeling from racial and socioeconomic divisions after the Civil War. By offering equal opportunities to children from all class backgrounds, Mann famously argued, common schools promised to be the "great equalizer of the conditions of men, the balance wheel of the social machinery."[4] Mann saw public schools as models of democracy where young citizens would be prepared for active participation in a civil society.[5]

By the beginning of the twentieth century, the demands of an industrializing economy required something different: a ready supply of workers. In addition to cultivating democratic values, public schools contributed to the nation's economic and labor needs by teaching children habits of discipline, self-control, and orderliness.[6] However, as the curricular emphasis shifted from the education of democratic citizens to the production of a reliable labor force, critics argued that the structure of schooling itself began to resemble a factory, with docile workers as its output. In the 1960s and '70s, theorists Paulo Freire, Samuel Bowles and Herbert Gintis, and Ivan Illich, among others, criticized the uniformity and standardization of public schools, arguing that schooling served the economic and nation-building interests of the state rather than the personalized needs of individual students. They called for a radical restructuring, or in Illich's case a complete dismantling, of an education system that reproduced class hierarchies and mirrored the oppressive structure of the capitalist economy.[7] Rather than cultivating children's love of learning, they argued, schools reward subservience to authority, promote capitalist values of efficiency and competition, turn students into compliant corporate and bureaucratic pawns, and ultimately prepare them to take their place in a class-divided society. According to Bowles and Gintis, rather than remedying class divisions, as Horace Mann had hoped, schools reproduce and naturalize oppressive hierarchies and perpetuate the economic interests of the dominant class.[8]

These critical theories solidified a countercultural perception of public education as an outdated and rigid institution bent on suppressing individual creativity and self-expression in service of state and corporate interests. In turn, this perception inspired widespread experimentation with innovative schooling models and teaching practices, both within and outside of existing public schools. Among these were school-based alternatives such as open schools, commune schools, and schools without walls, "freedom schools" established to serve black students and advance racial pride, and schools based on particular learning theories espoused by pioneering educators like Maria Montessori, Rudolf Steiner (Waldorf schools), and A. S. Niall (*Summerhill*-inspired free schools). While many of these alternative options reflected the left-leaning countercultural movements of the time, the 1970s also saw the proliferation of more conservative alternatives, such as religiously affiliated academies and Christian day schools.[9]

Today's worldschooling families often align themselves with some of the alternative educational philosophies and practices that emerged in the 1960s. However, they are especially drawn to alternatives that take learning beyond school altogether, such as homeschooling, a movement that expanded considerably during the 1960s and '70s. In her widely cited 1988 study of homeschoolers, Jane Van Galen found that the movement was growing, but not necessarily along coherent ideological lines.[10] Homeschoolers, she argued, tended to fall into two camps: *ideologues*, primarily conservative religious parents who protested the secularization of the public schools; and *pedagogues*, parents who felt that institutional schools failed to prioritize their children's individual needs or cultivate their innate potential.[11] Of the families who fell into the pedagogue category, many subscribed to the ethos of unschooling, a form of child-directed learning through spontaneous play advocated by John Holt.[12] As we will see later in this chapter, many worldschooling parents today practice a contemporary form of unschooling that is deeply influenced by Holt's pedagogical philosophies of natural learning.[13]

While the countercultural and alternative education movements of the 1970s promoted individualized and child-centered learning, the 1980s brought a new set of geopolitical threats that pushed the reform pendulum back toward control and uniformity. The Cold War and the intensification of globalization kindled neoliberal anxieties about America's waning political and economic power on the global stage. Armed with reports of US students testing below their counterparts in other countries, neoliberal reformers called for stricter accountability throughout the nation's schools.[14] These calls were answered at the beginning of the twenty-first century with the No Child Left Behind (NCLB) Act. Passed by the US Congress in 2001 and enforced at the national level until 2015, NCLB expanded federal control of schools, homogenized curricula across states, and implemented standardized testing, all in the name of accountability. Proponents of the NCLB legislation applauded the bill for applying a consistent curriculum across the country and holding schools to high academic standards. But critics worried that classroom teachers were overly focused on mandated standardized tests that prioritized one particular skillset and ignored the myriad other intelligences and talents that children express. Plus, the students found the tests very stressful.[15]

Not far behind NCLB were policies that essentially privatized local public schools, handing underperforming schools over to for-profit management organizations and paving the way for private charter schools, school choice, and vouchers that channeled taxpayer funds to private schools. If public education embodies the tension between collective and individual interests, these neoliberal reforms played both sides of the debate. They implemented centralized standards and measures of accountability while simultaneously framing education as a matter of personal choice.

The discourse about public schooling that circulated in the aftermath of NCLB fed into a perception of schools as rigidly standardized, even factory-like in their models of instruction, but it also endorsed the belief that free market principles, and especially consumer choice, were the solution for a failing school system. According to education scholar Marta Baltodano, "education is no longer a public good offered and protected by the government; it has become a commodity that can be traded in the market."[16]

These developments set the scene for the resurgence of alternative education we have witnessed since the beginning of the twenty-first century. Under these conditions, it is perhaps no surprise that a growing number of families are rejecting conventional classrooms and exercising their freedom to choose alternative options for their children. What is somewhat surprising, however, is that the uptick in alternative education like homeschooling and worldschooling is taking place among professional, middle-class, progressive families, the very same people who have traditionally championed the institution of public education.[17] This trend is especially evident in places like Silicon Valley, where alternative education has become particularly fashionable among tech-savvy and entrepreneurially minded parents.[18] Disillusioned with mainstream schools and skeptical of government institutions, but armed with new educational technologies and empowered by a discourse of choice, wealthy and middle-class families are opting out of conventional schools in unprecedented numbers to pursue a kaleidoscopic range of alternative practices such as homeschooling, unschooling, microschooling, gameschooling, and hackschooling.

It is here that we find worldschooling, as well, an alternative education approach that appeals to middle-class parents' sensibilities about child-centered learning, their growing skepticism of institutional conformity, and their ability to leverage technological and class resources to create a future-oriented learning experience for their children. From this historical backdrop, we can now return to worldschoolers' concerns about their children's spark of creativity, their fidgetiness, and their future to understand why they reject conventional schooling and adopt the world as their classroom.

Spark, Fidget, and the Future

Leah and Richard Reynolds are a white couple from the United States who have been traveling the world with their three sons for several years. After initially enrolling their oldest son in traditional preschool and kindergarten programs for two years, Leah decided to homeschool him. There was nothing technically wrong with his school or teacher, she explains, but she wanted more for him. "What more did I want?" she asks. "Room for independent thought, creativity, an ability to question things without being 'in trouble'—and the freedom to run our household without the demands of the school system intruding." What began as homeschooling soon evolved into unschooling, a philosophy and a practice that fit with Leah's desire for more freedom. Without the tether of school keeping them in their hometown, Leah and Richard decided to move their family and their online business to Central America, where they worked as digital nomads and unschooled their boys for a few years before deciding to travel more extensively. They have been traveling, working, and worldschooling their boys ever since.

Along the way, Leah has fielded a constant barrage of questions about her children's education. She addresses many of these questions in a separate section of her blog, where she expresses her dissatisfaction with conventional schooling. She writes on her blog that "kids are having creativity and diversity sucked out of their lives." Comparing schools to prisons, she complains that schools and classrooms are "overly institutional feeling, which is cold and unhealthy." This institutionalization is mental as much as it is physical according to Leah, who explains that it "stifles creativity and curiosity and makes our children accept the life of living in a box."

Like Leah, many parents describe the slow realization that the traditional school system is stifling their children's innate curiosity or pathologizing their natural tendencies to move and fidget. For Maggie Coates, a white mother of two from South Africa, this realization came when she gave her daughter Lola, who was enrolled in a local preschool at the time, a blank piece of paper and urged her to draw something. Lola didn't know what to draw and melted into tears when Maggie would not tell her what to do. As Maggie explains on her blog, Lola had already become accustomed to following strict directions, even in art class. Maggie gives the following example from a school worksheet:

> How to make a duckling: Cut out a circle of paper. Colour it in yellow. Cut a smaller circle out of paper. Colour it in yellow. Cut a small triangle out of paper. Colour it in orange. Stick the small triangle on to the edge of the small circle.

Maggie complains that "kids weren't simply allowed to . . . you know . . . just draw (or create) their own interpretation of what a duckling might look like." Even worse, she writes, "the children's versions were deemed messy and 'wrong.'" What Lola was really learning, Maggie concludes, is that "there were rules that needed to be obeyed."

This struck a nerve with Maggie, who candidly recounts her own negative experiences with formal schooling. She describes herself as a questioner who struggled to conform to the "correct answer" regime of schooling. She recalls constantly being in trouble for asking "why?" or for disagreeing with her teachers. "School taught us to be obedient and compliant," she writes. "We were not allowed to talk in class. [. . .] We were never taught creativity or critical thinking—and seldom (if ever) given the opportunity to think for ourselves—or decide for ourselves." The drawing episode with her daughter encapsulated Maggie's growing displeasure with the school's emphasis on obedience, compliance, and standardized tests over creativity and critical thinking, ultimately leading her to pull her son and daughter out of school.

When worldschooling parents explain why they are taking their children out of conventional schools, or when they feel the need to justify their decision to disapproving relatives or skeptical friends, they often turn to Sir Ken Robinson to help them articulate what is wrong with today's educational system. Robinson is a British education advisor who, in 2006, delivered a TED talk titled "Do Schools Kill Creativity?" The talk has since been viewed more than 65 million times, making it the most-watched TED talk of all time. Four years later, in 2010, Robinson delivered a second talk titled "Changing Educational Paradigms," with more than 15 million views and counting.

Leah and Maggie both include links to Robinson's talks on their blogs, as do many of the parents in my study. Clearly, Robinson's message resonates deeply with this group. I refer to his presentations here in part because so many of the parents in my study lean on his logic to express their own reasons for worldschooling, but also because Robinson so neatly distills the key critiques worldschooling parents repeat in their own blogs and in interviews: Schools kill creativity, endorse a narrow definition of success, and stifle natural movement and learning, all in service of an outdated mind-set about the role schools play in society.

One story, in particular, captures these sentiments. Robinson tells the audience about Gillian Lynn, a young girl growing up in the 1930s. Early on in her schooling, Lynn was labeled with a learning disorder because, as he explains it, "she couldn't concentrate; she was fidgeting." She was taken to see a specialist. Had the diagnosis been available at the time, Lynn probably would have been labeled with ADD/ADHD (Attention Deficit Hyperactivity Disorder), Robinson says. Instead, the specialist told her mother, "Gillian isn't sick; she's a dancer. Take her to dance school." And so her mother did. Robinson says that when he asked Lynn, who eventually went on to become a renowned dancer and choreographer, what happened when she got to dance school, she replied, "I can't tell you how wonderful it was. We walked in this room and it was full of people like me. People who couldn't sit still. People who had to move to think." Robinson concludes that schools are "educating people out of their creative capacities" by rewarding a single kind of academic intelligence, one based on job-ready subjects like math, reading, and writing, while punishing children like Lynn who display the disruptive signs of creativity.

This story about Gillian Lynn touches on the same concerns about creativity and fidgeting that led Cathryn and Mike Silva, a couple from the United States, to worldschool their three children. Isabella, William, and Callie were ten, seven, and four, respectively, when the family spent a year traveling the world during Mike's sabbatical from his job as a high school teacher. Cathryn was a career educator but had left her teaching position ten years earlier to stay at home with the children. The family lived on the outskirts of a large city in the eastern United States, where Mike taught and where Isabella and William were enrolled in a traditional public school.

On the family's travel blog, Cathryn describes her growing dissatisfaction with Isabella's and William's early experiences in their local school and in the public school system overall. She blames the experience not on the school itself or on the teachers, whom she describes as "phenomenal," but rather on a broken system that no longer grants teachers or children the freedom to teach and learn at their own pace. She explains:

> A major angst-factor that nudged me toward this trip was EDUCATION. In a nutshell:
> 1. Our kids' school experiences have been heavy on paper-pencil rigor/ quantity of content, and light on choice/open-ended learning.
> 2. Our public school system prioritizes standardization/high-stakes tests.
> 3. My own teaching/parenting style conflicts with the current priorities of public school, *but*, I believe in public education—that it should be and can be the best education for all kids.

When Cathryn talked to friends whose kids attended other schools, the story of rigid curricula and high-stakes testing was the same. "This is not a commentary on school or teacher quality," Cathryn clarifies. She explains that these problems are not confined to her children's school but rather are endemic in the public school system. "Unfortunately, schools and teachers are evaluated based on test scores; many public schools do the best they can in the current environment."

Cathryn laments that the freedom she had as a teacher more than a decade ago no longer exists in today's public schools. Teachers simply do not have "the same freedom to follow their students' hearts and minds because they have to follow the top-down, content-heavy curriculum that will yield the best scores on The Big Tests," she observes. "There are some brilliant, skilled teachers in our schools, but they have to work their magic under the weight of a political agenda that is rooted in standardization and fill-in-the-bubble data." By framing the problem as a systemic one, Cathryn justifies her family's decision to take the children out of school. If even the best schools and best teachers are constrained by a dysfunctional system, the only viable option seems to be to escape the system altogether.

For Cathryn, this dysfunctional system failed her two children in different ways. When her daughter Isabella started kindergarten in 2009, Cathryn was shocked by how little recess and how much homework Isabella had. By the time Isabella entered third grade, Cathryn was again shocked, this time over how much time was spent preparing for the standardized state test. "I must admit," Cathryn writes on her blog, Isabella "handled it well (aside from the chronic stomachaches) and got great grades (which is not the same as thriving)." Even though Isabella performed well under the pressures of a system focused almost entirely on standardized testing, Cathryn notes that her daughter's well-being suffered for the sake of academic success.

Whereas Isabella was able to meet these narrow expectations, Cathryn worried that her son, William, simply would not "fit the mold." She tells his story on her blog:

> When [William] hit kindergarten and could not sit still or keep quiet for hours on end—because he is a silly, social, scrumptious boy—my anxiety increased. How was this kid going to fit the mold? When that squirmy boy got to 1st grade, and I requested that his class of 33 kids be given more than 15 minutes of recess in a 6 hour day, the response was, *They are in 1st grade now, and there's a lot to cover, but we'll try to give them more recess*

when we can. I don't know if I was sadder for the kids or for their sweet teacher who had to blaze through curriculum with all those 6 yr olds.

Cathryn's anxiety about her son's inability to "sit still or keep quiet for hours on end" echoes the concerns about fidgeting that Ken Robinson touches on in his talks and that many worldschooling parents express.

The topic of ADD/ADHD frequently cropped up in my interviews with worldschoolers, in their blogs, and in an online forum for world-schooling parents. For several of the families in my study, a diagnosis of ADD/ADHD was the catalyst for pulling their children out of formal schooling. Others never enrolled their children in the first place out of fear that a child's fidgetiness would quickly be medicalized in the in-stitutional school setting. Sarah and David Milken, a couple from the United States whom I interviewed in Argentina, were worried that their son Colin, who struggled to sit still for long periods, would be diagnosed with ADD if they enrolled him in a regular school. Instead, they placed him first in a Montessori school, later homeschooling and then world-schooling him, with the intention of eventually moving to a country where rates of diagnosis were not as high as in the United States.

One mother turned to the online forum with a request for help deal-ing with her extended family who, due to the child's ADHD and dyslexia diagnoses, opposed her plans to worldschool her son. Parents on the forum weighed in with a range of responses. One mother observed that any child who doesn't fit the "quiet learner/child that is demanded" by the modern classroom is likely to receive the ADHD label. "This is my fear," she writes, "that if I ever send my child to a 'regular' school setting that his energy and curiosity will be quickly labelled." She adds that he is currently thriving through worldschooling, "where he can explore, experiment and learn by doing [which] most traditional school systems do not allow." Another mother agrees, writing that "my son would likely be diagnosed if in a traditional public school but out here in the world labels mean nothing." As she sees it, "ADD only exists when it interferes with someone else's agenda." To this, another commenter replies that public school "causes the self-esteem to plummet for these children! The[y] become self-conscious and made to feel stupid, even though they are often the brightest kids in class!" She goes on to commend the other parents on the forum for taking an alternative path: "As a homeschool/

worldschooler, you are allowing children with unique minds to grown [*sic*] and blossom without having the negative stress and pressure of trying to mold into the standard shape the school insists upon."

As these responses indicate, a common theme in worldschoolers' discussion of ADD/ADHD is that the disorder is an effect of systemic and structural arrangements, not an inherent flaw in the individual child. As one respondent points out, labels such as ADD/ADHD or dyslexia "mean nothing" outside of the school setting. Instead of medicating their children, these parents embrace movement—both micro-level embodied movements and macro-level movements of world travel—as a pedagogical experience. Through the physical and mental freedom of worldschooling, "unique minds" can "grow and blossom."

What becomes clear is that parents feel as though institutional education systems are a rigid one-size-fits-all solution to a dizzying array of individual needs, passions, and talents. The tension between standardization and individual self-expression has long been a defining feature of debates about public education, only now, following neoliberal reforms that have further standardized curricula and accountability regimes, the problem seems more urgent to parents. At the same time, more and more middle-class parents also feel empowered to reject the standardized model of conventional schools and make their own choices about their children's education. And the alternatives are endless. As one mother observes on her blog, "there's no perfect choice, but there's a thousand good ones."

Worldschooling parents acknowledge that traditional education serves some students, but certainly not all. For them, trying to squeeze children into the box of compulsory classroom-based education is deeply damaging. As the forum commenter cited above puts it, the narrow confines of proper behavior and intellectual achievement make the brightest kids seem stupid. What's worse, they argue, is that this educational paradigm—one that stifles creativity and requires behavioral conformity—is premised on an era that is long past. In this sense, they echo another critique that has been around for generations: modern public schooling is based on an outdated factory model of education that is failing to prepare children for the future.

The image of schools as factories stems from the nineteenth-century Prussian model of education that inspired Horace Mann to establish compulsory schooling in the United States. It is easy to see why the Prussian schools might be associated with factories; they were, by all accounts, rigidly organized institutions intended to produce mass education through a state-controlled curriculum, uniform modes of instruction, and obedience to authority. When critics refer to schools as factories, however, they are not just condemning conformity, compliance, and mass outputs, they are suggesting that the school system reflects an outdated way of thinking. This critique is hardly new. Traditional schools have long been criticized for their inability to keep pace with a changing world. A 1973 report on the state of education in the United States claimed, for example, that the primary problem with the educational system is that "though youth is no longer the same, and the world is no longer the same . . . schools are essentially unchanged from what they were at the beginning of the century."[19] More than four decades later, critics are repeating the same refrain about education in the twenty-first century. The world has changed, but education hasn't.

Not everyone buys into this narrative. Education historians note that the development of mass education has never mapped neatly onto the rise of industrialism or the actual structure of factories. They suggest that the narrative overstates the extent to which public education, in the United Sates at least, has become a centralized and standardized institution. And yet reformers, many of whom come from the worlds of private enterprise, politics, or corporate philanthropy rather than classrooms, have latched on to this narrative, in part because it paves a tidy path to ever more technical and privatized solutions.[20] Whether or not the factory model narrative is accurate or defensible, the parents in my study are profoundly compelled by the idea that the institutional arrangements of today's educational system remain rooted in this old-fashioned model and that only a disruptive approach to learning can put us on the path to the future.

Many worldschooling parents dip into the rhetoric and symbolism of factories, assembly lines, and industrial-era production to paint a picture of an outdated educational system that they are happy to leave behind. Julia Porter, who worldschooled her four children for more than ten years, explains at length on her blog how an outdated educational system fails to prepare children for the future:

The world is changing, and along with it the rules of the economic game and the job market. [. . .] We're still pushing kids through an educational process that was designed for a bygone era. The industrial revolution is over. Nobody gets a job and holds it until they retire any more. Very few corporations exist in a nationalistic bubble any more. The game has changed. The game is constantly changing. Our schools aren't doing a very good job of keeping up with this reality.

Leah echoes this sentiment on her blog: "Our children deserve new ideas to help guide them into the quickly changing future. Our school systems are deeply rooted in an archaic mind-set and it is vital that we change that sooner rather than later." Worldschoolers like Julia and Maggie reject the notion that all children should receive essentially the same education and be measured by the same standards. They chafe at the idea of a one-size-fits-all education geared toward outdated values and skills more suited to factory work than to the new global economy. According to sociologists, these concerns about preparing children for a global future are commonplace among upper- and middle-class parents, especially in the United States. One of the upper-income mothers Marianne Cooper interviewed in her study, for example, notes that "math, science, and technology [is] where the economy is going" and laments that her children's skills are not keeping pace with those of students in other countries.[21] Aware that the rules of the economic game are changing, parents worry that their children won't be prepared.

In his talk on educational paradigms, Ken Robinson argues that the current model of education fails to equip children with the kinds of skills—skills like creativity, communication, collaboration, independent thinking, risk-taking, or self-directed learning—needed for tomorrow's world. Robinson claims that education is "meant to take us into this future that we can't grasp. [. . .] Nobody has a clue what the world will look like in five years' time. And yet we're meant to be educating [children] for it."[22] The solution he offers is not to narrow the focus of education to a small number of career-ready skills such as math and reading, but rather to cultivate children's creativity and "educate their whole being, so they can face this future."

Whereas in previous centuries, governments, factories, or large corporations provided secure employment over the course of a worker's career, today's economy is more flexible and casualized. Workers are often hired on part-time contracts, moving from project to project as needed. When Julia claims that "Nobody gets a job and holds it until they retire anymore," she is referring to the fact that we are now living and working in an economy that values a freelance mind-set and portable entrepreneurial skills. As we will see in the chapters that follow, worldschoolers are adapting to new economic arrangements that are less solid and predictable and more precarious, mobile, and flexible. Succeeding in this new economy requires an altogether different set of skills and sensibilities than those required in the bygone industrial economy, a fact that fuels parents' anxieties over traditional schooling.

Worldschoolers' critiques of conventional schools as the place where creativity goes to die, where children's natural movements are deemed abnormal, and where students are prepared for an economic era that has come and gone belie an imagined future that is quickly changing and profoundly uncertain. Under these conditions, the parents in my study justify their decision to opt out of the collective project of public education and turn, instead, toward a freer, more personalized, and forward-looking model of worldschooling. As Robinson reminds his audience: "We may not see this future, but they will."[23] If formal schooling stifles creativity, pathologizes children's natural exuberance, and imprisons students in an outdated factory model of education, travel does just the opposite. It sparks children's sense of curiosity, celebrates mobility, and equips children with the knowledge and skills they will need to thrive in the twenty-first century.

Travel Is Our Teacher

Worldschooling allows sparks of inspiration. Once we've climbed a mountain, we now want to know about global warming and we want to know about the history, the astronomy and the mythology—all of these things are sparked because [of] the world providing these sorts of stimulus for us.
—Ella, blog post

From an educational perspective, worldschooling appears to offer an antidote to almost all of the problems parents attribute to mainstream schooling. If conventional schooling extinguishes children's spark of creativity or natural curiosity, worldschooling ignites it. If conventional schooling pathologizes children's embodied movement, worldschooling celebrates it. And if conventional schooling is stuck in an outdated model of learning, worldschooling equips children with the skills they need for the future.

The key to worldschooling is the deeply held belief that travel itself is inherently educational. Worldschoolers' blogs are peppered with inspirational maxims from Mark Twain, St. Augustine, and Seneca attesting to the idea that travel cures prejudice, broadens the mind, and enlightens the individual to the ways of the world. This belief builds on a legacy that stretches back to the Greek scholar Herodotus who traveled throughout the ancient world learning the myths and legends that would be retold in his foundational work, *The Histories*.[24] But the popular notion that travel is educational really took hold during the seventeenth and eighteenth centuries, with Enlightenment thinkers like John Locke and Jean-Jacques Rousseau insisting that travel enhances intellectual development and British aristocrats dispatching their sons (and a few daughters) to Europe on a Grand Tour that was meant to complete their scholarly training.[25] After World War II, educational travel found a new form in the study abroad and study tour programs offered by high schools, colleges, and universities.[26] In recent decades, gap years have also become increasingly fashionable in the United States and Europe, where a new industry is emerging to help young adults enlist travel as a way of learning about themselves and the world.[27]

The rising number of students participating in study abroad and gap year programs is evidence of an abiding confidence in travel's educational outcomes, but it also reflects a growing sense that the kinds of things students learn from studying abroad—such as flexibility, creativity, or the ability to navigate across multiple cultures—are precisely the skills and sensibilities they will need to succeed in the global economy of the future. Of course, the extent to which traveling or studying abroad actually achieves these outcomes is the subject of some debate, with scholars questioning whether these international experiences actually reinforce stereotypes, reproduce systems of postcolonial "otherness," and affirm the privilege of students from the Global North.[28]

Nevertheless, worldschooling parents emphasize the educational outcome of travel. In a blog post titled "Long Term Travel as Education," a piece she composed back when her family's journey was still new and she was still grappling with the ever-present question about her children's schooling, Julia Porter explains how travel gives children the inspiration, freedom, and learning experiences that outdated educational models fail to supply. Travel teaches these things, Julia writes, by exposing "children to diverse cultures and individuals who light the sparks of their imaginations in ways that are impossible in the mainstream school mentality." While traveling, children "learn to live and work in a range of paradigms, with shifting sets of data and resources." This becomes especially important, Julia suggests, as children begin charting their future career paths. She continues:

> They often learn to support themselves in outside-of-the-box ways, and they develop a confidence in their own creativity that will allow them to rise to the top in any vocation they choose. The business world is driven by the movers and the shakers, not the minions. Flexibility and creativity aren't two things you can work into a lesson plan three times a week and check them off the list. They are developed through doing hard things, through things going badly sometimes, through coping with the unexpected, through taking what you've got, which is perhaps not enough, and making the best of it, making it work, making something happen.

According to Julia, traditional schooling teaches kids to be followers, when what the future will really require are unconventional thinkers and creative problem solvers. The skills kids will really need, like flexibility and creativity, are best developed through the kinds of experiences, hardships, and uncertainties afforded by long-term global travel.

Julia is far from alone in her advocacy of travel's educational outcomes. On their blogs and in interviews, worldschooling parents recount stories of their children's imaginations coming alive as they scramble over Mayan ruins, cycle through Vietnam, try to communicate in Spanish with kids at a park in Buenos Aires, or grapple with real-world math problems. They write lists of all the academic, social, and emotional lessons their children are learning—ranging from lessons in algebra and climate science to how to say "thank you" in eight languages to problem solving and tolerance—some of which may be taught in a formal classroom but many of which they presume are not. Parents also deflect worries about what children might be missing in the curriculum back home by highlighting the invaluable life lessons their children are learning on the road.

What is striking about worldschoolers, however, is not just their belief that travel teaches children what they need to know for the future, but also their embrace of an alternative, some would say radical, pedagogical philosophy: unschooling. I was somewhat surprised to learn that many of the families in my sample were unschoolers, something I associated with a fairly extreme countercultural movement, and I was even more surprised to find myself going down the same path not long into my family's journey. Unschooling is so prevalent in worldschoolers' accounts and so tightly interwoven with their beliefs about travel and education that it is impossible to ignore. But what accounts for the fact that so many worldschooling parents, intentionally or not, end up taking an unschooling approach to their children's education?

Accidental Unschoolers

Elliot was ten when my husband and I took him out of school. We planned to travel and educate him while I also conducted fieldwork with worldschooling families during my sabbatical leave. We had every intention of keeping Elliot on track with his grade-level curriculum. In preparation for this undertaking, I requested a copy of our school district's fifth-grade math and reading standards, downloaded electronic versions of his textbooks, and loaded our digital tablet with electronic versions of the books his class would be reading while we were away. As required by the state, we wrote a letter of intent to our district superintendent outlining our plans to cover and assess the relevant content in math, reading, writing, and history. And off we went.

For the first few weeks of our journey, we conscientiously set aside time each day for Elliot to do math problems, read chapters in his history textbook, and write about his travel experiences. But staying on track got harder and harder, especially as we spent entire days on trains or in airports, moving every few days or weeks from one place to another. It also made little sense to force him to read chapters about the Wampanoag tribe in New England just to stay on track with his class when the Roman forum or a Buddhist temple was just outside our hostel. So we started skipping around in the world history tome I had downloaded on our tablet, reading about ancient Rome while we were in Italy and about the Australian bushranger Ned Kelly while we were in Sydney and about Al-Qarawiyyin, the world's first library, during our time in Marrakesh. We also began to neglect the math worksheets and instead had Elliot calculate things we were dealing with each day, like exchanging currencies or converting metric measurements. Soon, we were hardly referring to any of the textbooks or curricular standards at all. Like Kim Hoffmeyer, who described her struggle with living up to homeschooling expectations, I became increasingly anxious about Elliot's academic progress. I was torn between forcing him to do something that at least looked like schoolwork and letting him just play and explore wherever we were. Eventually, the latter won out.

It turned out we were not alone. Just as we were abandoning our curricular ambitions, I began to notice a similar story appearing in the blogs I was following online and in interviews with other worldschooling families. Parents who were trying to hold their children to prescribed curricular goals or to a certain number of schooling hours per day often ended up with kids—or themselves—in tears. This was the case for Elaine, a writer and mother from New York who traveled with her two school-aged children. When Elaine and her husband decided to take their family on the road for nine months during her husband's sabbatical, Elaine dutifully administered the curriculum they had selected for the trip. In an article she published on an educational website, Elaine admits that things didn't go to plan. She describes sitting on the patio of a guesthouse with her eight-year-old daughter, both of them crying. Elaine was trying to get her daughter to write an essay, and her daughter was refusing to do it. They were just at the start of their nine-month trip around the world, Elaine recalls, and she had already lost her patience with homeschooling. Every time Elaine sat down with her daughter to "do school," as she puts it, "there was more resistance, and now tears."

Disheartened by her daughter's refusal to cooperate with the home-school agenda, Elaine sought advice online from other worldschooling families. Their unanimous recommendation was to set aside the prede-

termined curriculum, worksheets, and assessments. Instead, they coun-
seled her to follow her child's natural desire to learn and to trust the
process. Above all, they advised her to have confidence that the world
would be "the best classroom one could ever hope for." Encouraged by
other worldschooling parents, Elaine stopped trying to replicate school
on the road. Like so many worldschooling parents who eventually forego
their educational plans and go with the flow, Elaine and I had become
what one mother calls "accidental unschoolers."

Unschooling is a pedagogical philosophy inspired by the work of John
Holt, a teacher, writer, and early proponent of natural, child-led learning. In the 1960s and '70s, long before Ken Robinson's condemnation of
the current education system, Holt published a series of books critiqu-
ing the shortcomings of traditional schools and laying the groundwork
for a radical rethinking of what childhood learning should look like.[29]
According to Holt, children are born with an innate sense of curiosity
and desire to learn, which schools slowly destroy. Given the freedom
to think independently and explore their own interests, children would
learn from their environment what they need to know when they are
ready to learn it.

Holt's philosophy found an eager audience among homeschooling
families in the 1970s, many of whom relied on his books to guide their
free approach to learning. Despite its reputation as a kind of hippie hold-
over from the countercultural movement of the 1960s, unschooling has
made something of a comeback lately. Statistics are hard to come by,
however, researchers estimate that roughly 10 percent of homeschoolers adopt an unschooling approach.[30] Among worldschoolers, a group
already predisposed to experimenting with innovative educational strategies, this pattern appears to be even more pronounced. Nearly half of
the fifty families whose blogs I analyzed explicitly refer to themselves
as unschoolers and many more incorporate unschooling principles to
some extent in their educational approach.

Leah and Richard Reynolds, who have been unschooling their three
boys, first while living in Central America and now while traveling
around the world, describe the approach like this: "Mostly we guide our
boys, help them seek out what interests them, provide the tools, and let
them make their own path." Leah describes what this looks like in the
context of worldschooling:

They swim, play badminton, soccer, build sand castles at the beach, go on hikes, and talk to people of all ages. They speak multiple languages, observe different cultures and religions in practice, and seek out answers to the questions they formulate.

As the family travels from place to place, Leah explains, her sons become curious about where they are going and begin reading about the next destination. They figure out how to deal with problems as they arise and how to make do with the few things they can fit in their backpacks. They learn Spanish through cultural immersion. They practice math by setting budgets and exchanging currency and figuring out time zones. In this sense, Leah and Richard let their sons' interests in the world around them direct their attention and learning.

This is what Ella Tyree, a single mother from the United States who travels with her son Vincent, also discovered. Ella had never heard of unschooling before she started traveling, as she explains on her blog:

> As we started our trip, I had no idea such a thing called "unschooling" even existed. However I noticed [Vincent] was talking about the things we wrap into neat packages within the formal educational system such as geography, sociology, history, economics, mythology, language and second language, literature, math, science within the context of our travels. I sat back one night and realized how brilliant the idea of having the world teach my son was!

Ella has since become a vocal proponent of taking an unschooling approach to worldschooling. Inspired by the work of John Holt, as well as Ivan Illich, Alfie Kohn, and John Taylor Gatto, she writes extensively about the benefits of unschooling on the road, dispensing advice to other parents, hosting guest posts by unschooling worldschoolers, and recording interviews with other traveling families describing how they happened upon unschooling.[31]

Ella's site now hosts a fairly large repository of stories describing how families became "accidental unschoolers." These archives include dozens of examples of travel-inspired moments of "organic" learning. One father describes how experiencing the midnight sun with his kids in the Arctic Circle brought up a discussion of the Earth's rotation around the

Sun, how a chance meeting with a man in a restaurant in Norway led to an in-depth conversation about World War II, and how attending Easter Mass at the Vatican prompted his kids to learn about the history of the Catholic Church. These conversations unfold naturally, he adds. No tests, no exams, just learning for the sake of learning. Parents tell stories of visiting museums and looking at artifacts, exploring caves, volcanoes, and other geological formations, learning about local handicrafts and culinary traditions, and absorbing history through archeological ruins, all evidence that the world can be trusted to spark children's curiosity and promote their natural tendency to learn if parents just let it.

To be clear, not all worldschoolers are unschoolers, and not even all unschooling worldschoolers identify themselves in these terms. Some parents combine some unschooling principles with other more conventional educational practices. Families who know their children will return to formal schooling, for example, are more likely to try to keep their children in step with their school's grade-level curriculum. Some parents refuse to put any labels on their pedagogical practice. And of course, unschooling has its own discontents. Some of the readers who respond to parents' blog posts about unschooling claim that it is essentially a lazy form of "unparenting," while others worry that children with diagnosed learning differences might fall even further behind if their special needs aren't carefully monitored. Still others point out that not all children are self-directed learners. Is watching TV or playing video games all day really educational? The list goes on. How do kids get socialized? What happens when they apply to college and have no transcripts or test scores to their name? How do they learn advanced-level math and science? What if they want to become engineers or chemists or doctors? And of course, without tests or exams, how can parents be confident that children really are acquiring the skills and knowledge they believe follows "naturally" from traveling?

Many parents reply sympathetically to these criticisms, admitting that they, too, were skeptical about unschooling until they tried it. Leah, for example, notes that she thought unschooling seemed crazy, lazy, and neglectful. But now that she has traveled extensively with her sons and experimented with various types of homeschooling, she has "discovered the mind opening experience that is unschooling." And now, she writes, "I can't imagine living my life in anything but this 'extreme' way." Like so many of the accidental unschoolers I encountered in my research, Leah is practically evangelical about the benefits of unschooling her children in the "real world."

Why is unschooling so appealing to so many worldschoolers? If we unpack the "accidental unschooler" narrative a bit more, we see that there are several reasons. To begin with, unschooling fits fairly easily into the logistics of long-term travel. In fact, many families report that they initially adopted an unschooling approach as a way of coping with the practicalities of life on the road. In my family's case, we never did settle into a daily schedule that allowed us to dedicate a certain number of hours per day to math or reading or social studies. Even during those periods when we were settled for a few weeks at a time, we often abandoned regular schoolwork in order to take advantage of other opportunities, like a day trip to the ruins of Volubilis in Morocco or an opportunity to visit the Elephant Nature Park in Chiang Mai. Like many other worldschooling parents, we rationalized our decision to prioritize these hands-on learning opportunities over math worksheets or history textbooks until, eventually, we stopped thinking about the worksheets and textbooks altogether. This shift can feel like such a natural offshoot of traveling that it is quite common for parents to discover only later, as Ella did, that there is actually an extensive literature behind this educational approach.

Another reason for the affinity between unschooling and worldschooling relates to the fact that this literature validates worldschoolers' practical choices with pedagogical reasoning. While many parents describe just knowing, in a visceral way, that travel is profoundly educational, work by John Holt, John Taylor Gatto, and others arms them with the vocabulary and rationale to support their claim that the world is their child's best classroom. One worldschooler posted the following quote, attributed to John Holt, to drive home this point:

> What children need is not new and better curricula but access to more and more of the real world; plenty of time and space to think over their experiences, and to use fantasy and play to make meaning out of them; and advice, road maps, guidebooks, to make it easier for them to get where they want to go (not where we think they ought to go), and to find out what they want to find out.[32]

For worldschooling parents, Holt's mobile metaphors of road maps and guidebooks justify their rejection of structured schooling and formal assessments in favor of learning on the move. Instead of quashing children's spark of curiosity, they argue, unschooling fosters it. Instead of being punished for fidgeting, children are free to move and explore. And instead of delivering top-down content-driven training in subjects children may never use in their "real lives," proponents argue that unschooling teaches children problem-solving skills, develops their sense of independence and self-reliance, and cultivates the intercultural competencies that will enable them to move fluidly in a global economy and diverse world.

The affinity between unschooling and worldschooling is not just practical or pedagogical, however. It is also philosophical. The turn toward unschooling, like the turn toward worldschooling more generally, requires parents to make a paradigm shift in the way they think, not just about learning, but about the role of education in society and in their own lives. According to Leah, unschooling "may be the most powerful form of revolt against an establishment which is terrified of individuals that question authority and refuse to be good little worker bees." This also holds true for unschoolers' attitudes about assessing their children's learning. While many parents in my study expressed intense concerns about high-stakes standardized tests, unschoolers are not categorically against assessment. Nevertheless, they rarely administered tests to their children, claiming instead that they knew what their children were learning because they were so closely attuned to their kids' questions, interests, and curiosity. Inspired by Holt's writings, Leah encourages her readers to "look outside the box for solutions" and to "trust our own abilities as parents to guide our children toward happiness and independence, not to blindly trust the failed government standards that have resulted in anxiety and stress conditioning." After all, what could be better than a bespoke education designed to meet each child's individual needs and monitor each child's unique achievements?

In her comments, Leah touches on underlying concerns that many worldschooling parents share regarding institutional schooling. At the same time, she also highlights some common hopes, such as the desire to raise happy, self-reliant children, a yearning to break out of the box of convention, and the conviction that being out in the world, not confined to the four walls of a classroom, is the best learning environment for a young child. Unschooling thus reflects not just parents' pedagogical leanings, but the kinds of lives they want to live and the kinds of people they want their children to become. In particular, it signals a life philosophy that prioritizes rebellious, self-reliant, free-thinking individualism.

Conclusion

In this chapter, I have explored what motivates parents to worldschool their children, showing how they weigh their concerns about conventional schooling against their confidence in the educational benefits of traveling and unschooling, even in the absence of formal assessment of such learning. This analysis brings to light several important points that I develop further in the chapters that follow. First, it begins to give us some sense of exactly what it is that worldschoolers are looking for in their pursuit of the good life. In their study of why parents choose to homeschool, sociologists Janice Aurini and Scott Davies argue that the defining trait of homeschooling is its "expressive logic."[33] They find that parents choose their children's educational experience not merely on the basis of specific skills or knowledge they want their kids to attain, but as an expression of the parents' cultural values. Key among these values, Aurini and Davies note, is parents' desire to provide a "customized experience to enhance a child's personality, idiosyncratic talents and sense of self."[34] Worldschoolers make a similar calculation. When parents opt to worldschool and unschool their children, they are not making an isolated decision about education; they are making a lifestyle choice. Leah makes this clear when she writes that unschooling "reaches beyond schooling and into our lives on every level." Their decisions about the right academic setting for their children are actually expressing their personal identities, their lifestyle aspirations, and their political and philosophical values about individual freedom.

When worldschooling parents lament standardized testing and conformity in the classroom, institutional control over children's embodied movements, or outdated models of conventional schooling, they are echoing a tension between individual and collective aspirations about the future that has long defined the complicated role of education in society. Should education be treated as a communal project serving shared social and economic interests or as an individual pursuit of self-actualization?[35] As the discussion in this chapter has made clear, worldschoolers land on the individual side of that debate. Indeed, there is very little discussion of the students, classrooms, schools, and communities these families leave behind. From the practicalities of allowing children to follow their own interests rather than a prescribed curriculum, to the pedagogical emphasis on experiential learning in the real world, to the philosophical rationale for rejecting institutional education, unschooling aligns with worldschoolers' vision of a good life defined by individual freedom, autonomy, and self-reliance.

Unschooling's emphasis on personalized, child-centered learning is thus part of a more prevalent celebration of individualism, and even rebellion, in the face of what many worldschoolers perceive as explicit institutional control and implicit social pressures that govern their lives. In this regard, worldschooling is really no different than any other kind of school choice parents make, from conservative religious families choosing to homeschool their children in line with their faith values to upper-class families sending their children to elite prep schools to Silicon Valley entrepreneurs experimenting with microschooling or hackschooling. Whatever else children learn from worldschooling, they learn that their unique needs, talents, and passions merit individual attention. That is the kind of personalized education that will set them up for the future.

This brings us to a second point, which has to do with the way worldschoolers' aspirations for the good life are premised on the future they imagine for their children. To hear the parents in my study describe it, worldschooling and unschooling are oriented toward the future in ways that conventional schooling is not. Whether or not the characterization is deserved, these parents frame institutional schools as hopelessly stuck in an outdated factory model of education that churns out "worker bees," as Leah puts it, whereas worldschooling prepares children for a future that parents imagine as complex, fast-paced, and unpredictable. As Julia points out in her praise of long-term travel, worldschooling teaches things like creativity, flexibility, and problem solving, precisely the kinds of skills kids will need to navigate their future careers in a rapidly changing economy. This is a theme I will return to again and again in the chapters that follow as I describe the various strategies parents use to prepare their children to thrive in this uncertain future.

A third point that I carry forward from the analysis in this chapter relates to the implicit workings of power and privilege that underpin families' educational choices. As is always the case with the decisions parents make about their children's schooling, choosing to worldschool is a matter of class distinction. We know from Annette Lareau's influential study, *Unequal Childhoods*, that a child's experiences and outcomes in school are largely determined by their parents' social class status, not merely because of the financial disparities between poor, working-class, and middle-class families, but because of the different ways these parents convey cultural capital to their children.[36] Her study illustrates in vivid detail the way middle-class cultural dispositions translate into advantages for middle-class children at school, but what about families who reject school entirely?

As decisions about where and how to educate one's child become less a matter of civic engagement in the collective project of public schooling and more a function of one's lifestyle, the very act of rejecting conventional schooling can be read as an expression of cultural capital. Middle-class parents have long critiqued public education in the United States, but to flatly reject conventional schooling—which for a vast majority of poor and underserved children remains their best shot at upward social mobility—requires a significant level of privilege. It is no coincidence that most of the parents in my study are, themselves, products of the traditional education system, and quite a few of them are former classroom teachers. Having gone through the system means that these predominantly white, middle-class parents know how institutional schooling fails students and teachers, but it also means that they are fluent in the dominant discourse of education. They know how to navigate the bureaucratic and legal system that governs compulsory education, they have the necessary resources to guide their children's learning outside of the traditional classroom, and they know what kind of learning matters. Even those families who become unschoolers, whether accidentally or deliberately, express a fairly orthodox list of the kinds of literacies and skills they want their children to master. Leaving school is far easier and carries fewer repercussions for these middle-class families who have the economic, cultural, and social resources to frame their rejection of school as an informed choice and their travels as educational.

What children learn and *how* they learn both align with the broader contours of a worldschooling lifestyle, and in turn the worldschooling lifestyle pivots around the children's education. To put it another way, the way children learn is intimately interwoven with the family's way of life. In the chapters that follow, I argue that, along with education, worldschooling families are making choices—about the kind of work they do, how they parent their children, the sorts of communities they join, and the way they express their citizenship—that line up with their vision of the good life. In the next chapter, I will explain in more detail how recent technological innovations and social transformations have paved the way for worldschooling families to live, work, and learn on the road.

HACKSCHOOLING

In February 2013, Logan LaPlante, a fresh-faced, newly minted teen-ager in a pink knit hat, stood in front of the audience at the University of Nevada and delivered a TED talk titled "Hackschooling Makes Me Happy."[1] In the talk, Logan describes his family's unschooling-inspired approach to his education, which included a combination of online resources, hands-on learning opportunities, and internships with local businesses that allowed him to explore his own interests at his own pace. This, Logan declares, is hackschooling.

Two years later, *Wired* magazine published an article titled "The Te-chies Who Are Hacking Education by Homeschooling Their Kids."[2] The article reports on the rise of "microschools" and "hackerspaces" designed for the homeschooled children of Silicon Valley tech work-ers who find traditional schools rigid and outdated. According to one parent interviewed for the article, "The world is changing. It's looking for people who are creative and entrepreneurial, and that's not going to happen in a system that tells kids what to do all day."

Links to Logan's TED talk and the *Wired* magazine article made the rounds on the worldschooling blogs and discussion forums, which is where I discovered them. Although neither Logan nor the Silicon Valley families were traveling the world, exactly, their stories struck a chord with worldschooling parents, who pointed to them as further proof that our broken education system requires creative solutions.

In his talk, Logan points out that the connotation of "hacking" has shifted from shady images of malevolent computer programmers to something far more positive. "A lot of people think of hackers as geeky computer nerds who live in their parents' basement and spread com-puter viruses," Logan explains from the stage. But he sees the term dif-ferently. "Hackers are innovators. Hackers are people who challenge and change the systems to make them work differently, to make them work better. It's just how they think. It's a mind-set."[3]

"Hacking," together with its cousin buzzword "disrupting," has become the leitmotif for the kind of technology-fueled entrepreneurial logic prized by today's business world. We now use these terms to describe clever techniques that get a job done in an unconventional way or to refer to an ingenious solution, often one that utilizes new technologies to produce better, cheaper, more creative, or more efficient outcomes.[4] This logic is not confined to Silicon Valley startups and corporate boardrooms. It has now spilled over into every aspect of our lives. As Logan observes in his talk, "I'm growing up in a world that needs more people with a hacker mind-set. And not just technology. Everything is up for being hacked. Even education."

Following Logan, many worldschooling parents started adopting the terminology of "hacking" to describe their out-of-the-box approach to educating their children. Among them were Leah and Richard Reynolds, whose family I introduced in chapter 1. On their blog, they posted a link to Logan's talk alongside a few inspirational quotes. One of these quotes, from columnist J. P. Hicks, reads: "The most innovative entrepreneurs of the future will be people who are able to hack the current system and create something new." And another, attributed to inventor Buckminster Fuller, reads: "You never change things by fighting the existing reality. To change something, build a new model that makes the existing model obsolete." For Leah and Richard, and many other parents in my study, quotes like these are a clarion call to hack and disrupt not just institutional education, but the whole taken-for-granted version of success that society has laid out for them. That version is too scripted, too predictable: go to a good college, get a good job, get married, buy a house, have kids, save for retirement, work for thirty years.

And then what?

This is the question that prompts many parents to steer their lives in a new direction. What starts with an impulse to hack their children's education often evolves into a thorough disruption of their middle-class lifestyle. Armed with new technological resources that enable them and their children to work, learn, and live on the road, families like the Reynolds set out to create a more deliberate, more meaningful, and better way of life that is untethered, both physically and existentially, from the plodding status quo.

2

Hack and Disrupt

Making Mobile Lifestyles

If taking your kids out of school to pursue an alternative educational approach sounds extreme, imagine upending your entire life. Imagine selling your house, quitting your job, and abandoning your comfortable suburban lifestyle. Imagine getting rid of almost everything you own and hitting the road with just a faint notion of where you and your kids might be sleeping in a week or a month. Imagine breaking all the rules and writing new ones along the way.

Once the parents in my study started to question the structure and rationale of institutional education, they often found themselves questioning other aspects of their lives, too. They began to wonder why they were enduring long commutes to dull offices, chauffeuring their kids to scheduled activities instead of spending quality time together, or making mortgage payments on houses they were just filling with frivolous stuff. Many of them came to the realization that they had mindlessly fallen into habits of thought and action that were not moving them toward being their best selves or living their happiest lives. It soon dawned on them that the sweeping technological innovations and increasingly globalized economy that were making conventional educational models obsolete were precisely the things that could make a radically different lifestyle possible for their families.

In this chapter, I explore what happens when worldschoolers apply the logics of disruption and hacking not just to their children's educations, but to other aspects of their lives as well. As I argue, many parents approach their new lifestyles not just as an alternative to institutional education, but as an enterprise to be managed, crafted, and capitalized through entrepreneurial techniques. The worldschooling parents I profile in this chapter are primarily those who decided to become online entrepreneurs to fund their families' mobile lifestyles. For these parents, exercising an entrepreneurial mind-set, and cultivating such a mind-set in their children, is a key strategy for navigating their families through the shifting labor conditions of late modernity. In a neoliberal society that encourages—and even requires—individuals to bear the risks of the free market and shoulder the responsibility for their own well-being, adopting an entrepreneurial approach to life is evidence that one has mastered the ability "to be secure with insecurity."[1] As I illustrate below, this entrepreneurial mind-set is not limited to the realm of work, but spills over into the way parents manage their families, relate to their children, and prepare for a precarious future. Rejecting convention to launch a mobile lifestyle, then, is a way of reinventing themselves and their children as entrepreneurs of their own lives.

Not all worldschooling families launch businesses or work online while traveling, but those who do are part of a new wave of tech-savvy, location-independent workers known as "digital nomads." The phenomenon of digital nomadism is one outcome of the shifting arrangements of work fueled by the Internet. The labor landscape now looks very different than it did for previous generations. Jobs that did not exist just two decades ago, from virtual assistants and mobile app developers to travel bloggers, social media influencers, and mobile life coaches, are now common occupations for today's digital nomads.[2] The structure of these jobs is also changing. Instead of long-term employment with a single company, this kind of work tends to be episodic and freelance, based on short-term contracts that are often coordinated via online platforms. In this emerging "gig economy," workers, especially those in the creative, digital, and knowledge industries, are increasingly encouraged to think of themselves and their individual careers as portable start-ups. Which begs the question: If you don't need to stay in a particular place to do your job, why not travel while you work?

This is the world that Tsugio Makimoto and David Manners foresaw in their 1997 book, *Digital Nomad*. In the book, Makimoto and Manners argue that humans are nomadic by nature, and that the Internet, mobile telephony, and other technological advances have rekindled our natural urge to roam. They projected that "for a sharply increasing number of workers—those who are selling individual skills—the new wave of technology will have a big impact because it will make them location-independent."[3] As new technologies unleashed employees from their desks and offices, they argued, people would overwhelmingly opt to work remotely and on the move. As I revisited their book twenty years on, I was struck by how many of the social and technological developments Makimoto and Manners anticipated have come to fruition. The image of a twenty-something traveler working on a laptop from a hammock in some exotic beach locale has become commonplace. But this one exception in Makimoto and Manners's future scenario caught my eye: "There is one group of people for whom the nomadic lifestyle does not seem to loom—parents. Schools are a geographic tie from which it seems impossible to break free."[4] On that point, worldschoolers are proving them wrong.

It is true that worldschoolers are unlike their nomadic lifestyle counterparts in many ways. They are not single, twenty-something digital nomads launching their technology careers from a beachside hammock. Instead, they are predominantly mid-career, middle-aged parents traveling with school-aged children, a demographic profile we have rarely seen in the media or scholarship on digital nomads. However, what many worldschooling parents do share in common with other digital nomads, besides the fact that they tend to be white, well-educated, and technologically savvy, is a vision of the good life that equates mobility with freedom. Like the digital nomads who are "on a quest for holistic freedom,"[5] worldschoolers, too, are explicitly motivated by a desire for freedom. In the previous chapter, we saw how this desire for freedom influenced the decisions parents made about their children's schooling. In this chapter, I explore how it translates into the kind of work they do to fund their traveling lifestyles.

Affluent parents in the Global North are acutely aware of the impact large-scale economic and labor changes will have on their children's futures. In her study of families in the United States, for example, Marianne Cooper interviews one father who acknowledges that the path to a successful career is no longer a matter of going to college, getting a job, and plodding along for decades with the same company. Instead, he recognizes that financial stability "requires 'graduate degrees,' 'entrepreneurship,' and familiarity with a global and diverse world."[6] Whereas the upper-income parents in Cooper's study are anxious about carving out a secure path for their kids within this unpredictable economy, worldschoolers do not see an employment landscape rendered precarious by the shift toward short-term, freelance, and mobile work as a threat to their livelihoods. Instead, the emergence of new kinds of work and more flexible ways of working is an exciting development that grants new freedom in the pursuit of their lifestyle aspirations.

As I noted in the previous chapter, freedom is one of the most important values driving families' pursuit of the worldschooling lifestyle. In her study of location-independent families, many of whom are also worldschoolers, Fabiola Mancinelli describes the way these families express their desire for freedom in terms of freedom *from* and freedom *to*. Drawing on philosopher Isaiah Berlin's two concepts of liberty, she explains that "negative freedom centers on freedom from obstacles or restrictions, whereas positive freedom is the capacity to choose and act accordingly."[7] For traveling families, pursuing the good life requires both. They must liberate themselves from an undesirable lifestyle in order to, as Mancinelli puts it, "celebrate a new beginning: the possibility of a 'different story.'"[8]

This chapter unfolds along similar lines. Using the concepts of hack and disrupt to chart this dual notion of freedom, the chapter begins with the stories worldschoolers tell about abandoning the mundane routine of their previous lives, or what I refer to as disrupting the *doxa*. It then outlines their strategies for hacking the good life. Worldschoolers seek freedom *from* the prescribed routines, consumerist attitudes, and alienating work rhythms of their normal lives. But they also want to exercise the freedom *to* create the lifestyle of their dreams, appealing to physical mobility, new technologies, and entrepreneurial strategies to craft more fulfilling lives for themselves and their families. As we will see, however, what looks like freedom may also be interpreted as a form of acquiescence to the market logic of neoliberal society.

Declaring Independence

Leah and Richard Reynolds open their blog with a story they call the "Moment of Realization." It is a tale of the various incidents and insights that eventually prompted them to completely change their lives. In this story, they describe themselves in their previous lives as "rat racers through and through" who had thoroughly bought into the illusion that the American Dream equated to accumulating material things. By all accounts, they had everything they were supposed to want—a big house, two cars, toys, full-time jobs—but instead of feeling happy, they felt trapped.

By this point, they had taken their eldest son out of school to home-school him and were planning to do the same with their two younger children, but they still felt that something was awry. "We were already sick of the rat race," they write. "Sick of the house that was too big for us and sick of watching society degrade to the point that children and adults alike didn't know the difference between needs and wants." It dawned on them that what they were racing toward was retirement, and that was decades away. They calculated that even if they worked at this pace for the next thirty-five years, they would still feel like they had gotten nowhere. "Talk about a hamster wheel!" they exclaimed on their blog post. As they describe it, this was the "wake-up call" that catalyzed their decision to leave behind their overworked and materialistic lifestyle.[9]

Leah and Richard's origin story is by no means unique. In blog after blog, interview after interview, worldschoolers tell similar stories, usually starting with an epiphany as one or both parents come to realize that the socially acceptable road to success is not necessarily a path to happiness. After the initial moment of realization, the story often moves on to a declaration of independence from the status quo and a proclamation about living more deliberate, vibrant lives. We see this in a post from Jay, a white, middle-class father from the United States who left his salaried job to travel with his family:

> We are getting away from our over-scheduled, overstimulated, suburban-American lifestyle. [. . .] We are escaping the stresses that clouded and weighed down our daily lives. It had become clear that we weren't our happiest selves, that the kids were growing up too quickly, that we needed to change our path and pace.

When Mark, a white father from Texas, realized how quickly life was flying by with his two young sons, he became determined to take a more deliberate path. He writes on his blog:

> I'm sure some of our friends reading this secretly think that we are wrecking our (and our children's) lives. In a sense they are right. Our aim is to

intentionally abandon a life that we have, frankly, both come to realize
is less than what we want for ourselves and our children. I know it is a
cliché, but this isn't a dress rehearsal for our lives: This is it. One shot.

As Mark puts it, the intention is to "wreck" and "abandon" a less-than-
fulfilling lifestyle in exchange for a more deliberately chosen life. He
hopes the journey will set his family on an entirely different path in life,
but figures that even if they end up back where they started, "at least it
will be due to a choice rather than inertia."

Maggie and her husband Trevor came to a similar conclusion, which
prompted them to leave their home in South Africa and travel the world
with their two sons. On her blog, Maggie explains that once she and
Trevor decided to homeschool their children, they realized that they
wanted to live differently on a larger scale. They were tired of what Maggie calls their "rat-race existence" and eager to "live DELIBERATELY."
As Maggie describes it, life was just happening to them in the suburbs
of Johannesburg. She admits that they "wasted a lot of life simply plodding along to the march of the Status Quo." They decided to steer their
lives in a new direction by making "on-purpose choices about where we
want to be."

It may be difficult to muster sympathy for the sense of alienation
these parents express. By all accounts, as predominantly white, upper-
middle-class, and heteronormative families, they occupy a very comfortable corner of the society they claim to loathe. So why are they so
dissatisfied? And what can we understand about life in a neoliberal society by examining their response to this dissatisfaction? Many of us
will be familiar with this particular litany of complaints about the way
everyday life feels in the industrialized societies of the Global North.
Essentially, these stories are an indictment of the sense of acceleration,
fragmentation, and anomie that is the hallmark of so-called modern
progress. The notion of traveling to escape the stresses of modern life
is certainly not new. Tourism is usually only a temporary break in the
normal, daily routine of things, but with worldschooling, the rupture is
somewhat more extreme.[10]

These stories and others like them read like existential crises. It turns
out that questioning the conventional school system is just the beginning of what many worldschoolers describe as a tectonic shift in the way

they think about the taken-for-grantedness of their socially acceptable but unfulfilling lifestyles and how they imagine their possible mobile futures. Instead of "living life by default, watching the years pass and the regrets add up" and spending every free moment wondering if "there was more to life," as one mother writes on her blog, worldschoolers embrace a life philosophy that they describe with phrases such as "no regrets," "carpe diem," and "YOLO" (You Only Live Once). To put it in sociological terms, selling everything, quitting steady jobs, and pulling the kids out of school to travel amounts to a disruption of the *doxa*.

Disrupting the *Doxa*

The term *doxa* comes from French sociologist Pierre Bourdieu, who introduced the concept to indicate the utterly taken-for-granted rules of the social fields we inhabit. Doxa refers to the institutional structures, social expectations, and daily routines that feel so natural as to be beyond question. For many of the worldschoolers in my study, the mortgaged house with a two-car garage in a respectable suburb, the daily commutes to work and school, and the weekends spent shopping in big box stores are all part of the doxa of middle-class life in the Global North. As doxa, the social world seems natural and self-evident rather than what it really is: an arbitrary construction of social arrangements. These tacit, often unconscious, assumptions about the seemingly commonsense arrangements of social life persist through the logic that, as Bourdieu puts it, "what is essential *goes without saying because it comes without saying*."[11] In other words, the doxa is the background hum of social norms against which we live our lives.

Worldschoolers illustrate these unacknowledged norms through a recurring set of metaphors: the rat race, the hamster wheel, the box, and the ticking clock. With these metaphors, worldschoolers declare their desire for freedom, which takes shape as both freedom *from* a frenetic and materialistic life of mindless conformity and the freedom *to* create a slower, more deliberate, and more meaningful life of purposeful mobility. Like Leah and Richard, many worldschooling parents use the images of the hamster wheel and the rat race to capture the sense of monotony, competition, and limitation they associate with their prototypical corporate work lives and modern lifestyles. More to the point, the hamster wheel and the rat race are both suggestive of being on the move but going nowhere. Norman Huang, a father of two young daughters, writes that after ten years of living in the "rat race of the working world [. . .] this is my chance to get off the spinning wheel for a while and venture out of the comforts of my cage." These metaphors imply a kind of imprisonment not just in a routine, but in a mind-set. This mobility is monotonous, not transformative; imposed, not chosen.

Worldschoolers want no part of a good life that boils down to material success. As Leah and Richard describe it, they felt trapped by the exhausting routine of a rat race that had them working full-time jobs just to pay for their house, cars, and toys. They explain in more detail why they rejected the materialism of the American Dream and the "box" it comes in:

> Life should be a collection of experiences, not a collection of shiny trinkets that mean nothing on our deathbeds. If we seek a life outside of the proverbial box—a life of travel, of passion, of adventure, of independence—then societal pressures and college debt become a prison that locks us into a narrow range of experiences. Once we step out of the box and realize this, the floodgates of alternatives to the "normal" path open wide.

Here, Leah and Richard acknowledge the many alternative paths to the good life that are made invisible by a narrowly consumerist definition of success. Like the Reynoldses, many parents write in slightly embarrassed tones about the sheer amount of stuff they have accumulated and confess that an "overweight anchor" of material possessions has prevented them from living a light and free life.

The realization that time is fleeting is another theme that threads through many of these origin stories. Mark laments that "the boys are growing up so fast and it seems to us like we are missing it." His declaration that "It's now or never," and other parents' frequent references to "carpe diem," suggest a sense of urgency. You only live once, children grow up so fast, and dreams can quickly become regrets. On her blog, Astrid Clark, the mother of eleven-year-old twins who were "hurtling into tweenhood," as she puts it, talks of her "desire to slow the clock, quiet the tick tock of the daily grind and expand all of our horizons."

And Maggie writes: "Life is just too damned short and precious to fritter away on meaningless, nothingless-nothing, purposeless CRAP. It is too precious. And too short. And the older I get—the more I realise how precious and short life actually is."

Instead of accepting the realities of daily rhythms, children growing up, and parents growing older as the natural order of the life cycle, parents experience these temporalities as an existential wake-up call. Mark's story continues this sense of urgency:

> You only live once. The phrase is so overused. But if you really stop and think about it, you realize that you had better make the most of life because chances are pretty good that this is the only one you're going to get. [. . .] I know we can't live like there's no tomorrow but we're also not going to live like we know there is.

These parents' desire to free themselves from the accelerated tempo of working life and the anchor of material comforts can be interpreted as an attempt to assert control over the pace of life. Adopting a mobile lifestyle is thus an appealing strategy for regaining what sociologist Judy Wajcman calls "temporal sovereignty," which is a crucial measure of a good life.[12]

These efforts are also evidence of the reflexive techniques that Anthony Giddens associates with late-modern lifestyle projects.[13] In comments like Mark's, we see parents coming to the realization that they can't just live life; they have to create it, cultivate it, and make it amazing—and do the same for their children's lives, too. The ways these families organize their work, time, and material possessions are all deliberate choices in the constitution of a lifestyle of freedom rather than unintended habit.

For Bourdieu, however, doxa is more than an anodyne metaphor for the status quo; it is an exercise in power. It represents a kind of soft discipline that holds people in their proper place in society by making expectations, limits, and hierarchies that are arbitrary seem like self-evident truths. Certain social arrangements, such as socioeconomic class structures, are thus placed beyond question as a way of imposing dominant systems of classification on more vulnerable groups in a society. As he explains, "the established cosmological and political order is perceived not as arbitrary, i.e. as one possible order among others, but as a self-evident and natural order which goes without saying and therefore goes unquestioned."[14] What adds to the power of doxa, Bourdieu tells us, is the fact that other possible truths become unimaginable.

Because doxa is about power, Bourdieu sees it as an object and instrument of class struggle. The dominant classes defend the integrity of doxa in order to legitimize prevailing power hierarchies, while the subjugated classes seek to disrupt the doxa and reveal those power inequalities as invented, not natural, divisions between people. When worldschoolers uproot from the prescribed version of how life should be to deliberately craft a life they desire, they reveal the fragility of the taken-for-granted social order and open up alternative possibilities.

It is important to point out, however, that in the case of worldschooling, the extent of this disruption is limited. The decision to cast off an unfulfilling lifestyle to travel the world is not really a case of the oppressed classes overthrowing the imposition of dominant hierarchies.[15] Worldschoolers may be disrupting the doxa that underpins traditional definitions of middle-class success, but this does not mean they are invested in undoing the doxa of global and class hierarchies from which many of them still benefit, as we will see in more detail later. At best, these disruptions—reclaiming quality family time or emphasizing autonomy over career success, for example—might feel transformative at an individual level, but without necessarily dismantling structural inequalities. In imagining and creating other possible arrangements of social life, then, worldschoolers are not promoting the radical overhaul of an oppressive system, but rather sidestepping the system altogether. In this sense, their disruption of the status quo is more akin to the connotation of disruption as an innovative workaround that upends traditional ways of doing business. This sets the scene for the entrepreneurial strategies I describe in the next section.

Hacking the Good Life

If liberating themselves from the "trap" of their previous lifestyles was the first step in creating a new lifestyle better aligned with worldschoolers' values of autonomy, intentionality, and self-reliance, figuring out how to afford it was the second. Very few of the families in my study were wealthy enough to fund indefinite travel outright. Some were traveling on savings or with proceeds from selling a home or, as I did, during a career sabbatical. However, many families make their traveling lifestyles financially viable by using a variety of creative "hacks."

Affording It

We aren't rich. We can't afford to do this. We couldn't afford
not to.
—Amy, blog post

After the question about children's schooling, the second most frequently asked question worldschoolers get is, "How do you afford it?" It is in response to this question that we see how worldschoolers mobilize the power of the Internet alongside an entrepreneurial logic in their efforts to hack the good life. A case in point is Maggie, who abandoned the status quo of her suburban lifestyle in Johannesburg. Maggie tackles the question of money on her blog's FAQ page, highlighting three strategies for making her family's lifestyle financially sustainable.

First, Maggie and her husband Trevor found ways to earn an income online while traveling. Maggie, a social entrepreneur, and Trevor, a filmmaker and video editor, were already conducting much of their professional work online for clients all over the world. According to Maggie, as long as they had their computers, digital cameras, and an Internet connection, they could continue to work for a geographically dispersed clientele. Without a doubt, the most powerful tool worldschoolers have for hacking their new mobile lifestyles is the Internet. Like Maggie and Trevor, a number of families in my study joined the world of digital nomadism by launching online media and marketing businesses that could be managed from anywhere. Other parents, those with advanced technological skills, took on contract development work that could be completed entirely online. And many found ways to earn an income through their blogs, through freelance teaching and writing gigs, or, as I will describe in more detail later, by offering various intermediary products and services to other worldschooling families.

Second, Maggie notes that she and Trevor recalibrated their approach to spending. Instead of wasting money on things, they decided to invest in their family life and personal happiness: "We want to spend our money on experiences rather than "stuff" . . . and we want to invest in our family and make memories with our kids—rather than purchase more things (that only drain us—and don't make us happy in the long-term)." Here, Maggie aims to rewrite the script of consumer society by defining the good life as an investment in her family's happiness rather than in the accumulation of material goods.

Third, Maggie describes the measures she and Trevor took to minimize the cost of their new lifestyle. Many families find that they can live much more cheaply on the road than they could while shouldering the overhead costs of their stationary middle-class lifestyles. Maggie notes that they effectively did away with all of the costs associated with their "normal" lives: "car repayments, household security, gardener, housekeeper, phone bills, property rates & taxes, school fees, credit card debt, satellite TV. [. . .] By the time we leave—all those expenses will no longer exist." Clearly, Maggie's and Trevor's comfortable lives in suburban Johannesburg left quite a bit of room for downsizing.

Maggie also points out that, thanks to the Internet, she has access to money-saving tips and resources now that she is "connected to a group of over 250 travelling families who have been living like this for many years (they have excellent connections and resources for us— everything from cheap, clean accommodation—to the best markets to shop for food)." What Maggie gleaned from this advice was that traveling "doesn't need to be excessively expensive." With tips from other families, she and Trevor stuck closely to destinations in the Global South where daily expenses are considerably lower. "In places like Central and South America—the cost of living is very reasonable. Same for South East Asia," she writes. With this itinerary, Maggie and her family tapped into something called "geoarbitrage," a popular hack among digital nomads.[16] As Beth Altringer points out in her report on the rise of digital nomadism, "salaries that would allow for a modest existence in top global cities allow for living like royalty in nomad hubs like Indonesia and Thailand."[17] Whether these travelers recognize it or not, the legacy of colonialism coupled with more recent neoliberal economic policies has ensured that desirable destinations in the Global South remain affordable for digital nomads, worldschoolers, and other lifestyle migrants.[18] Being from an industrialized nation with a strong currency usually means global political and economic conditions work in their favor.

The advice worldschoolers offer one another typically boils down to these three strategies: minimize costs, maximize income, invest in returns. If this sounds like a page out of a business textbook, that is no coincidence. The more I studied worldschoolers' stories about abandoning old, entrenched lifestyles in their quest for a better life, the more I noticed the extent to which their stories draw on a language of management and enterprise. We see this language in the points Maggie makes in her post: reducing costs by traveling to inexpensive destinations, tapping into a resource-rich social network, investing in her family rather than in things, and leveraging technology to earn money on the road. The ability to work online enables the physical freedom worldschoolers seek, but it is through becoming entrepreneurs and applying entrepreneurial thinking to their lifestyles that they are also able to achieve the kind of existential freedom they desire. This was certainly the case for worldschoolers who were launching businesses and pursuing self-directed, freelance online work as a source of income, but this language extended beyond the realm of work to frame an entrepreneurial approach toward a traveling lifestyle more generally.

Entrepreneurial Freedom: Beyond Work

Many worldschoolers apply an entrepreneurial mind-set not just to funding their mobile lives, but to lifestyle itself. They adopt the language of enterprise to talk about their children's education, their travels, their families, and their hopes for the future. Mitch, a white father from California, illustrates this conflation between entrepreneurial thinking and his family's new lifestyle, which he refers to as a "start-up." When he and his wife Carolyn exhausted their travel budget after six months on the road, they both quickly realized that they couldn't bear to return to their "normal" and "respectable" lives. "Ever since then," Mitch writes, "we've been figuring out one step at a time how to sustain our lifestyle. At first, it was kind of crazy. We were entrepreneurs and our life was like a start-up company."

Mitch echoes this notion of a start-up life elsewhere on his blog. In one post, he publishes his checklist for living a good life that looks strikingly similar to the strategies Maggie listed on her website. With entries like "minimizing financial commitments" and generating "location-independent income," as well as things like feeding his family's "unquenchable thirst for travel" and "hack-schooling our kids using the world as our classroom," Mitch extends his entrepreneurial impulse beyond financial viability and into investments like his family's travels and the children's education. This is common among many worldschooling parents who express their desire to cultivate their own entrepreneurial skills as part of a larger project of self-reinvention, and to draw out an entrepreneurial mind-set in their kids as well.

Educating Entrepreneurs

If worldschooling is about turning every experience into a "teachable moment," then many of those moments and lessons are dedicated to developing children's entrepreneurial skills. When Maggie's two children, Lola and Isaiah, started a small business designing stationery and selling postcards online, Maggie encouraged their budding entrepreneurialism because she saw it as an opportunity for the two to "learn how to work with money . . . how to budget (so they can print more cards with their profit) . . . to explore and try new things." She writes of their endeavor: "I want them to initiate . . . create . . . invent . . . and problem-solve!" Maggie describes Lola and Isaiah's foray into business as a learning opportunity that promotes the entrepreneurial skills and sensibilities she, and many worldschooling parents, hope to impart to their children.

This became clear to me during an interview with the Harts, a family of four from the United States. Byron and Elsa had left their corporate jobs in the United States and moved to Spain for a couple of years before setting off on their round-the-world journey with their son, Erik, and daughter, Marisa. Erik and Marisa were close in age to Elliot, and while I talked with Byron and Elsa, the kids played together with one of our digital tablets. After a while, they came over to show us what they had been doing: Shooting and editing a short film. "Hey, if they publish that, we get half the royalties," joked Byron. When I pressed him to say more about his response, he explained that he and Elsa had been encouraging both of their children to make and post short videos on the family's travel blog, which had become an important source of income. By helping generate content for the blog, the children were learning useful lessons about running an online business.

Many parents claim that through worldschooling, they are raising children to utilize the resources around them to solve problems, to take the initiative in their own learning, and to see themselves as entrepreneurs. Rose, a mother from Australia, interprets her son Kairo's entrepreneurial thinking as an inevitable result of an unschooling and worldschooling approach. "Learning is a natural consequence of Kairo's life because he is interested & passionate about what he is doing in each moment," she writes on her blog. Because children naturally want to learn, she explains, "they will do what needs to be done to have their needs met. I can see that I'm raising a free-thinking entrepreneur." For Rose, the decision to let Kairo follow his natural curiosity awakens his entrepreneurial resourcefulness.

While Rose cultivates Kairo's entrepreneurial mind-set through unschooling, other parents opt for a more directed approach. In a social media forum for worldschooling families, members often share advice and seek information about conferences, workshops, or online classes that train kids to become entrepreneurs. One worldschooling mother on the forum posted an article she wrote titled "7 Entrepreneurial Skills Kids Can Learn to Lead a Successful Life."[19] In the article, originally published on a life-hacking website, she predicts that her son "will enjoy more success if he develops a solid entrepreneurial mind-set at a young age."

Among the seven skills on her list are self-confidence, resilience, problem solving, creativity, and initiative. It is no coincidence that these entrepreneurial skills align quite closely with the lessons parents hope their children will learn from traveling more generally. Lauren and Edward Falk, two enterprising worldschooling parents who host a blog to support other nomadic families, explain that many entrepreneurial families "desire to travel, have adventures and explore the world" precisely because they "want to raise children who are flexible, risk takers, big dreamers, confident, savvy, humble, holistically-educated, globally-minded, creative, compassionate." In a word: entrepreneurs.

Parents often refer to their travels as an investment in their children's entrepreneurial outlook and future ability to pursue meaningful, self-directed work, free from the constraints of nine-to-five employment. Johanna and Reed Keogh, both self-proclaimed entrepreneurs who escaped the corporate rat race, took their children traveling precisely because they wanted to raise them to be entrepreneurs, not the rule-following employees that conventional schools produce. They write on their blog:

[A]re we raising employees or entrepreneurs? It's entirely different skill sets and I do think that public school is wise to prepare children [for] the real world, which for most of them will include working for other people. But is that our goal? And since we loathed that life so much, and love the freedom of what we're doing now, wouldn't it be sort of hypocritical of us to put our kids through a system that made us unhappy?

In comments like these, it is evident that parents believe children will need entrepreneurial skills like creativity, leadership, and self-reliance not just to weather an uncertain labor market, but to thrive in it. But if worldschooling is an investment in children's future entrepreneurial selves, it is also an investment that positions the family as an enterprise.

Family as Enterprise

In the mobile lifestyle of worldschooling, family life sometimes becomes the object of an entrepreneurial logic that frames parenting as a managerial role and the family as a business. In some cases, this appears through the language of investment, as we see in the way Iris, a worldschooling mother from the UK, responds in an online debate about the wisdom of taking children out of school:

To those that have said we are mortgaging the future of our children, we would say it is quite the opposite! We have made a very calculated and conscious choice to invest fully in our family's overall development, that takes into account every family member's needs and to build something, that is now, after seven years of investment, starting to bear wonderful fruit!

With expressions like "mortgaging" the future or "investing" in the family, some parents draw explicit parallels between businesses and families, arguing that similar management practices can create more productive, more connected, and happier families.[20]

Among these are the Baronettis, a white, middle-class family from California. On his blog, Kyle Baronetti expressly applies such strategies to his family and their worldschooling journey. "Just as organizations and businesses need a mission statement, families also need rules to live by," he claims. And this is especially true on the road, he notes, where in the absence of a daily routine both kids and adults need "something to remind us what our goals are as a family." That "something" is the Baronetti family's round-the-world mission statement, a set of principles that echo entrepreneurial sensibilities like the importance of teamwork, learning from mistakes, and maintaining a positive attitude in the face of adversity.[21]

Kyle continues this theme elsewhere on his blog, publishing posts about the qualities and habits of successful families and explaining how he applies a managerial approach to his own family's effectiveness. Kyle's method is inspired by authors like Stephen Covey, a management consultant best known for his *7 Habits of Highly Effective People* series, and Tim Ferriss, a lifestyle guru famous for his *4-Hour Work Week* book and productivity hacks for entrepreneurs.[22] Kyle explains that he hopes these guiding principles will help his family maximize the educational benefits of their travel experience and the quality of their time together.

Ruth and Adam Abbot, a white couple from the United States, reiterate this advice in a family improvement webinar broadcast on their website. In the inaugural episode of the webinar, Ruth explains that families, like businesses, need a plan:

> We need to make a plan. We'll start a business, and we'll create a business plan, and we'll go into all this detail down to what are we going to put on twitter on this day? [...] But do any of us even have a family plan? Have we thought about it? What is the plan for making my family fantastic? What are the step-by-step things I'm going to do?

She laments that when it comes to family life, "too many people just let their families function on default. It's not planned or structured in a way that's going to help them achieve long-term goals." Instead, she encourages her viewers to "focus" and "do things on purpose" to create the family culture they want for themselves and their children. Ruth's advice positions the family as a goal-oriented corporate entity that can and should be constantly striving to be more productive. From this perspective, the family is an enterprise whose corporate culture and operational structure can be effectively managed to produce responsible and resilient entrepreneurial selves.

Looking to corporate managerial techniques for inspiration, these parents engage in family improvement strategies as an investment in children's future ability to work and flourish in a global economy. In other words, the family itself is folded into a kind of free market rationality. This should hardly be a surprising development in a neoliberal society that seeks to align all realms of life within a market-based framework. The discourse of entrepreneurialism may have had its origins in the world of business, but it has by now "effectively colonized other aspects of the lifeworld, including intimate family relations," as scholars Leanne Eleff and Angela Trethewey argue in their research on modern parenting practices.[23] And where better than within the intimate fold of the family to cultivate children's enterprising habits of risk taking, savvy investing, and above all, self-improvement?

The parenting advice worldschoolers share with one another doesn't always draw on such explicitly managerial language, but in some notable cases it becomes difficult to find the line between family life and enterprise. This is especially true in those instances where advice about parenting and family is both informed by entrepreneurial strategies *and* packaged as a product. The Abbots are a case in point. Ten years ago, when Ruth and Adam Abbot left their jobs in the United States—as a web designer and high school teacher, respectively—and began traveling, they had four small children. Since then, they have welcomed three more children to their family and continued to travel the world.

Ruth and Adam fund their family's mobile lifestyle with income from their online business, a motivational lifestyle-design enterprise that offers "transformational" guided expeditions for youth and families along with online classes and mentoring sessions. Theirs is a one-stop self-help shop for parents who want to live—like the Abbots do—a deliberate lifestyle that combines travel and education with intentional family development and online business. The couple earns income from the guided expeditions, e-books, video podcasts, and webinars that promise to take your family to "the next level," facilitate family bonding, or help launch your online business. They package their lifestyle—a combination of intentional parenting and nomadic entrepreneurialism—as the product they sell. In other words, their lifestyle has become their livelihood.

Lifestyle as Livelihood

Alongside the rise of digital nomadism is the emergence of a cottage industry of companies and consultants ready to help digital nomads navigate their mobile lives. These companies offer virtual hangouts where digital nomads can network with one another; co-working spaces; online platforms that connect digital nomads with freelance jobs; and remote working programs that smooth out the logistics of location independence.[24] Within this cottage industry is a subset of businesses catering to traveling families, with enterprising worldschoolers offering a range of freelance services and products to help other families live the worldschooling lifestyle. Among these are temporary learning communities for worldschooling teenagers, annual summits and conferences held in family-friendly destinations, and intentional co-working communities for mobile families, all of which I describe in more detail in chapter 4. These intermediary services also include curriculum consultants, e-books, print books, online magazines, websites, travel blogs, webinars, and other curated resources to support everything from travel planning to family improvement to lifestyle design to generating an income online. In these cases, enterprising families are both participants in and purveyors of a mobile lifestyle.

Leveraging the Internet and social media, individuals with a bit of entrepreneurial zeal can make a living by commodifying their mobile lifestyle into inspirational and technical know-how for others who want to make a living—and commodify their own mobile lifestyles—in precisely the same way. Lauren and Edward Falk are a good example of this recursive loop between lifestyle and livelihood. The Falks are a family of seven from Canada who spent a year traveling while worldschooling their children. Although they have since returned to a somewhat more settled life in Canada, they continue to promote themselves as location-independent homeschooling entrepreneurs whose mission is to help other families live a similar lifestyle. This is how Lauren and Edward introduce themselves and their website:

> I'm Lauren, (and I'm Edward), and together we run a gamut of businesses, while raising and educating our four kids. If you're anything like us, you're a dreamer, doer, & risk taker. You're audacious, intentional, hard working, and just a little bit irreverent. We created this site so that family-minded entrepreneurs could come together to build a business *and* family life they love.

In this opening paragraph, Lauren and Edward merge their work (running a gamut of businesses) with their identities (as irreverent, risk-taking dreamers) and their family life (as family-minded entrepreneurs raising and educating their kids). The tagline for their site, "Lead an uncommon life: life and business hacks for family-minded entrepreneurs," captures both a sense of disrupting the doxa of a common life and hacking the good life. In keeping with Giddens's notion that modern subjects constitute themselves through reflexive techniques like lifestyle design, the Falks embrace the idea that their lives and identities are projects to be developed and improved. Helping other families engage in this kind of intentional lifestyle design work is, as they put it, their "true passion project."

Among the many businesses Lauren and Edward run is this very travel blog, which not only features stories and photos from the Falk family's travels but is also dedicated to helping other families launch online businesses to fund their own worldschooling journeys. As they describe it:

> We cherish the life that we've been able to design—where work and family and travel and education all mingle into one, and flow together to create this beautiful, uncommon life we're blessed to lead. Sharing our own journey together with all of you—what we've learned, how we've grown, where we've failed, what we're still figuring out, and how we're enjoying the ride—well, this is a dream come true and we're grateful to be a part of this community of outside-the-box dreamers and doers.

With stories, images, and advice from their own entrepreneurial-family-travel-education lifestyle, Lauren and Edward are able to attract an aspirational audience of like-minded entrepreneurial and nomadic families who pay a fee to subscribe to their website, social media feeds, and online newsletter. In other words, what they describe as their "community of outside-the-box dreamers and doers" is actually their target market, one that can be monetized for advertising, affiliate sponsorship, or paid content.

What we see in Lauren's and Edward's enterprise is a lifestyle confluence of travel, education, self-improvement, entrepreneurialism, and family life. As they write on their website: "We're a family that loves to do everything together—work, play, learn, and have incredible adventures. You'll find all of us sharing about our integrated life here." This notion of a "mingled" and "integrated" life suggests that worldschooling is far more than merely an alternative approach to education; it is an altogether alternative lifestyle. What may previously have been distinct domains of social life—home and school; work and leisure; public and private; consumption and production—seamlessly blend to create a worldschooling lifestyle. Travel and learning become a lifestyle; families become enterprises; communities become markets; and leisure becomes a livelihood.

To hear worldschoolers like the Falks describe it, this "mingling" of one's personal, work, and family life is an authentic and exciting way to pursue the freedoms they desire. However, there are two questions that are rarely posed in these conversations. The first is a question about starting conditions that tends to get lost among the stories of bootstrap heroism. Who gets to pick up, take off, and invent a new digital nomad life? I do not think it is a coincidence that many of the entrepreneurial parents in my study, like the broader demographic of digital nomads, tend to be white, well-educated professionals equipped with the technical know-how that makes remote online work possible.[25] The second question that few of these parents ask is this: Integrating one's lifestyle and one's livelihood sounds appealing, but at what cost? What happens when even the most private aspects of our social lives are subjected to the logic of market rationality? What happens to individuals, and to society more generally, when people are expected to become entrepreneurial selves?[26]

Enterprising Parents, Entrepreneurial Kids

As the origin stories I outlined earlier in this chapter suggest, many worldschoolers see themselves as pioneers of a radical new lifestyle movement, which may explain why they accentuate an entrepreneurial streak in their stories. This streak is not unique to worldschoolers, however. Entrepreneurialism has become a prevailing social logic, accompanied by a new form of subjectivity: the entrepreneurial self.[27] The entrepreneurial self is one who constantly seeks self-development and self-improvement through market-based possibilities. Peter Miller and Nikolas Rose explain that individuals act as "entrepreneurs of themselves, seeking to maximize their 'quality of life' through the artful assembly of a 'life-style' put together through the world of goods."[28] In the examples I have discussed, parents seek to improve their family's quality of life not merely through practices of material consumption—on the contrary, they deliberately reject a consumer-oriented lifestyle—but rather by applying entrepreneurial techniques to all aspects of their lives.

According to Michel Foucault, "the stake in all neoliberal analyses is the replacement every time of *homo oeconomicus* as partner of exchange with a *homo oeconomicus* as entrepreneur of himself."[29] In this sense, market rationality is not limited to the realms of production and consumption, but extends "across the entire social field into the deepest crevices of individuality."[30] The mobile lifestyle of worldschooling is a case in point, where parents apply management techniques and a market logic not just in the kind of work they do, but in the way they raise and educate their children, in their philosophies of family togetherness, in their pursuit of lifestyle-aligned work, and in their self-constitution.

The entrepreneurial self is the central protagonist in the drama of contemporary neoliberal life. The rollout of neoliberal economic policies transferring responsibility for personal health, wealth, and well-being away from the state and onto individuals has been accompanied by modes of governance that encourage individuals to be self-sufficient and savvy consumers who assume responsibility for their own welfare by acting as competitive players in a free market landscape. According to neoliberal doctrine, government programs and social services coddle people into complacency, but the free market promotes individual initiative, personal choice, and self-reliance.[31]

As Wanda Vrasti observes, neoliberal policies and ideologies, above all, encourage individuals "to give their lives an entrepreneurial shape."[32] Vrasti acknowledges that in many ways, this shift toward entrepreneurial subjectivities is cause for celebration. After all, as the parents I've profiled in this chapter seem to suggest, an entrepreneurial orientation can lead to more fulfilling, meaningful, and autonomous lives. However, Vrasti also sees it as reason for concern. She explains that, as a model of subject formation, entrepreneurial selfhood "introduces new selection criteria for political membership and economic security that in many ways is more stringent and more ambiguous than ever before."[33] In other words, rather than expanding political participation and economic stability to larger swathes of people, the imperative to be entrepreneurial limits security to those who are willing and able to embrace change, exhibit business sense, and embody self-reliance. Entrepreneurialism is an avenue to economic well-being for those individuals who can already handle the risks and responsibilities of life in an uncertain world.

While these critical accounts have tended to describe the entrepreneurial self in purely individual terms, we can see that the world-schooling parents I've profiled in this chapter extend this logic to their children and families, whom they also see as objects of entrepreneurial management and improvement.[34] They are cultivating not only their own entrepreneurial skills, sensibilities, and subjectivities, but also their children's. They encourage their children to think of themselves as entrepreneurs of their own lives, taking advantage of technology, disrupting "inside-the-box" thinking, and hacking their learning. The "entrepreneurial selves" parents hope to foster are ones who are autonomous, nimble, and willing to question the doxa of modern life. They are also shrewd and self-reliant. As the social safety nets in their home countries deteriorate and economic and social conditions become more uncertain, these entrepreneurial families take matters into their own hands, embracing these uncertain conditions as opportunities for self-reinvention, creativity, and profit. Becoming an entrepreneur is the ultimate lifestyle hack for families committed to principles of freedom, autonomy, and self-reliance.

Conclusion

In this chapter, I have used the concepts of "hack" and "disrupt" to ges-
ture toward the interrelated themes of freedom and entrepreneurialism
that underpin worldschoolers' vision of the good life. These terms capture worldschoolers' desires to upend the preconceived script of how
they should live and instead adopt a more deliberate and meaningful
way of living. The narrative worldschoolers tell is one in which they
declare freedom from the tyrannies of modern life in a consumer society in order to exercise the freedom to craft an alternative lifestyle for
themselves and their children. They contrast a life of mindless habit, one
symbolized by the hamster wheel, the ticking clock, and the anchor of
consumer goods, against a purpose-driven and vibrant life, one that is
intentionally designed to make their families happier and more productive. In this sense, mobility is the ultimate life hack in the pursuit of the
good life.

Drawn from the corporate lexicon of disruptive business models and
productivity hacks, these terms also bring attention to the value worldschoolers place on entrepreneurial thinking.[35] Throughout this chapter,
I have illustrated how worldschoolers become enterprising managers of
their own lives, engaging in freelance digital work and employing hacks
such as geoarbitrage to afford their lifestyles. As I have suggested, this
entrepreneurial logic is not confined to generating income, but reaches
into the way parents raise their children, conduct their family life, and
craft their lives and selves. In some cases, the line between work and lifestyle becomes indistinguishable as social media–savvy worldschoolers
commodify their mobile lifestyles. And as with their children's education, these parents reframe work not as an externally imposed obligation, but as a personal choice in a larger lifestyle project.

To hear worldschoolers describe it, their alternative lifestyle is a radical and risky departure from rigid social norms and their newfound autonomy is a result of their bold and rebellious actions. As I read these
narratives, however, I was struck by the extent to which worldschoolers
acquiesce to the norms of neoliberal ideology. One of neoliberal capitalism's defining features is its ability to saturate all corners of social
life. This is evident in the way many of the entrepreneurial families in
this chapter readily open every aspect of their lives to market rational-

ity, blurring the intimate sphere of family life with the public sphere of production and industry. Things we might have assumed to be private, personal, or merely intrinsically valuable—such as a family's leisure pursuits or parents' relationship with their child or, as I will discuss in chapter 4, friendships and communities—become commodified as lifestyle content. When worldschoolers launch online businesses to fund their travels, and especially when they capitalize on their mobile lifestyles in the form of blogs, webinars, and resources that teach other families how to do the same thing, as we saw with the Falks and the Abbots, they are effectively parlaying their new freedom into a marketable commodity. While there is something appealing about the creativity, autonomy, and self-actualization that worldschoolers describe in these moments, there is also something troubling about the ease with which capitalism reduces human lives and social relations to a consumerist logic.

These stories of entrepreneurial pluck must also be understood against a backdrop of globalization, the rise of the service economy and precarious work, and neoliberal policies that have shifted the public burdens of health care, education, and retirement onto individuals. This new economic order rewards those who are flexible, risk-savvy, and self-reliant. Families at the top end of the socioeconomic ladder, including many of the worldschoolers in my study, are well equipped to grapple with the risks that this new economy throws their way, but even wealthy and middle-class families fret about the very real possibility of their children's downward mobility.[36] Under these conditions, it makes sense that parents should encourage their kids to develop the entrepreneurial skills and sensibilities that will help them hedge against economic insecurity.

To worldschoolers, launching a mobile lifestyle is a creative, and even courageous, workaround to the confining expectations of a respectable middle-class life. But in these stories of worldschoolers commodifying their lifestyles and cultivating their children's entrepreneurial sensibilities, we do not see a radical challenge to the capitalist structures and neoliberal policies that have led to such rampant social and economic insecurity in the first place. Instead, we see families who are vying to position themselves favorably within that uncertainty. In a social and economic landscape that prizes individual freedom, parents who are entrepreneurial and autonomous, kids who are nimble and self-reliant, and families that run like miniature start-ups are well situated to weather the uncertainties wrought by neoliberal rationality.

In this chapter, I have described how parents try to instill entrepreneurial values in their children and, in some cases, even manage their families like enterprises as part of a new lifestyle that embraces freedom, invests in self-reliance, and capitalizes on uncertainty. I return to these themes in the next chapter, where I explore the way worldschoolers navigate risk as part of their parenting philosophy. As we will see, teaching children to embrace risk is yet another strategy for coping with current and future uncertainties.

ARCADE

"Let's try to do something educational for the kids," Sarah's message read. Sarah Milken and her husband David were from the United States and had been traveling for several months with their eight-year-old son, Colin. We happened to be in Buenos Aires, Argentina at the same time, and I was trying to set up a research interview that could double as a playdate for Colin and Elliot. I suggested a children's science museum, but it turned out to be closed for renovations. Maybe a park where the kids could play outside? The forecast promised torrential rain. We finally agreed on the Abasto shopping center. The building, at least, had some historical significance.

Martin, Elliot, and I waited for the Milkens downstairs near the mall's main entrance. The atrium was busy with shoppers escaping the rain, but we found one another among the crowds. We headed upstairs to look for something to eat and a place to talk. The boys were thrilled to discover an enormous arcade just across from the food court and immediately asked if they could go play. "Do you mind if they play while we talk?" I asked Sarah and David, pointing out that we wouldn't be able to see them from the table. "No, not at all," Sarah said. "In fact," she added, "one of the things we love about traveling is how much more independent Colin can be."

Money in hand, the boys ran off to the arcade. We bought some snacks and coffee for ourselves, and as we sat down to talk, I asked Sarah to tell me more about her comment regarding Colin's independence while traveling. She responded with a story about visiting the Legoland resort in Denmark. "When we arrived, all of the kids were getting ready to head out on a scavenger hunt in the park. The hotel said write your room number on their arm and then let them go and enjoy the scavenger hunt without you. It was very clear!" Sarah recounted. "They were running free," David added with a laugh.

Later, in Barcelona, they rented an apartment that was about two blocks away from a playground. Sarah and David would let Colin head down there for an hour or so each day to play with some local friends he had met. "I mean, he's eight. So we don't let him go out without us too much," David said. "I think once he's ten, we'll let him go more." As if on cue, the boys reappeared, this time wanting the digital tablet and more money. David gave Colin another handful of coins but refused to let him take the tablet. "Enough screen time for today," he said, echoing, I imagined, thousands of exasperated parents around the world, myself included.

After the boys ran off again, we talked about how much free rein kids should be given at what age, and how much children's independence had been curtailed in recent decades. "Wasn't there just a story on the worldschooling forum about this kind of thing?" Sarah asked. "About those parents who got in trouble because the ten-year-old boy and his six-year-old sister were just walking home from the park?"

In fact, there had been several such news stories posted on the world-schooling forum and they had generated outrage among the forum members. The story Sarah was referring to involved Alexander and Danielle Meitiv, a couple from Silver Spring, Maryland whose two children were picked up by the police after being spotted walking home unsupervised from a local park. "It seems a little over the top," Sarah sighed.

When the story about the Meitivs broke, the response on world-schooling blogs and social media forums was almost unanimous in its indignation. There was an outpouring of support for the family along with declarations of solidarity from worldschooling parents who similarly let their kids roam free. Several parents referenced Lenore Skenazy's popular book on free-range parenting and linked to an article titled "The Overprotected Kid" published in *The Atlantic* the year before by Hanna Rosin.[1] In it, Rosin describes a free-range playground in Wales where kids can play with tools, old pallets, and fire.

Many parents on the forum made the point that, statistically speaking, kids are safer and require less protection than they did a generation ago. Some of the more conservative commenters used the Meitiv story as an opportunity to express a general distrust of any government intervention in family affairs, warning that the case was taking us down the slippery slope toward things like government control of home education or state-mandated vaccinations. Others rebutted that there are enough horrific cases of child abuse and neglect to justify government protections, but they agreed that calling the cops on the Meitiv kids constituted a collapse of common sense. To many parents, the Meitiv case was disturbing but not surprising. It merely symbolized a culture that coddled children to the point of dysfunction, and it validated their decision to leave the United States to raise their kids on the move and in places where they could cultivate their children's independence and self-reliance without fear of legal repercussions.

Throughout the course of my research, there were several mobile families whose intrepid and highly publicized escapades captured worldschoolers' imaginations. One was the Kaufman family from San Diego, who set off to sail around the world with their two small daughters. The Kaufmans made the news in 2014 when their sailboat, *Rebel Heart*, had to be rescued at sea by the Air National Guard after their youngest daughter became seriously ill. The family returned home to a media maelstrom, with critics accusing them of wasting taxpayer dollars due to their selfish and irresponsible decision to set sail with small children. In her defense, Charlotte Kaufman reminded people that it "is far, far more dangerous to drive every day on the freeway than it is to sail from San Diego to Mexico, or even around the world." Worldschoolers, some who were themselves sailing around the world with their own kids, vocally supported the family's decision to follow the path of adventure despite the risks and the naysayers.

While parents on the online forum rallied around the Meitiv and Kaufman families, they were also inspired by another family who was making a 13,000-mile overland journey from Canada to India. In 2015, Bruce Kirkby, his wife Christine, and their two young sons embarked on a three-month trek to a Himalayan monastery. The family's trip was featured on a Travel Channel program called *Big Crazy Family Adventure*, which in turn was enthusiastically parsed and promoted on the worldschooling discussion forum. Worldschoolers admired Kirkby's bold approach to traveling with kids. They praised his logic that rigorous travel built character, that a bit of dirt boosted kids' immune systems, and that disconnecting from modern technologies fostered family togetherness.

The documentary portrayed the ups and downs of family travel with a generous emphasis on these character-building and family-bonding aspects of the trip, but Kirkby later published an article in *Outside* magazine recounting what happened after the trip. When a racking cough landed him in the hospital with a possible diagnosis of tuberculosis, Kirkby began to question the wisdom of what he calls this "experiment in extreme parenting."[2] Lying in quarantine awaiting the results of his TB test, Kirkby wondered if the trip had exposed his wife and sons to the disease, too. Was it worth it?

In the article, he calculates the relative forces of fear and love, freedom and joy. As he looked through the hospital room window at his sandy-haired son, he writes, "a wave of love swept across me, an immensity of feeling I suspect only a parent knows. Then, on its heels, a fleeting shadow. Fear." In the end, and even before the TB test came back negative, Kirkby reached the conclusion that he would do it all again if it meant teaching his boys to reject fear and embrace the joys of freedom. All he wants is for his sons to be free "to live the life they were meant to live," he writes. "And the only way I know to teach freedom is to live it myself."[3] Worldschoolers make a similar calculation, trading fear for freedom in their own experiments with extreme parenting.

By now, Colin and Elliot had exhausted the last batch of coins and were back at the table, ready for whatever was next on the itinerary. The rain had stopped, and so we all headed out to do a bit of sightseeing in the city, with Colin and Elliot leading the way through the crowded sidewalks and across busy intersections.

3

Fear and Joy

Adventures in Extreme Parenting

Security is mostly a superstition. It does not exist in nature,
nor do the children of men as a whole experience it. Avoiding danger is no safer in the long run than outright exposure. Life is either a daring adventure, or nothing.
—Helen Keller

If you think adventure is dangerous, try routine; it is fatal.
—Paulo Coelho
(Quotes posted on worldschooling blogs)

Early in my research process, and before I started traveling with my
own family, I contacted Julia Porter, the Canadian mother of four whose
story I have recounted in previous chapters. A former teacher and pro-
lific writer, Julia had been traveling and educating her kids on the road
for several years when I got in touch with her. I first found her online,
where she was documenting her family's journey on her popular blog.
The Porters happened to be renting a farmhouse just a few hours' drive
from where we lived, and Julia promptly invited Martin, Elliot, and me
to come up and spend a day with them.

We arrived mid-morning to find the family temporarily settled into
a quaint house on the banks of a scenic river, complete with barns, live-
stock, and snow-covered fields. We shed our coats and snow boots on
the landing as Julia ushered us into a cozy kitchen where she was bak-
ing a ham. She laid out homemade pickles and local cheese to snack on
while we chatted, but before we settled in to talk about travel and education, Julia's youngest two sons invited Elliot to go sledding with them
outside. "That's okay with you, isn't it?" Julia asked. "They have a whole
forest to play in," she said, casually waving her hand toward a frosted

window. Send my young son out into a frozen forest with two older boys I had never met? Why not?

Perhaps seeing the shadow of worry that crossed my face as Elliot climbed back into his snow gear and headed outside, Julia explained that her educational philosophy and her parenting philosophy were cut from the same cloth. Her number one goal was to raise independent, self-reliant adults, which meant practicing a kind of deliberate detachment. This was no helicopter mother, but rather a self-proclaimed "traveling mama," one for whom risk was something to be welcomed, not avoided. As Julia explained, education is not about preparing for a job, but learning how to be the person you are and will become—and learning how to take risks is a key step in that process.

It was during this conversation that I learned that the family's traveling lifestyle, one they had been following for almost seven years at that point, was a testament to Julia's risk-embracing mind-set. When the family launched their trip, it was originally meant to be a one-year sabbatical funded by a healthy nest egg invested in the stock market. Just months into the trip, the stock market crashed. Julia and her husband Scott, a database engineer, found themselves unemployed and their savings decimated. Instead of giving up on their dream of travel, they embraced these events as an opportunity to reinvent themselves and their journey. Scott and Julia revised their travel budget and began to do freelance work for online clients. Instead of one year off from their "normal" lives, their journey became an indefinite way of life for the family.

For other families considering a similar leap, Julia offered the following advice in a blog post:

> If there's one thing I'd like to say to parents who have the dream of traveling with their kids but are afraid to for some reason (education, socialization, relationship issues, whatever) it's that they should step back from the fears and walk forward toward their dreams. [...] Life is meant to be an epic Technicolor adventure, not a greyscale photocopy. If my life broadcasts one message, I hope that's it: Don't be afraid, LIVE your dreams.

Later, in the car on the drive home, I asked Elliot how he had enjoyed the sledding. "It was fun. We had a big crash," he replied. "A big crash?" I prodded. "Yep, we crashed into a tree!" As inspired as I had been by

Julia's approach to parenting, I have to admit that in that moment, as I pictured Elliot flying toward a tree trunk, I had the fleeting thought: "Am I a bad mother?"

* * *

The contemporary world of parenting is a confounding place. Modern parents enjoy unprecedented leeway in deciding how to care for their children and conduct their family life, but they exercise that freedom in an environment where personal experiences, professional advice, and cultural prescriptions often clash. In part, this is because things like expert opinions about the "right" way to raise kids or the legal line between independence and neglect are in constant flux. In a generation, the approach that we now refer to as free-range parenting has gone from a perfectly acceptable way to raise kids in the United States, to a culturally suspect—if not explicitly criminal—way to parent, back to the latest trend in alternative parenting. In this chapter, I explore the way worldschooling parents navigate this shifting cultural landscape by leveraging the risks involved in raising their children on the move.

If the prioritization of freedom over security is the experiment Bruce Kirkby was referring to when he wrote about "extreme parenting," then many worldschoolers are surely near the extreme end of the spectrum as well. But what, exactly, is extreme about it? Is it the duration of the journey, the remoteness of the destination, or the severity of the risks involved? Is it the decision to forego an apparently stable lifestyle in favor of an uncertain but exhilarating one? Is it the willingness to push children out of their comfort zones in order to foster a sense of independence? In the case of worldschooling, it is a combination of all of these factors. In this chapter, I show how worldschoolers frame their mobile lifestyles not just as an exercise in risky living, full of unpredictable events and environments, but also as a strategy for teaching children to live and thrive in a turbulent world.

To call worldschooling an adventure in extreme parenting puts it in opposition to other ways of parenting. The prevailing culture of parenting among upper- and middle-class families in the Global North, and especially in the United States, has curved toward a form of intensive parenting popularly known as "helicopter parenting."[1] In many ways, this approach, with its emphasis on monitoring and shielding children, could not be more different from the Kaufmans' sailing expedition or the Meitivs' free-range parenting or the Kirkby family's perilous journey to the Himalayas, but it is also a form of extreme parenting. The difference is that helicopter parenting is at the *other* extreme, the one that prioritizes safety and protection over freedom and independence. Worldschoolers often position themselves in contrast to helicopter parenting, which they see as a form of fear-based parenting. Instead, their approach to parenting involves rejecting fear and embracing risk as a conduit to the good life they are seeking for themselves and their children. However, as we will see, worldschooling parents are subject to the same external pressures and internal anxieties as their helicopter counterparts. And in many ways, their response is just as intensive.

I begin here by exploring the way worldschoolers invoke joy and fear as the emotional poles around which extreme parenting revolves. As worldschoolers describe it, traveling is an attempt to recapture a sense of joy in parenting and family life. Some of the stories I shared in the previous chapter depicted suburban lifestyles that left parents overworked, distracted, and unable to connect meaningfully with their children. According to worldschoolers, however, a mobile lifestyle offers the opportunity to create a happier and more joyful life together. Getting there, however, also requires engaging with another emotion that shapes contemporary parenting: fear. Traveling the world with kids is a daunting prospect for many of these parents, but facing those fears is crucial for crafting the lives and identities they desire.

To understand the way this tension between joy and fear informs worldschoolers' parenting choices, I situate the discussion within the broader context of the risk society. Worldschoolers and free-range parents are not so different from helicopter parents in the sense that all of these parents are figuring out how to navigate the uncertainties of life in a risk society. However, unlike helicopter parents, who respond to risk by avoiding or mitigating it, worldschoolers tend to see risk as a "good thing." Throughout the rest of the chapter, I detail the way worldschoolers orient themselves and their children toward risk as an opportunity for growth and learning. Worldschoolers frame their own experiments in extreme parenting not just as a way of coping with the immediate risks of global travel, but as a way of preparing their children for the social and economic uncertainties they will encounter in the future.

All Joy and No Fear?

In her 2015 book, *All Joy and No Fun*, Jennifer Senior pinpoints the fundamental paradox of modern parenthood: Children are the source of indescribably profound joy, but parenting requires such a massive outlay of emotional and physical labor that, on a day-to-day level, it doesn't feel like much fun.[2] As she describes it, parenthood may bring unimaginable delights, but it also requires parents to constantly navigate the fears that come with each stage of childhood, from knowing which foods to feed their kids, to selecting the right extracurricular activities, to monitoring their technology use, to worrying about whether their children are becoming moral, sensible, and capable individuals.[3] Making the wrong move on any of these questions can quickly brand a parent as "bad" or "irresponsible," a kind of cultural policing that carries its own set of fears.

Senior argues that this knot of joy, fun, and fear stems from the notion that childhood is a period of innocence and vulnerability, which turns out to be a relatively new idea. Today, Senior explains, parents' lives revolve around their children, but it used to be the other way around. Just two or three generations ago children's lives would have been subject to the economic needs of the family. If they were not working in factories or textile mills, they would have been caring for younger siblings or helping on the family farm. Children were expected to be useful to their parents. In late modern society, however, children are "economically worthless but emotionally priceless," as sociologist Viviana Zelizer puts it.[4] In other words, children have become an emotional rather than an economic investment.

Worldschooling parents derive immense joy from spending time together with their families. The chance to bond with their children, to create treasured memories together, and to rediscover a sense of joy as a family are among the top reasons worldschoolers give for adopting a mobile lifestyle. Ella Tyree, the mother from California who traveled with her son Vincent, reflects on the benefits of traveling together as a family: "We've traveled together, had adventures together, learned together, and enjoyed life together. Through travel, [Vincent] and I have created a bond based on trust, being present for one another, and the joy life has granted us."

This intersection of quality time, togetherness, and joy comes through again and again. Bryce, a mother from the United States who traveled with her son and daughter, reflects in an interview on another world-schooler's blog that the greatest gift she and her husband, Randy, discovered during their journey was time with their children. Away from the scheduling pressures of work, school, and sporting events, she observes, "our kids know that they pretty much have our full attention. [...] What a joy to just BE!" And Elsa Hart, another white mother from the United States, writes that having time to slow down and be present means she and her husband "can appreciate and enjoy each and every moment with our kids. Really watch them learn and grow and think!"

Because children are perceived as an emotional investment, they become closely associated with parents' quality of life. The reason that parents like Ella, Bryce, and Elsa cherish time with their families and delight so fully in their children's growth and development is because, like many modern middle-class parents from the Global North, they are personally and emotionally invested in their children's well-being. This means that the decision to have children and follow-on decisions about how to raise them are no longer bound by traditional models of parenting, but instead have become choices that reflect parents' individual lifestyle aspirations.

Today's parents are free to experiment with different ways of raising and relating to their children. And in the absence of a definitive road map for parenting, they are encouraged to choose from a dizzying array of parenting possibilities that match their lifestyle values: attachment parenting, child-centered parenting, conscious parenting, free-range parenting, holistic parenting, natural parenting, permissive parenting, positive parenting, slow parenting, and the list goes on. This revolving menu du jour of parenting trends is often curated from other cultures that appear to be doing this whole parenting thing better. In 2011, Amy Chua got the ball rolling—and the debates roiling—with her best-selling book, *Battle Hymn of the Tiger Mother*. In this book, Chua promotes strict Chinese parenting principles that instill a strong work ethic, self-confidence, and the competitive edge children will need for a successful future.[5] Pamela Druckerman's book, *Bringing Up Bébé: One American Mother Discovers the Wisdom of French Parenting*, appeared in 2014, tempering the debate with anecdotes from French parents' more laissez-faire approach to raising children. A spate of similar books hit the shelves soon after. In 2016, Jessica Alexander published *The Danish Way of Parenting: What the Happiest People in the World Know About Raising Confident, Capable Kids*, followed by Rina Acosta's 2017 work, *The Happiest Kids in the World: How Dutch Parents Help Their Kids (and Themselves) by Doing Less*, and Sara Zaske's *Achtung Baby! The German Art of Raising Self-Reliant Children* in 2018. Drawing on parenting insights from other cultures but aimed at a predominantly American audience, these books captured a world of anxiety in their subtitles. How on Earth do parents raise happy, self-reliant, confident, and capable kids without exhausting themselves in the process?

Many of these authors position their parenting advice as an antidote to the predominant trend toward what sociologist Sharon Hays originally called "intensive mothering," and which is now popularly known as "helicopter parenting." Among them is Julie Lythcott-Haims, whose 2015 book, *How to Raise an Adult: Break Free of the Overparenting Trap and Prepare Your Kid for Success*, became a bestseller. From her position as a dean of first-year students at Stanford University, Lythcott-Haims watched with growing alarm as parents hovered, covered for, and intervened in their college-aged children's lives while their sons and daughters, for their part, displayed fewer and fewer resources for coping with life's challenges. Lythcott-Haims recognizes that overinvolved parenting is really a function of fear, and it seems that affluent parents have a lot to be afraid of. Fear of "stranger danger," fear of kids making bad choices, fear of what *could* happen, and fear of downward class mobility all drive these parents to monitor and meddle in their kids' lives.

Even among worldschoolers, fear, more than joy, is the emotion that dominates stories about contemporary parenting. But don't get me wrong. On their blogs and in interviews, worldschoolers write and talk frequently about fear, not because they are succumbing to it, but because they see their approach to parenting—and indeed, to life—as an explicit rejection of fear. In this sense, worldschoolers take a decidedly different approach to parenting than their helicoptering counterparts.

Fearlessness

Leah Reynolds describes her fearless approach to parenting in a blog post titled "Changing the Cycle of Fear for Our Children." We met Leah in previous chapters. She is from the United States and travels the world with her husband, Richard, with whom she publishes an extensive travel blog, and their three sons. Leah's story about the cycle of fear starts, as many of these stories do, with the stark contrast between her own much freer childhood and the current state of affairs. She recalls that as a child she took the bus alone, walked by herself to a friend's house, and even talked to strangers sometimes, a confession she punctuates with a "**gasp**" to indicate how unacceptable that would be today. "Flash forward to the present and almost every news story is encouraging fear," she writes, noting that stories about shootings, violence, and kidnappings "keep us scared, worried, and in a constant state of reacting to things through emotion alone."

This culture of fear felt normal to Leah until it dawned on her that fear is actually about control. And just as the state uses fear to control its citizens, so, too, do parents "sometimes use fear to control our children," she explains. "Usually it is in the name of safety but a lot of times it stretches far beyond safety and more towards just getting our children to do what we want." This realization led Leah to rethink her approach to parenting, as she describes on her blog:

> Is it worth scaring our children, making them fearful, and capable of being controlled through their emotions? I don't think that it is. My youngest 2 sons have always been daredevils, scaring people where ever we go. And I am sure some people look at my reaction to the things they do and wonder where I am, why I am not yelling at them.

Leah admits that, like these onlookers, she too is often petrified when she sees her boys climbing cliffs, jumping off rocks, or careening across a busy road on their own.

> But just when I am about to yell, "be careful," I think, what is worse, a broken arm or a crushed spirit? Is it worse overall for their lives to have a cut that needs stitches or to be crippled by fear? A concussion or the feeling that your parents do not believe in you and so the belief in yourself wanes? I[n] my opinion, the latter of each is far worse, especially in the long run.

As Leah sees it, parenting through fear actually makes children more vulnerable and less able to handle life's challenges. She worries that children who are not free to explore on their own, test their own capabilities, climb things, and, yes, fall down, will never become the fullest version of themselves. They will develop a worldview and a sense of self limited by fear. They will be susceptible to being controlled by others. Despite the cuts and bruises they may suffer today, she writes, "in the long run my boys feel confident and proud of themselves where a lot of children have replaced those things with fear and low self-esteem."

The way fear shows up in Leah's story is key to understanding worldschoolers' approach to parenting. In one sense, Leah is focusing on the physical dangers her boys face and her own tolerance for their bruises, stitches, and broken bones. In another sense, she sees fear as an existential obstacle; as something that can fundamentally stunt a child's healthy development into an independent, fully formed self. What might ensure her sons' physical safety in the moment is precisely what threatens their emotional and existential freedom in the long run.

Leah also imagines herself as resisting a broader culture of fear and judgment, one that disciplines parents into safeguarding their children no matter the cost. Her own experience, and the advice she offers to other worldschooling parents, captures the difficult paradox in which they find themselves. It is her job to keep her children safe, she concedes, but safety gained through fear can backfire by making children easier to manipulate, and less safe. Leah navigates the extremes of this spectrum, ultimately choosing freedom over safety, despite the disapproval she perceives from others. It is worth noting, however, that Leah's apparent aloofness is actually quite attentive and calculated. As her story suggests, she is present with her children and carefully monitors their activities, even though she elects not to intervene. In this case, free-range parenting is far from disinterested. Through this kind of deliberate detachment, worldschooling parents remain intensely focused on what kids are doing and how they turn out.

Leah's story about breaking the cycle of fear suggests that being a good parent requires parents to account for risk. For some parents, this means hovering and protecting children from danger; for others, it means encouraging children to take risks. The worldschooling parents in my study tend to fall in the latter category. This is not to say that all worldschoolers subscribe to the same philosophy of parenting, but Leah represents a notable inclination among worldschoolers toward a freer approach to parenting. In this corner of the parenting debates, risk is not a bad thing that needs to be avoided or mitigated, but a good thing that can lead to a life of greater joy.

Parenting in a Risky World

Today's parenting landscape may be suspended between two extremes, with helicoptering at one end and free-range parenting at the other, but both sides are a response to life in a "risk society." The concept of the risk society comes from sociologist Ulrich Beck, who argues that whether or not the world has actually become riskier, it feels like it has. We are more conscious than ever before of the environmental, economic, political, and biological risks that threaten us on a daily basis. According to Beck, decisions about how to live our lives now revolve not just around the statistical probability of negative outcomes, but around the atmosphere of uncertainty those probabilities breed.[6] The hazards of pandemics, rising sea levels, nuclear war, inflation, government corruption, unemployment, online scams, kidnapping, mosquito-borne diseases, and so on are part of our everyday conversations and concerns. Because we are constantly made aware of these risks, we arrange our individual and collective lives around anticipating, avoiding, and coping with them. In other words, risk, more so than any other factor, has become the organizing logic of modern society.

It is no surprise, then, that risk is a defining feature of modern parenting as well. Scholars have found that parents today are more attuned to the potential risks that threaten their children and bear a heightened sense of individual responsibility for dealing with them.[7] In his book, *Paranoid Parenting*, for example, Frank Furedi describes how a constant barrage of media stories about new dangers puts parents on high alert and prompts increasingly intensive vigilance regarding children's whereabouts and well-being. Despite the fact that children are statistically unlikely to be hurt or abducted while playing outside, Furedi argues, the idea that the world is more dangerous and that children are more vulnerable than ever before holds a powerful grip on the public's imagination.[8] Gill Valentine's study of parenting in the United Kingdom bears out Furedi's claim that public space has become a site of fear and "stranger danger" for parents and children.[9] Children's mobility in public spaces, especially if it is unsupervised, is seen as particularly risky, both because it exposes them to dangers farther afield and because it creates an opportunity for children to wreak havoc themselves.[10] The assumption that unchecked mobility is a danger to children and threatens to disrupt family life justifies parents' decisions to keep children close to home.[11]

While Furedi's and Valentine's studies focus on immediate threats, the risk society also imposes a future-oriented worldview on parents. As Ulrich Beck argues, through risk, i.e., something that has not happened yet, "the future somehow determines the present."[12] This is the focus of sociologist Margaret Nelson's book, *Parenting Out of Control*, which reveals how the specter of a risky and uncertain future shapes modern parenting.[13] The professional upper- and middle-class parents in Nelson's study acknowledge that they are primarily worried about the economic and employment uncertainties that their children will face in the future. Driven by a desire to "secure their children's competitive advantage in a world that is marked by increasing anxiety about college acceptance and increasing economic inequality (and perhaps shrinking options for elite status)," parents practice an extremely intensive, even all-consuming, form of oversight to safeguard their children from an elusive and unknowable future.[14] The affluent parents in Marianne Cooper's study expressed a similar fear that their children might lose their footing as "haves" in a society polarized between "haves" and "have-nots." The result, Cooper observes, is that these parents suffer from a "never-resolved anxiety about goalposts that are constantly receding."[15]

These studies and others like them tend to identify helicopter parenting as the most prevalent response to raising children in the risk society, resulting in a generation of "managed" children and "cotton wool" kids.[16] In fact, given such risky conditions, helicopter parenting makes sense. Ulrich Beck and Elisabeth Beck-Gernsheim explain that what looks like parenting "gone mad" is actually a "logical outcome when one interlocks loving a child with feeling responsible for its welfare and being uncertain on how to achieve this."[17] For parents bound by this logic, risk becomes unacceptable. "Modern thinking says parents are responsible for their children and leaves them no margin for mistakes or revisions," Beck and Beck-Gernsheim argue. "[L]oving a child is an asymmetrical arrangement with all the decisions one-sidedly on the parents' shoulders and every mistake likely to interfere with the child's chances in life."[18] The parent-child relationship has become so integral to parents' sense of self and way of life that it is simply too risky to leave children to their own devices.[19] Helicopter parents' intentions are good, and even understandable. After all, given the conflation of children's outcomes with parents' identities, the insecurities of global capitalism, and the unraveling of social safety nets that no longer promise to catch kids when they stumble, parents must be vigilant about their children's futures.

There is another response to parenting in a risky world, however, one that is common among worldschoolers. Rather than intervening in their children's affairs in an effort to minimize risk, worldschoolers see risk as an inevitable and even welcome part of their children's lives. This is not to say that worldschoolers are any less emotionally invested in their children or any less worried about their socioeconomic futures than helicopter parents. But the way they express this emotional investment and plan for the future orients these families toward risk in a very different way. As Leah describes in her story, exposing children to danger and staying out of their way while they explore the world means withstanding a certain level of risk today in order to build kids' tolerance for the uncertainties that face them in the future. From this perspective, teaching children to reject fear, to display resilience in response to failure, or to assert their independence, which are key to the character-building experience of worldschooling, requires facing up to risk rather than avoiding it.

Both the worldschooling and helicopter parenting approaches can be interpreted as a response to upper- and middle-class anxieties about securing children's privilege in a shifting economic landscape. Whereas helicopter parents seek to secure their children's future socioeconomic status by intervening in their schooling, extracurricular activities, and career planning, however, worldschoolers seek to give their kids a competitive advantage by exposing them to risk. In the sections that follow, I detail the strategies worldschooling parents employ to frame risk as a "good thing."

Good Risk

In an age of constant change, we are doing our children a disservice by insulating them from all risk. By imploring them to play it safe, they'll be all thumbs in a future world where only taking risks will be the key to prosperity.
—Comment on Katya's blog

While the notion of good risk may seem counterintuitive in the contemporary landscape of intensive parenting, it is actually quite common in the context of travel and tourism. In tourism studies, scholars have long understood that many tourists, especially adventure travelers, see risk as a pleasurable and desirable experience. Encountering risk is what makes an experience feel authentic and life-affirming.[20] Risk is also seen as a necessary gateway to genuine encounters with others and meaningful experiences of cultural difference.[21] And in the context of tourism, risk-taking is a vital component in tourists' reflexive narratives of self-transformation.[22] In interviews with volunteer tourists, sociologist Amie Matthews found that her respondents believed that "there have to be risks to face, or dangers to survive and obstacles to overcome, if one is to have an authentic adventure and, importantly, to learn and grow from that."[23] As we will see, the risks entailed in travel are part of the identity work, or "pedagogy of the self," that brings out desirable characteristics like confidence and self-reliance.[24]

This is the backdrop against which worldschoolers understand their relationship to risk as both travelers *and* parents. The way they assess risk and help their children engage with and manage it taps into the idea that risk is good for cultivating a particular kind of self and a particular kind of life. More to the point, exposure to risk produces the characteristics of adaptability, resilience, and self-reliance that are so celebrated in a neoliberal capitalist society. I found that worldschoolers framed travel-related risk as a good thing for themselves and their children in four ways: as a way of learning about the world and oneself, as a desirable learning outcome, as a conduit to joy, and as a way of expanding children's worldviews.

Risk as a Way of Learning

The findings of a widely cited study by researchers Ellen Sandseter and Leif Kennair support worldschoolers' claim that children's learning and healthy development require taking risks. After observing and interviewing children on playgrounds in Norway, Sandseter and Kennair distilled six categories of risky play: play with dangerous heights, play with high speed (like skating or skiing), rough-and-tumble play (such as wrestling with other kids), play with dangerous tools (like sharp knives), play near dangerous elements (such as a fire pit or a steep cliff), and walking off alone or getting lost in unfamiliar environments. They explain that these "thrilling experiences" teach children important lessons such as physical and motor skills, object manipulation, and depth and movement perception. Perhaps more important, they argue, exposure to these risks in early childhood "provide[s] a desensitizing or habituating experience" that staves off phobias related to the physical environment—such as a fear of heights—later in life.[25]

In her post about breaking the cycle of fear, Leah writes explicitly about what her sons learn from trying, climbing, jumping, and falling in various physical environments. In response to her post, a reader and fellow worldschooler commented with her own similar story:

Just yesterday at the beach I was given many dirty looks because I let my 22-month-old splash and play in the wavers [sic] without me intervening. He would get knocked down but always got up and if he were to get in real trouble I was close enough to help. I really believe that in order to have self-assured adults that they need this time as kids to explore, figure out gravity and the workings of the world around them. So I will also keep doing what I am doing, dirty looks and all.

This mother affirms her commitment to allowing her children to pursue risky endeavors, despite judgmental looks and comments from other adults, precisely because they were learning about the world around them on their way to becoming self-assured adults.

Allowing children to take these kinds of physical risks is part of worldschoolers' commitment to self-directed, hands-on, experiential learning that I described in chapter 1. Learning about gravity with one's body rather than from a book may require a few falls. This applies to the risks involved in discovering social knowledge and self-knowledge as well. While most of the forms of risky play Sandseter and Kennair identified in their study are related to taking physical risks, like jumping off of rocks or playing in the waves, the last form of play, wandering off alone in an unfamiliar environment, is more about taking social and emotional risks. The lessons children derive from wandering alone include learning about a new environment, of course, but Sandseter and Kennair suggest that it is really a child's "way of exploring their world and becoming at home in it."[26] In this case, the researchers say, exploring undiscovered environments alone seems to be a way for children to "inoculate" themselves from separation anxiety and assert a larger degree of individuality.[27]

Worldschooling parents also recognize the learning potential of allowing their children to explore on their own. In an online conversation on this topic, one worldschooling father posted the following comment:

> The places we [. . .] really enjoyed were the ones where the kids could go and roam outside unsupervised, making up games with what they find and meeting other kids. I really love seeing them be creative and enjoying freedom to explore, a big part in fostering independence and confidence. Society's pressure to constantly supervise your kids in case something happens or to cover someone's back does make me seethe.

In this comment, we see how a form of risky play, unsupervised exploration, is associated not just with physical learning but with developing independence and confidence. Similarly, Ella Tyree, who takes an unschooling approach to her son's education, explains that "life learning is experiential, I must give [my son] permission to make mistakes. This involves taking risks and through these risks, discovering a thing or two about one's self." These comments and others like them reflect worldschoolers' belief that risk is a good, and indeed necessary, avenue through which children learn about the physical world, test their embodied abilities, develop their social and emotional capacities, and learn to feel at home in the world.

Another insight we can draw from these parents' comments is that it is not just children who are learning through risk, but parents too. In her post about fear, Leah goes on to say that letting children take risks is a learning process for parents: "It is possibly the hardest part of parenting," she writes, but it is one of "the most imperative gifts we can give." Leah encourages parents to be aware of how they use fear to control their children, to use risky situations as a chance to "get your own emotions and fears in check," and to "trust your child to make good decisions."

In her account, she describes the emotional labor it takes to break the cycle of fear. If, as sociologist Arlie Hochschild defines it, emotional labor is the work we do to generate or suppress the feelings that a particular social situation calls for, then Leah is doing double duty.[28] She stifles her desire to yell at her boys while also shaking off others' expectations that she *should* display some fear on their behalf. In this sense, she navigates between competing goals (social expectations of conformity and safety versus her children's confidence and independence) and competing audiences ("some people" versus her sons). She resists external social pressure to be a certain kind of parent or to give in to fear and the internal pressure of her own parental impulses by taking a long view that prioritizes her sons' future self-confidence over their short-term physical safety. And she describes all of this as part of the work of learning how to parent through risk.

As challenging as it is to step back from the impulse to hover, Leah writes, "I find children are far more capable if we let them live and learn on their own. They know their capabilities better than we do in most instances." She ends her post by suggesting that parents and children can use risk as a way of learning together how to be—and how to let children be—in the world. "Guide them, but let them cook, let them climb, let them jump, and let them explore and you will see the changes starting," she writes. "The change has to start with you, the parent—but they end with a confident child!"

The risks Leah and other blog commenters describe—cooking alone, climbing, jumping, bike riding, splashing in waves, and just generally being unsupervised (or lightly supervised)—are hardly reckless endeavors. The fact that parents use these small forays into the world as examples of dangerous activities is a testament to just how far the conditioning to a "fear-based mentality," as Leah puts it, has reached. But for Leah, and other worldschooling parents, it is less about the actual physical risks children undertake and more about cultivating a particular mind-set toward risk. They want to cultivate in their children the opposite of a fear-based mentality: a risk-inclined self. In this sense, risk is not just a way of learning, it is also a learning outcome.

Risk as a Learning Outcome

That risk-taking is a learning outcome parents desire for their children is evident in an article Julia Porter published on her blog following the news of the Meitiv case. In the piece, she provocatively suggests that "parenting from a place of fear is what is wrong with America." She writes:

> *Is it our responsibility to protect our children?* Yes. *Do bad things happen?* Yes, but very, very rarely.
> Which is a better response?

- To legislate against children, and parents, cowing them into fear-based submission with police investigations over lovely afternoon walks to the park?
- To cause our children to believe that the world is a frightening place and no one can be trusted?
- To keep our kids so sheltered that they are always safe but then lack independence when "the time comes" for them to brave the real world?

> Or

- To encourage parents to wisely, sanely, carefully prepare those little people to become as independent as they can?
- Teaching them to manage independence in graduated doses, with safety nets in place, so that they learn intelligent risk-benefit analysis, develop the ability to assess a given social situation and make a wise choice, and grow slowly and naturally into their ability to handle what the world throws at them?

In this critique, Julia discusses knowing how to conduct risk-benefit analyses as important learning outcomes of a free-range approach to parenting. In chapter 1, I suggested that one of the critiques world-schooling parents direct toward conventional schooling and traditional curricula is that they reward conformity and therefore tend to reproduce compliant, inside-the-box thinkers. Their critique of helicopter parenting turns on similar anxieties. They argue that this parenting approach produces children who are more frightened, less independent, and completely unprepared to face the world. Worldschooling parents, on the other hand, want their children to think freely, to challenge assumptions, and to try new things. More to the point, they want their children to *want* to try new things.

For worldschoolers, risk is intimately tied to a "pedagogy of the self." Sociologists Majid Yar and Rodanthi Tzanelli introduce the concept of the pedagogy of the self in their analysis of simulated kidnappings as a new kind of tourist experience.[29] In trying to understand what is so appealing about faking a traumatic event like being kidnapped, they find that participants come away from the experience having faced their fears and with a renewed sense of "mental toughness," "survival capacity," and "exhilaration and omnipotence."[30] The pedagogy of the self is a form of physical and psychological identity work that uses encounters with risk to bring about these outcomes of enhanced confidence and capability.

Yar and Tzanelli suggest that diving headfirst into risky situations—even in the midst of a risk-conscious society that publicly and constantly reminds us to do everything we can to *avoid* risks—may be a way to cope with "the sense of existential dread in the face of proliferating uncertainty" that pervades contemporary society.[31] Living with daily exposure to such uncertainty requires us to learn how to become confident, resilient selves, able to generate creative responses to inhospitable conditions in order to live well in a risk society. In other words, we must learn to "manage the vicissitudes and challenges of a shifting and unpredictable lifeworld."[32] This is the goal of the pedagogy of the self. Worldschooling parents want to train their children to be creative and resilient, risk-savvy and fearless. And that training includes equipping them with the skills, knowledge, and sensibilities they need to capitalize on risk.

It is no coincidence that these learning outcomes of good risk align with the kind of entrepreneurial spirit parents want to instill in their children. An entrepreneurial self is not a victim of circumstance, but an agent of change who embraces risk as an opportunity. In this sense, the lessons children learn from taking "good risks" are about preparing them for the future; in another sense, though, they are about learning how to live in the moment.

Risk as a Conduit to Joy

In the case of worldschooling, allowing children to undertake physical and social risks is part of a much larger risk-taking exercise: leaving behind stable, familiar lives to pursue an unpredictable mobile lifestyle. As worldschoolers navigate the tensions between fear, on the one hand, and their desire to live a freer, more joyful lifestyle, on the other, they frame risk and fear as crucibles that must be faced in order to come out on the other side in a world of new possibilities and potential joy. As I described in the previous chapter, embracing the financial, social, and physical risks of a traveling lifestyle—in spite of fear—is part of a necessary ritual that initiates worldschoolers into a new, more joyful lifestyle.

Comments weighing the risk-to-reward ratios are common on worldschooling blogs, such as Mark's observation that "No great thing was ever done without some risk," or Kim's note that "It's a risky ride, but it's worth it—living your life according to who you really are simply takes a little intention." And Kevin Clark, looking back on his family's year of worldschooling, enthuses in one of his final blog posts:

> The last year has been one of the best in our lives. It was all about change, risk, adventure, and discovery. We took, what some would consider, a crazy leap of faith, and although we can't say what the future holds, we wouldn't change a thing. The experiences that we've had in the last year are more than most could hope for in a lifetime. We are amazed and so grateful when we look back on it all.

When worldschoolers write about handling their worries over family travel, they often point to the happiness and freedom that lie on the other side, thereby convincing themselves, perhaps, as much as their readers, that facing fear is what eventually leads to joy.

We see this logic in a blog post by Hallie, a mother of two girls from Australia, published while she was still in the planning phase of her family's trip. In her post, she admits that "it can become scary and daunting, thinking about all that can go wrong and trying to think of ways to avoid it." But more clearly than the potential pitfalls of traveling, Hallie also recognizes the risk of bucking social convention. She writes, "As much as dropping everything and setting off gallivanting around the world sounds dreamy, it is also against all the rules for what a pair of responsible adults or good parents are supposed to do, especially when they are not financially set up." She concedes that what she and her husband *should* be doing is pursuing respectable careers and paying off their house note, explaining that:

> As much as I don't seem to have a problem with curbing societal pressures, what we are doing is risky and [my husband] and I have had late night chats about our fears and doubts. So no, we are not constantly buzzing about like silly, grinning with glee idiots. Not constantly, but most of the time, because shortly after we feel the gnawing teeth of doubt eating at our excitement, all we have to say to each other is "But this is what we always dreamed of" and we get the clarity we need.

Hallie points to a number of vague fears in terms of what "can go wrong" on the trip, but her post ends with a twist that takes Hallie through fear and toward happiness. When she and her husband face their doubts, she says, they become joyful, "silly, grinning with glee idiots."

Julia Porter has something to say about fear, as well, in an interview she gave for another worldschooler's blog. In response to a request for advice about overcoming fears, she writes that fear can have a "crippling" effect on people's lives. "Far too many people are paralyzed and settling for marginal existence instead of living their real dreams because of their fears," she says. "There is no easy way through." If mobility is normally associated with risk, Julia turns this around to equate fear with paralysis. She continues her post, encouraging others not to be stopped by fear:

> The reality is that life is better than we could have possibly imagined, and we wouldn't go back to our previous "normal" (which we were very happy in, by the way) for anything. We've had the great joy of living an adventure with our children through their middle childhood that reads like a storybook. It has been worth every bit of struggle, difficulty, uncer-

tainty and night spent awake and sweating through the present trouble. If your dream is hanging out there in front of you, I encourage you, with my whole heart, to chase it. Assess the fears, take the risks and give this life your absolute all. We only get one chance at greatness and one chance at our dreams. Today is your day.

The fact that the Porters' savings evaporated in the financial recession just months after they started traveling gives Julia's advice a substantial amount of credibility. Here is a woman whose worst fears did materialize, and yet she continues to encourage other families to chase their dreams anyway. By overcoming their fears, she and her husband were able to experience what Julia calls "the great joy" of a worldschooling lifestyle.

Worldschoolers also argue that *not* following your dreams is even riskier than following them. This is how Angela Carter, a mother of two daughters and a son from the United States, justifies her family's trip while on the road:

> SO, ARE WE RECKLESS? To some, absolutely. Could it have gone absolutely wrong? You bet. And it still could. But know this, it could have gone wrong had we stayed on the most risk-free path in life. People lose their jobs and their houses all the time, even while playing it safe.

In her post, Angela poses another rhetorical question to her readers: "Have you ever gotten to the point where: you didn't fear the consequences of taking the risk as much as you did the thought of staying in the same place, not changing, just existing?" She explains that she and her husband realized that they were no longer willing to trade decades of working, commuting, nine-to-five misery waiting for the promised "utopia" of retirement. Similar to the stories of disruption I presented in chapter 2, Angela says that she "experienced an awakening of sorts." She writes: "I started making life decisions as if I truly believed the following statement: Life is much less about taking the safest road, and more about, well, just living the hell out of it."

A corollary to the argument that the safe path doesn't necessarily lead to happiness is the argument that the safe path isn't necessarily safe, either. As worldschoolers point out, risk is relative and it is everywhere.

This means that, rather than cocooning children in a protective bubble, they should expand their exposure to the wider world.

Expanding Children's Risky Worlds

In her study of children and public spaces, geographer Gill Valentine introduces the concept of "geographies of fear" to describe the way media representations map risk onto specific spaces, in particular designating private space as safer and public space as more dangerous for children, even when statistical evidence shows the opposite to be true. Through the media, parents become more aware of the potential risks around them, with the paradoxical result, Valentine argues, that "as parents' knowledge of the world expands, so their children's experiences of their local worlds contract."[33] In fact, further studies have shown that children's sphere of independent play has narrowed significantly in recent decades, a development Valentine attributes to the increasing "terror talk" in the media and among parents.[34]

Like the parents in Valentine's research, worldschoolers are also processing media messages about a world of trouble, which are often conveyed to them by concerned friends or worried family members, by mapping them onto a geography of fear. But theirs is an alternative geography of fear, one in which children's worlds are expanded despite, or because of, risk. In a somewhat paradoxical move, worldschoolers tend to diminish risk by extending it to a global scale. They do this by rebutting claims that it isn't safe to travel abroad not by responding that it *is* safe, but by countering that home is just as unsafe as anywhere else.

I found this to be a common trope on worldschooling blogs and in interviews with worldschooling parents. One mother posted the following comment on a social media forum for worldschooling parents:

> The idea that we can control everything that happens in our kids [sic] lives by making all of the "right" and "safe" choices is a feather that frightened parents hold in their trunks like Dumbo did when he was afraid to take the leap and believe he could fly. Bad things happen. Statistically speaking, they happen at home. [. . .] Things of a tragic nature happen, very rarely, when traveling too. You do your best, as a parent, to minimize risk, and you move on, just like at home.

And when another mother published a blog entry on fear and travel, one of her readers posted the following response:

> I think that LIVING is dangerous no matter where you are. Bad events are random, be it car crashes or earthquakes. You can't worry about lightning [strikes], so you just go with your big bad self. Absorb the beauty every day and roll with the punches, around the world or right at home. :)

Some parents give this trope a slightly different twist by referring to the dangers of a sedentary life, like the one many young people in the United States and other westernized societies lead. Obesity, diet-related illnesses, lack of physical exercise, loneliness, and an overabundance of screen time are all proposed as physical and mental health risks associated with staying home. Comments like these disrupt the intertwined assumptions that home is naturally safe and mobility is inherently dangerous. The message these parents are sending is that there are risks everywhere, which means avoiding them is impossible.

While preparing for her family's trip, Amy Devon Sharp, a Canadian writer who traveled around the world for a year with her husband, Mac, and their two sons who were ten and twelve at the time, began to reflect on how the news about natural disasters and political events abroad was hitting closer and closer to home. The Sharps, who were the only black family in my study sample, were in the process of planning their itinerary when Amy wrote in a pensive blog post: "Now that we're only months away from setting off the very thing that I wanted—to feel more connected to the planet—is raising fears in me that are surprising." She goes on to list a variety of incidents that seemed to line up with her family's proposed itinerary: "The bomb at the Moscow airport is closer now that the city is on our shortlist. The floods in Australia more real now that we could literally have been there when it happened. Turmoil in Northern Africa jumps off the newspaper page as we chat about whether or not to stop in Morocco and Egypt." These are no longer remote dangers threatening other people in other places. The incidents feel close and real now that these places are on her family's travel horizon.

Amy also hopes that exposure to risk will expand her and her children's scope of empathy. She continues:

The fear comes, but so does the increased compassion. I feel closer to the people who are living through the difficult times, more impressed by their strength and grace and in the end, when I weigh it all, it doesn't make me not want to go, it makes me want to go even more. And when the opening lines of a disaster story tell me that "luckily no Canadians were injured" I find myself increasingly annoyed. Does the death toll become less important because "We" are ok?

It's not what I want my kids to grow up believing. I am taking my children with me on a trip around the world. It will be fun and exciting and scary. We will stop in at amusement parks and orphanages. We will lie on the beach and we will worry crossing borders. If I do my job right we will all come back better human beings than we left as. And, even though stepping out the front door will be as scary as it will be exciting, I wouldn't change it for anything.

Annoyed by news reports that seem to give weight to disasters elsewhere only if they have impacted fellow Canadians, Amy feels herself becoming more connected to, and therefore impacted by the events in, other places. For Amy, this is an uncomfortable but desirable development since one of her explicit goals for the trip is to foster her boys' sense of global citizenship. As she writes, she wants her children to become "better human beings." If expanding their worldview and their sense of compassion means expanding their geography of risk, then that is a price she is willing to pay.

In their response to the risks of world travel, these worldschooling parents are not conveying the message that the world beyond one's home country is safe, but rather acknowledging that tragic events happen everywhere, even when you stay put. They claim that risk is an inescapable reality, which means that if children are to develop their sense of global citizenship, assert their independence, and feel at home in the world, they need to learn how to live with risk, wherever they are. In a global risk society, avoiding risk is a futile endeavor. The key to survival, worldschoolers would argue, is to embrace risk as an opportunity to learn and grow.

Cultivated Independence

Children's independence is often a casualty in the trade-off parents make between safety and freedom. In the United States, a society steeped in an ethos of rugged individualism, parenting has historically been an exercise in encouraging children's independence. In recent decades, this tendency has reversed. Young children's range of unsupervised activity has been vastly reduced due to parental fear, and middle-class parents often over-function for their teenage and even college-aged children. According to historian Paula Fass, this unprecedented level of monitoring and intervention in children's lives reveals a deeper concern about how to balance children's independence with securing their future success in a culture that demands both. She acknowledges that parents are deeply worried about "how the commitment to independence can be maintained in a highly competitive world without sacrificing the success that parents want for their children."[35] They are fearful that if children become too dependent, they will be unable to function in an adult world, but given too much free rein, they will make bad choices with long-lasting ramifications. Under these conditions, Fass explains, many parents appear to be willing to sacrifice their children's independence today to ensure their educational and economic security in the future.

Worldschooling parents see this trade-off in somewhat different terms. They claim that raising independent and self-reliant individuals is a primary goal of their parenting philosophy and the key to their children's future success. Learning how to handle the conditions of risk and uncertainty is vital to the reflexive project of self-making in contemporary society.[36] Therefore, instead of curbing children's independence, worldschoolers deliberately foster it.

Simona Knox, a single mother from the UK who traveled for several years with her son Leo, was starkly aware of this responsibility. On her blog, she describes an episode in which she watches ten-year-old Leo step off the side of the boat for an open water dive. She recalls the "slightly eerie feeling watching him descend the guideline into the murky blue and disappear." What Simona was feeling wasn't exactly worry, she explains, since she knew Leo had mastered the necessary diving skills and was a sensible child who would stay with his instructor. It was, she writes, more of "a sharp realisation of his ever-growing independence.

And a very visual realisation, too, as he disappeared from view." As Simona reflects on the moment, she writes:

> From birth, parenting's about enabling your children to go out into the world independently, do their own thing, manage their own risk. It is, and I'm aware how paradoxical this sounds given we spend so much time together now, a constant process of letting go. And watching your little boy disappear into the depths feels a very firm reminder of how much more letting go there is to come.

In this passage, Simona captures a central contradiction of worldschooling family life: Parents want to teach children to manage their own risks and become independent, but they do so in the context of an extraordinarily intensive pattern of family togetherness.

What Simona describes is an approach to parenting that I call "cultivated independence." The concept of cultivated independence is inspired by Annette Lareau's work on the way race, class, and gender intersect with parenting styles. As I explained in the introduction to this book, Lareau's ethnographic research with a dozen families across the class spectrum revealed two distinct approaches to parenting: the accomplishment of natural growth, a style practiced primarily by poor and working-class parents, and concerted cultivation, an approach more common among middle-class parents.[37] To put it in Lareau's terms, worldschoolers may adopt the techniques of natural growth, such as allowing children to learn and play free of adult direction, but they maintain an ethos of concerted cultivation by deliberately fostering children's independence.

As Simona's post suggests, there is something inherently paradoxical about cultivated independence. For one thing, it rests on the idea that children's independence cannot be left to its own devices but must be actively developed. Just as worldschoolers intentionally design their lifestyles, so, too, do they take a concerted approach to developing their children's autonomy as free-thinking individuals. For another, worldschooling parents cultivate their children's independence within the context of tight-knit, full-time family togetherness.

Families on the move are usually together all day, every day, living in small spaces like caravans, hotel rooms, or rented apartments. Worldschoolers write frequently about the constant, inescapable togetherness that is a fundamental feature of life on the road. In these stories, they present family togetherness as both a nuisance and a source of the joy they hoped to feel in their new lives. Judy and Dean Willis, a white couple from Oregon who traveled with their eight-year-old daughter Addie, capture both the joy and the frustration of family togetherness in respective blog posts on the topic of family togetherness. In her post, Judy writes:

> I am sure the real question that everyone really wants to know about, are you sick of each other yet? Overall, No! I wake up most days thinking that I really love our life and appreciate the time that we have together. True, some days I do get frustrated or annoyed with [Dean] or [Addie] over something trivial [. . .] Despite the annoyances, it is all worth it. I am enjoying the fact that I have so much time to spend with my family. I feel like I am learning so much more about [Addie] and [Dean] that I never knew. [. . .] I also feel that my relationship with [Dean] has deepened and that we [are] much more intimate with each other.

Dean weighs in later with his own perspective on how traveling brought his family closer. He observes that during their four months on the road, his relationship with Judy has been "enriched" and writes that "being together 24 hours a day, 7 days a week, has helped us become closer." As for their daughter Addie, however, he admits, "I often feel bad that she is stuck with us all the time and has no friends to play with."

In these posts, Judy and Dean echo the ambivalent emotions many worldschoolers experience about their new pattern of family life. Judy enjoys the intimacy of their time together, but also admits to feelings of frustration and annoyance. In his blog post, Dean worries about Addie being "stuck" with her parents all the time, but still prefers their full-time family life to their previous working life that pulled them in different directions.[38] Perhaps more important, though, both Judy and Dean frame this family togetherness as the backdrop against which their daughter learns to exercise her independence. Judy explains that being together all the time allows her to really observe their daughter. She writes: "I love seeing how [Addie] thinks, how she learns and what makes her laugh. I also love watching her become increasingly independent of us." Dean echoes this sentiment in his post:

Watching [Addie] become more independent and confident every day is something every parent should experience. Before we left I would see [Addie] for less than an hour in the morning and for about 2 hours in the evening on weekdays. Our weekends were filled with racing around to different lessons for [Addie] and doing house projects and it left no time to ask her how she was feeling and what her hopes and dreams were. Homeschooling her everyday gives me instant feedback about what she knows and what she needs to learn.

It is striking that both parents use the topic of family togetherness to highlight Addie's burgeoning independence, which they are able to detect precisely because they are now so attuned to her learning style, her hopes and dreams, and her daily behaviors.[39] By remaining closely focused on Addie, they are able to anticipate and facilitate these sparks of independence.

To return to an observation I made earlier, worldschoolers claim to reject the intensive parenting style associated with helicopter parenting, yet they are undertaking a form of parenting—one in which they serve as their children's full-time teachers and parents and co-learners in the context of almost constant family togetherness—that could hardly be more involved or resource-intensive for the parent(s). In fact, unlike many professional middle-class families, worldschooling families outsource almost none of the work of caring for or educating their children.[40] In many ways, they are more present, more conscious, and more attuned to their children at every turn, not least of all so that they can take advantage of opportunities to develop their children's sense of independence. It is precisely this constant attention that makes Dean and Judy aware of their daughter's increasing independence and puts them in a position to develop it even further.

In a culture that holds parents responsible for children's outcomes, there is a narrow sliver of moral high ground between the extremes of being overinvolved, as we see with helicopter parenting, and negligent, as Alexander and Danielle Meitiv discovered. Worldschoolers' strategy of cultivated independence navigates this moral landscape by deliberately fostering their children's independence, but by doing so with what looks like a laissez-faire approach to raising their children. It may appear that worldschoolers give their children free rein to explore and experience the world around them, and to a large extent they do, but that freedom and the lessons it teaches are carefully curated and choreographed by parents. The natural learning and free play that worldschooled children enjoy is not unsupervised, as it is in Lareau's examples of the accomplishment of natural growth. As we saw in Leah's and other parents' comments earlier, worldschooling parents are not *not* paying attention; they are actually very closely attuned to their children's physical and emotional states. But, as Leah describes, they may be suppressing their impulse to intervene in a concerted effort to let their kids learn their own lessons. In other words, parents calibrate their supervision to allow risk-taking to do its work.

Conclusion

In this chapter, I have described how worldschoolers parent their children through a complex nexus of joy, fear, risk, and independence. From the "leap of faith" they take in abandoning their stable lives to the dangerous play that teaches children about the world and themselves, worldschoolers court risk as part of their mobile lives and identities. The epiphanies and aspirations that lead parents to embrace a worldschooling lifestyle in the first place—a realization that time is precious and fleeting, a yearning for freedom, a willingness to take big risks, and a desire for a family that is untethered but tight-knit—all funnel into the way parents relate to and rear their children. In their quest to become free, worldly, risk-taking, entrepreneurial, self-sufficient adventurers who "live the hell out of life," as Angela puts it, worldschoolers adopt a philosophy of life *and* a philosophy of parenting that promote the same qualities in their children.

With parents' identities and lifestyles wrapped up in their children's lives, it makes sense that worldschoolers' choices about parenting should become intertwined with other lifestyle choices as well. For example, parents adopt educational philosophies and strategies, like unschooling, that align with their parenting philosophies, like free-range parenting. They play overlapping roles for their children as parents, teachers, co-learners, and travel companions. They take on freelance or online work specifically to fund and facilitate the kind of mobile lifestyle that affords the family bonding they desire. And in many cases, the work they do capitalizes on the intersection of their family life with their travel life-style, as I explained in the previous chapter.

The good life worldschoolers seek is thus intimately tied up with being a "good parent." In a broader cultural context, the decisions worldschool-ers make about how to assess and manage risk are weighted with moral significance and policed according to an implicit code of conduct for good parenting. The Meitiv case, for example, illustrates a moral climate in which concerned neighbors, other parents, and government agencies feel compelled to enforce intensive parenting, while free-range parents like Alexander and Danielle Meitiv feel compelled to resist it. Sociologist Ellie Lee points out that contemporary parenting is profoundly shaped by this conflation of risk and morality. In a context where morality func-tions through proxies of risk, she argues, "good" parents are those who are vigilant about anticipating dangers, avoiding harm, and "keeping us safe."[41] She traces this development to two causes. First, parenting has be-come a more individualized practice. Raising children is no longer seen as a communal duty, but rather as a responsibility that falls to individual parents. Second, there has also been an increase in "parental determin-ism." By this, Lee means that we believe that what parents do today de-termines a child's future happiness, healthiness, and well-being.[42] Given that everyday life in a risk society is perceived to be rife with potential hazards, parental action needs to be focused on assessing and managing those risks. And the moral stakes—children's future happiness, health, productivity, and well-being—could hardly be higher.

This moralization of risk may explain why worldschoolers go to such lengths to put a positive spin on risk. The work worldschooling parents do to frame risk as a good thing is really about framing their extreme parenting and lifestyle choices as morally justifiable. As they describe it, their refusal to be paralyzed by fear and their willingness to face risk head on could be interpreted as even *more* responsible than other par-ents' avoidance of it. Furthermore, worldschoolers' embrace of risk is a strategic move made with their children's future character and capaci-ties in mind. As Margaret Nelson notes in her critique of intensive par-enting, one of the things that stokes parental anxiety is not knowing what the future holds in store or how, precisely, to prepare children for that future. In the case of helicopter parenting, upper- and middle-class parents' intervention in their children's lives is a fairly transparent effort to guarantee their children's future socioeconomic standing. With worldschoolers, the aim may be similar, but the strategy is more nuanced. Whereas the parents in Nelson's study attempt to stave off risk, worldschooling parents embrace it as a way for a child to become a self-reliant, globally minded, and enterprising self with the emotional and intellectual capacity to handle uncertainty. Despite worldschoolers' explicit rejection of helicopter parenting, they practice an equally—if not more—intensive form of parenting, with the same goal of securing their children's future prospects.

Wherever parents land on this spectrum, then, their choices about risk, safety, and freedom reflect a certain level of privilege. What I have described in this chapter, as in previous chapters, should be understood against a backdrop of racial and class privilege. Take, for example, the comparison to the forms of parenting outlined in Annette Lareau's book, *Unequal Childhoods*. Even though worldschoolers prefer to think of themselves as giving their children plenty of leeway for independent exploration, their approach to parenting is closer to the concerted cultivation practiced by the middle-class parents in Lareau's study than the accomplishment of natural growth favored by poor and working-class families. The key difference relates to choice. The poor and working-class families Lareau describes often adopted a laissez-faire approach to child rearing, not out of choice, but out of economic necessity. Worldschoolers, most of whom come from a middle-class background, exercise far more choice around the kinds of risks their children experience and how they respond to them.

When placed in historical and global context, the terminology of "extreme parenting" even seems a bit hyperbolic. Every day, thousands of parents make similar calculations about how to balance risk and security in their children's lives. We don't call it "helicopter" or "free-range" parenting when Syrian refugees bundle their children into unseaworthy boats to flee war zones, when immigrants take their children across borders to escape economic or environmental catastrophe, or when poor working parents are forced to leave their children unsupervised while they go to their jobs. These parents are also taking extreme measures to make a better life for their families, but they do so without the trendy labels. Worldschoolers, on the other hand, are able to position themselves and their children not as victims of risk, but as beneficiaries of it.

Those worldschoolers who lean toward the risk-taking, free-range extreme of the parenting continuum align their approach to parenting with their aspirations to live a free, mobile, and independent lifestyle. Embracing risk and encouraging independence, but within the fold of family togetherness, is a key mechanism for achieving that lifestyle. It is also an important strategy for preparing their children for an uncertain future. By framing risk as a "pedagogy of the self" through which children can assert their independence, cultivate their global subjectivities, and make themselves at home in the world, these parents teach their children to be competent risk-takers who know how to leverage uncertainty to their advantage.

HOMESICK-ISH

Argentina was the last stop on our family's journey around the world. After being on the road for nearly seven months, we planned to spend the remaining several weeks of our trip in Buenos Aires. We had rented a small Airbnb apartment and were looking forward to shopping for our own groceries, cooking for ourselves, doing our laundry, and exploring the neighborhood. For the first week, though, we kept busy with a mandatory to-do list of tourist sights: Casa Rosada, Recoleta Cemetery, the Museo Evita, La Bombonera football stadium in the famous La Boca district, the watery neighborhoods of Tigre.

As our pace eventually slowed, however, we found ourselves feeling a little unsettled. A few episodes contributed to this feeling of disorientation. For one thing, Argentina was experiencing staggering hyperinflation. Our Airbnb host had tried diligently to explain the intricacies of the local economy, the legacy of postcolonialism and failed neoliberal policies, and the recent recession, but the complexity of it all turned out to be more than she could cover while pointing out how to use the hot water heater and start the washing machine. As she handed over the key, she also slipped us a nondescript business card with a phone number on it. "Just change your money with this guy and you'll be fine," she said.

On our second night there, long after dark, we were roused by a commotion outside. We stepped onto our apartment's small balcony to see the neighbors around us and in the nearby buildings, also on their balconies, holding up kitchen pots and banging on them with spoons. We hadn't turned on the television or read any news since arriving, so we had no idea what was happening or why. Only later did we discover that the clamor, a form of protest known as *cacerolazo*, had been prompted by news that a prominent prosecutor had apparently committed suicide just days after accusing a powerful politician of a cover-up. The timing was suspicious, to say the least, hence the outpouring of frustration. We watched and listened for a while before going back to bed, confused and clueless.

As visitors, we were unaware of the particular economic and political uncertainties that Porteños were dealing with on a daily basis, but we sensed the anxiety all the same. At the time, I wrote in my journal: "I think, for the first time on this trip, we're all feeling a little homesick. Even though this is the homiest situation we've had so far!" I then added: "A month is a long time to be a tourist in a place, but not enough time to forge any real connections or deep understandings." To be honest, I wasn't entirely sure what kinds of connections I wanted to feel. Was I hoping to deepen my understanding of the economic and political situation? Did I want to become friends with the neighbors? Or feel like a local, as Airbnb's marketing had promised? In reality, I felt detached from it all. And, I'll confess, it was kind of a pleasant detachment.

Anthropologist Bianca C. Williams describes a similar experience in her work on emotional transnationalism. In her ethnography, *The Pursuit of Happiness*, she follows a group of African American women who traveled frequently and repeatedly from the United States to spend time in Jamaica. On the one hand, these women wanted to feel a sense of kinship and belonging during their holidays in Jamaica, a paradise that offered them respite from the racist and sexist environments they regularly endured back in the United States. On the other hand, they didn't necessarily want to get too close or know too much about Jamaica's own race, gender, and class politics. As much as these women wanted an authentic experience of Jamaica beyond the tourist façade, they also wanted Jamaica to retain its sense of mystery. "If one stays too long, or engages in too many real-life, everyday discussions," Williams explains, "then the fantasy begins to fade away, like sand running quickly to the other side of the hourglass."[1] Knowing too much about the cultural politics of the place might shatter the fantasy or burden the women with unwanted obligations. Perhaps this is what we were also feeling. A desire to feel connected, to belong, but not necessarily to become tied up in someone else's social and political drama. After all, we were just passing through.

Either way, it was clear that we were not going to get through this journey emotionally unscathed. I didn't expect us to feel homesick at the end of our trip or in Buenos Aires, but there you have it. I suspect Elliot felt it most intensely. Back home, his friends had just returned to school after the winter break. Meanwhile, here he was walking around in a strange city in the summer heat while his friends messaged him with updates about snow days. Everything was fine, but everything felt just a little off.

We coped with these feelings in a number of ways that I recognized well from my previous research with long-term backpackers.[2] We carved out daily routines to feel, as Elliot put it, "more grounded." We walked to the same park every morning, shopped at the same grocery store each afternoon, and ran mundane errands like going to the post office or getting a haircut. We became regulars at a nearby restaurant where Elliot always ordered what he called a "real" hamburger: a beef patty topped with a slice of ham. We found a local bakery that catered to his allergies with gluten-free empanadas and pastries. Small comforts.

I tried to impose a bit more structure on our days by enrolling Elliot in Spanish classes. Someone on the worldschooling forum had recommended a language school just a short walk from our apartment and I had hoped we might meet other kids at the school. When we showed up, however, Elliot was the only one in the class. He would breeze through his worksheets and then build precarious little houses with the Spanish flashcards while I stumbled through basic conversations with Camila, his infinitely patient teacher.

Even though we were spending enormous amounts of time together as a family, I sensed that we were all also feeling a bit lonely. Elliot was missing his friends, so I went online to try to arrange some meetings with other families. The results were mixed. I was able to set up a play-date, which doubled as a research interview, with the Milkens, another worldschooling family who happened to be in Buenos Aires at the same time. I messaged with another mother on the forum, but it turned out that her family wasn't due to arrive in Buenos Aires until the day after we were scheduled to leave. I contacted a friend in New York who put us in touch with one of her work colleagues, a woman based in the Buenos Aires office who had three sons around Elliot's age. She kindly invited us to her home, where the kids spent a boisterous afternoon playing in the backyard. And I reached out to a fellow academic at the university in Buenos Aires, someone I knew well through email but had never met in person. It turned out he was on sabbatical, too, spending the semester in Boston, of all places. Mobile life is all about these (missed) connections, I thought.

From interviewing worldschoolers and reading their blogs, I knew that there was a particular emotional arc to family travel. It's not necessarily a roller coaster of constant ups and downs, but more like an unpredictable welling up of emotions and shifting intensities of excitement, boredom, loneliness. I was also beginning to understand that my impulse to reach out and the brief times we had with other families reflected common themes as well. Like us, many of the worldschooling families in my study wanted to feel connected, but not tethered. They wanted to feel a sense of belonging that wasn't suffocating. They wanted to craft meaningful social lives that fit in with the freedom and independence of their mobile lifestyles.

4

Rebel and Tribe

Life Politics in a Mobile Community

There's a tribe of rebels out there . . . slowly connecting . . .
and finding one another. And every time we do . . . we're
flooded with a sense of relief: *I'm not alone on this journey—
There are others who think—and feel—like me.*
—Maggie, blog post

Up to this point, I have described the good life worldschoolers seek in
terms of individual autonomy, personal choice, and self-actualization.
On their blogs, parents are quick to remind readers that worldschooling
is a deeply personal decision, one based on each family's unique needs,
desires, and circumstances. Jan, a mother from Australia, describes it
thus: "The thing about dreams is that they are incredibly personal. The
important part is knowing what *your* dream is, and chasing it." Johanna,
a mother from the United States, makes a similar point on her blog.
"Each family has their approach, and every child has their own needs,"
she writes. "I have no idea what's best *for everyone*, I'm just trying to figure out what's best *for us*." As the traditional prescriptions for how to live
one's life give way to a panoply of personal choices, worldschoolers turn
to individual dreams and desires for guidance. Which is why I became
curious when the worldschooling parents in my study started talking
about things like "tribes" and "community."

Alongside worldschoolers' quest for individual freedom, I discovered
an equally powerful desire to connect and belong. Many parents quickly
realized that the good life was not so good alone, so they sought out
a sense of community with others. But not just *any* others. Maggie, a
mother of two from South Africa whom I introduced in previous chapters, writes about her desire to connect with "like-minded people." She
expresses a sense of relief at finding what she calls her "tribe of rebels,"

an itinerant community of dream-following individuals. "I'm not alone. We're not alone," she writes: "There are many path-forgers out there, too. Pioneers. Machete-wielding Questioners and Truth-Seekers."

This chapter explores the paradox captured in Maggie's phrase "tribe of rebels." It examines how this tension between individual freedom and communal belonging gives shape and meaning to worldschoolers' search for the good life. The chapter starts by taking account of the emotional costs of a mobile lifestyle. A life of untethered mobility is exhilarating, but this lifestyle can be isolating, not least of all for teenagers who crave interaction with peers. It then details how parents help their children cope with loneliness and homesickness by developing new forms of community to anchor them in the midst of mobility. Children learn how to make and maintain friendships on the move and how to have a fulfilling social life with people who cycle in and out of one another's orbits. Perhaps more important, they learn how to create and sustain social relationships on their own terms, positioning community as a carefully curated component of their mobile lifestyle.

The Emotional Costs of a Mobile Lifestyle

"I just feel loosey goosey because I don't where home is anymore." Ten-year-old Daisy Cormier was suffering from a bout of homesickness and her mother, Holly, was blogging about it. She titled the post "Roots and Wings." "I know that feeling well," Holly writes. "I'd say I've had that feeling for years; [. . .] it's become quite a companion in my life." The Cormiers were in Australia, spending a few weeks at a friend's house in suburban Sydney, before heading on to Southeast Asia. Holly explains that in Sydney they had been indulging in the small comforts of quotidian routines, the "roots" part of her blog post's title, before spreading their "wings" again to backpack through Thailand. Something about all this made Daisy homesick. To console her, Holly gave her a hug and reminded her that "every now and then we just have down, homesick-ish moments." Part of the problem, Holly acknowledges, is that the family doesn't have a home to return to. They are completely free to go and live anywhere in the world. "Which sounds invigorating," Holly adds, "but really, it's not. It's like when you have too many toothpaste choices at the store, so you just stand there, flummoxed."

There is nothing more exhilarating than escaping from the stale routines of everyday life to chase adventure around the world, but the mobile lifestyle worldschoolers escape *to* comes with emotional costs as well, among them homesickness, loneliness, and rootlessness. We can attribute many of these troubles to the logistics of long-term travel. It is to be expected that children and their parents will experience pangs of nostalgia for a familiar home, miss dear friends, or feel at loose ends in a new place.[1] In response, parents who have left their stable lives behind for a life on the road often wax poetic on their blogs about the benefits of community and the enduring human desire to connect with others. As I listened to worldschoolers' accounts of coping with homesickness and loneliness on the road, however, I began to wonder to what extent these feelings were merely an effect of traveling and to what extent they were emblematic of the broader emotional contours of late modernity.

Sociologists Anthony Elliott and Charles Lemert have argued that late modernity has an emotional dark side, a melancholia they attribute to the new individualism that has taken hold in a post-traditional world. They suggest that in a society where we are utterly free to make and re-make our lives, individualism becomes woven into the social fabric itself:

> In the so-called do-it-yourself society, we are now all entrepreneurs of our own lives. What is unmistakable about the rise of individualist culture, in which constant risk-taking and an obsessive preoccupation with flexibility rules, is that individuals must continually strive to be more efficient, faster, leaner, inventive and self-actualizing than they were previously— not sporadically, but day-in day-out.[2]

Knowing what we do about worldschoolers' values, Elliott and Lemert's description of the contemporary world as a "do-it-yourself society" will sound familiar. From what we have seen so far, worldschoolers are among the rebels who embrace entrepreneurial risk-taking and flexibility in their own projects of lifestyle design and self-reinvention. They are the free-thinking cosmopolitans who dare to experiment with their children's educations, their parenting techniques, their careers, and their lifestyles, and they do so primarily in the private realm of family life rather than as part of a larger collective.

In such a world, where there are endless possibilities for self-reinvention but few moments of solidarity or belonging, Elliott and Lemert warn that "the lures and seductions of individualism reign supreme."[3] These seductions of individualism come at a steep price, however, and Elliott and Lemert's diagnosis of the emotional costs is a bleak one. They argue that the new individualism has "set the stage for a unique cultural constellation of anguish, anxiety, fear, disappointment and dread."[4] The free-floating anxiety of endless choice has left people increasingly isolated, adrift, and empty in a world that no longer anchors their sense of self or their relationships in solid ground. In his book, *The Global Soul*, travel writer Pico Iyer similarly describes the angst suffered by jetsetters, expatriates, and immigrants who live their lives in between cultures, consuming the fruits of cosmopolitan globalization but rooting nowhere.[5] Grappling with the potentially liberating and potentially catastrophic possibilities of this new individualism leaves people flummoxed by choice, as Holly puts it. They are deprived of a solid mooring, existentially (if not actually) homeless, and in a constant state of uncertainty. The global soul is a lonely soul.

The free-wheeling, joy-filled lifestyle of worldschooling is not exempt from the feelings of loneliness and isolation that plague late modern subjects. Tucked between the adventure narratives and stories of familial bliss are confessions of homesick children, sullen teenagers, and exasperated parents dealing with the emotional travails of a mobile lifestyle. As one mother confesses to the readers of her blog: "Sometimes we are homesick, sometimes we are tired of our own company, sometimes we are scared, [and] sometimes we really miss our family and friends." In the stories below, we will see how children's homesickness and loneliness expose the emotional limitations of mobile individualism, but we will also see how parents devise new strategies for coping with the emotional consequences of life on the road.

Homesick and Friendsick

Sometimes homesickness hits after families have been on the road for a while, but sometimes it sets in before they have even left. This was the case for Kyle Baronetti's six-year-old daughter. Kyle and his wife were packing up the last few items in their southern California home when their daughter proclaimed, "I'm not ready." Then she started crying. Kyle recounts the story on his blog:

> This was a mix of being overtired, over hungry and the fact that 12 hours earlier, she had to say goodbye to her cat and beloved friend. While we packed the house the kids played with our neighbors and their very close friends. Our daughter was realizing this would be the last of that for a year.

Kyle tried unsuccessfully to distract his daughter with promises of the adventures that await: "Ostriches, Kangaroos and Balinese beach shacks." Only a hug from her mother could calm her down.

Dismayed, Kyle says that he wanted his daughter to "toughen up." But he also confesses that he, too, has mixed emotions about the trip. "The stress of moving, leaving your job, your routine, going into the unknown and in our case, even underdeveloped parts of the world has been giving me an ulcer lately," he writes. What Kyle really wants to get across to his daughter is that these feelings of homesickness and insecurity are normal, but must be overcome. He concludes his blog post by saying that "security, as comfortable and anxiety relieving as it is, does not always mean we are growing and experiencing."

Sari Frisch's three children were older than Kyle's daughter when Sari and her husband Ben, both originally from Israel, decided to leave home to travel with their family. According to Sari, whose story was featured in an interview on a fellow worldschooler's blog, the children were initially enthusiastic about the journey, but as they approached their teenage years, they became increasingly resistant to their parents' travel plans. They had entered what Sari called a period of "teenage turmoil." And so, three years into their dream nomadic life, Sari and Ben decided to end the journey to appease their children's homesickness. As Sari explains it, "Ben and I would do this forever, but our kids have different dreams." She writes:

> Though they love traveling, make great friends everywhere we go and still gush over the coolest things they've seen and done, they want a normal childhood. They dream of going to school, birthday parties, and hanging out with their cousins and grandparents. And because we deeply value

those relationships and realize that all five of us need to lead fulfilling lives, we're hanging up our backpacks next summer.

Sari recognizes that as her kids grow, they "have different dreams," ones that revolve around a rooted, predictable lifestyle with extended family—quite the opposite of the carefree worldschooling lifestyle she and Ben have created for them.

Children's homesickness is a problem for parents who envision the good life as a life of mobile individualism. Sari and Ben, for example, were devastated to discover that their teenage children were no longer onboard for their nomadic lifestyle. Even parents who are empathetic to their children's distress often respond to homesickness with some version of Kyle's attitude that kids should "toughen up." In the industrialized societies of the Global North, homesickness is perceived as a sign of weakness and immaturity and it can be an obstacle to the kind of self-actualization worldschooling parents desire for themselves and their children.[6] As Kyle's comments suggest, parents see security and familiarity as impediments to "growing and experiencing," and especially to developing the kind of global characteristics parents hope for in their children.

This intersection between children's homesickness and their global subjectivities appears quite often in worldschoolers' blogs. Six months into her family's journey, Hallie reflected on her family's newfound homelessness and its effects on her, her husband, and their three children. She starts by listing the ways her children have changed and grown after 200 days on the road "without a home and living off a backpack":

> How are we going? We are proficient at living on the road—we can sleep anywhere [. . .] we can pack-up in nought [sic] point five seconds [. . .] we can chat to anybody about anything. [T]he kids' imaginary plays often include pretend guesthouses or hostels, as well as world travel and citizenship; not much fazes us in general.

Hallie is happy to see her children developing into world citizens. However, she also observes that this new lifestyle is hard on her oldest daughter, Michaela, who seems to "have hit a wall of some kind." Hallie concludes that "Michaela is feeling friendsick more often, I am still tired. I think we are all a bit edgy lately and probably ready for a bit of a break."

Marie Franco is a white mother from the United States who traveled with her husband, Charles, and their five children. She reports a similar difficulty with her oldest daughter, who was fourteen when they started traveling. When asked in an interview on a fellow worldschooler's blog whether she had any doubts about choosing a mobile lifestyle, she admits that one of her fears is that her "children won't be able to develop friendships as we move about." Marie was already finding this to be true for her oldest daughter, explaining that they "just haven't met many other families with older children that she's clicked with, so I think she feels a bit lonely at times." Nevertheless, Marie does not see her daughter's loneliness as a reason to stop traveling:

> As for doubts about whether to travel or not, absolutely not! We're 100% convinced that THIS is what we need to be doing as a family. Our family goal when we began this journey was to help our children (and ourselves) be comfortable around people who are very different than they are so they can build genuine relationships with them [. . .] We've seen how easy it is for our younger children to connect with other children and are filled with such joy to see how they can love others unconditionally and so easily.

From Marie's perspective, her daughter's loneliness is offset by the other, more worldly, feelings her children are developing, such as the ability to forge genuine relationships and feel unconditional love for people who are very different from them.

This was the case for Dean Willis's nine-year-old daughter, Addie, who also found it difficult to connect with children her age while on the road. On his blog, Dean laments that:

> Although our list of UNESCO World Heritage Sites that we have visited is impressive and we have visited places we have always dreamt of seeing, it hasn't always been fun. [O]ur 9-year old daughter, [Addie], really misses her friends and gets really lonely at times and wishes she had friends her own age to play with.

Homesickness seems to be the price to pay for exposing children first-hand to World Heritage Sites or for cultivating global sensibilities such as adaptability, flexibility, awareness of world citizenship, and comfort with cultural difference. These stories also reveal that children bear the emotional hazards of traveling differently than their parents. What parents experience as liberating, children may experience as a profound loss. In Kyle Baronetti's case, the complex set of hopes, dreams, and worries he harbors about the trip are quite distinct from his six-year-old daughter's feelings. At the point of departure, she is more upset about leaving dear friends, beloved pets, and a familiar environment.

To be precise, many of the passages above are not describing homesickness in terms of nostalgia for a particular house or place, but rather in terms of what Hallie calls "friendsickness," a desire for social connection with peers. Daisy, Michaela, and Addie are relatively young—all under ten years old—but once worldschooling children enter their teenage years, like Sari and Ben's children or like Marie's fourteen-year-old daughter, the sense of loneliness intensifies. In fact, this phase of "teenage turmoil" has generated many blog posts and social media threads as parents commiserate and share advice online when their teenagers complain of being lonely and, in some cases, ask to stop traveling.

Lonely and Unrooted

The experiences of two families, both of whom I introduced in previous chapters, illustrate a familiar story of loneliness among worldschooling teenagers. First is Ella Tyree, a single mother from California who left a stressful career in public relations to travel with her son Vincent, who was nine years old at the time. The idea was that the pair would travel for one year, push reset on their hectic lives, and then return to what they hoped would be a calmer and more deliberate lifestyle in the United States. Instead, they kept traveling for a second year. Then a third. Now, almost ten years later, they are still traveling. However, their mobile lifestyle almost came to an end when Vincent turned fourteen and experienced what Ella describes as an alarming mood shift. Normally carefree and loving, Vincent became agitated and despondent, snapping at his mother when he wasn't ignoring her. While Ella chalked much of this up to the hormonal upheavals of puberty, she was concerned and asked Vincent about his change in behavior. Vincent confessed to feeling unhappy, depressed, alone, and isolated. After they talked, Ella questioned whether their lifestyle was causing Vincent's feeling of isolation, as she explains in a blog post:

> Our lifestyle isn't easy. It certainly isn't [. . .] easy being an outsider in a foreign country. Nor is it easy being a teenager. [. . .] Knowing how intense feelings of loneliness can be, I have assured Vincent he is not alone. I get it. I really do. [. . .] But still, I wonder, has our lifestyle, [and] Vincent's unschooling journey helped lead to further isolation?

Ella concluded that a traveling lifestyle may have intensified Vincent's loneliness, but ultimately defends their decision to travel, arguing that teenagers suffer emotional ups and downs no matter where they are.

We find a similar story with Simona Knox, also a single mother and a writer from the UK, who traveled with her son Leo. When Leo turned thirteen, he began to express a similar desire to settle down and spend time with friends. Much like Ella and Vincent, Simona and Leo left their home in the UK when Leo was nine years old with the intention of traveling for a year. After that first year, however, they just kept going. That is, until Leo became a teenager. Simona had been preparing herself for this stage, as she writes in a blog post titled "When Travelling Kids Hit Their Teens":

> I'd heard that something happened to travelling kids when they hit their teens—that they became averse to long-term travel, unwilling to make new friends and desirous of (eek!) settling down. It happened to the [Bassett] family, who cycled from Alaska to Argentina. It appears to be happening now to my online friend [Mason] and his son. It's a topic of fervent discussion among the small and sometimes fractious community of travelling families. Because of this law, I'd thought we'd stop when [Leo] turned 13. But he agreed to carry on another year, so I hoped we'd beaten the jinx.

They hadn't. This became evident when Simona and Leo were in Egypt, staying in a beachside village where they had spent several months previously. Simona was curious to know why Leo hadn't looked up any of the friends he'd spent time with on their earlier stay. Her heart sank at his response:

[Leo] looks at me, instantly, agonizingly full of sorrow, and replies, "I just don't want to make new friends and leave them all the time, that's all." Ulp. [. . .] This is, for the record, something new. You'd think, from the outside, that travelling children would miss fixed friendships, and find the moving-on process tough. Historically, [Leo] hasn't. [. . .] But now he does. I'm at a loss for what to say.

Eventually, Simona found the words:

"You know, we can always stop travelling if you want to," I say, weakly.
"No, Mum," he lies. "It's fine. We can do another year."
But I realise, in my heart, that it isn't fine. What my son wants and what I want, and, more importantly, what is best for my son and what I want, are different.

Like Ella, Simona recognizes that her desire to live a life of "sheer freedom"—which she describes as having no commitments, no commute, and no morning alarm—is at odds with her son's desire to forge meaningful face-to-face friendships.

More to the point, as a freelance travel writer who writes about being a traveling mother, Simona happily embodies the concept of "lifestyle-as-livelihood" I described in chapter 2. Giving her son the "regular settled life" he wants jeopardizes the lifestyle and identity projects Simona has embraced, as she explains:

And when we stop travelling, I have to build a whole new identity. I'm no longer someone who's travelling and writes about it. I'll have to be someone else, something else, have a whole new set of answers to those questions. I'll have to settle, build a life, be a grownup that meets commitments like rent and school fees, and stays in one place much of the time—goddam it, LIVES SOMEWHERE—and likely owns more than the contents of two backpacks.

Simona concedes that they will need to establish themselves in one place for Leo's high school years, not just for his educational needs, but also, as Simona writes, "for the social thing that you need especially at that age, to break away from me as a parent and become his own person." She concludes: "The more I think on it, the more I think he'll need a 'home' to leave when he's 18."

In the end, Simona and Leo reached a compromise. They didn't move back to the UK, but they did settle in a small community abroad where Leo attended an international school for the remainder of his secondary education. Ella and Vincent also began to explore ways to alleviate Vincent's loneliness and sense of detachment. They briefly considered moving back to the United States and living a more settled lifestyle for a while but ultimately rejected the idea. Instead, they decided to continue living on the road, but to become more intentional about creating a sense of community for Vincent. They did this, initially, by reaching out to other mobile families with teenagers to create a virtual community online. Later, they launched a business organizing temporary learning communities for other worldschooled teenagers. These online and entrepreneurial strategies for dealing with loneliness point to worldschoolers' enduring, albeit ambivalent, desires for belonging and community.

Ambivalent Desires for Community

Although children often bear the emotional cost of homesickness, their parents also confess to feeling unrooted at times. For example, several months into his family's journey, Kyle admits to feeling a bit unmoored on the road. He explains that "however monotonous it may seem; home, a job, church, gym, school, grocery shopping, community," these things "provide more than just security, they deliver a sense of meaning and accomplishment that once removed can be difficult to replace." Likewise, Simona's friend Mason, a father from the United States who traveled with his teenage child Cal, writes that he is "in search of community [and] the experience of belonging." He confesses, "I miss that feeling of community and having neighbors drop by for a cup of coffee or whatever." And yet, in the same paragraph, he writes that he is eager to "embrace the unexpected" in the hopes that his "safe, dusty and static self-concept gets knocked off the shelf in ways that allow me to experience how better and stronger I actually am than I've allowed myself to believe." And Dean, also from the United States, captures these competing desires in a blog post about the trials of long-term travel:

> In our travels we have met the eternal nomads; the ones who can't choose a place to resettle and keep traveling. Eternally searching, and searching, and searching. The desire to have a permanent home and to be part of a community is strong, but so is the thrill of long-term travel and to explore new places.

He concludes by connecting these ambivalent feelings to lifestyle: "In the end, I think everyone is just searching for a home and a lifestyle that will make them happy."

Many worldschoolers talk and write about community in terms of these competing desires. To belong or to travel? To feel secure or to be challenged? To be accountable or to be free? As these fathers describe it, community threatens to devolve into monotony, stagnation, and obligation, but it also represents a sense of certainty and belonging that people ultimately desire. How do parents square their commitment to freedom with their children's homesickness and their own desires for rootedness and belonging? As we will see in the next section, worldschooling families experiment with new configurations of community that seek to balance mobility, freedom, and personal choice with camaraderie and a sense of belonging for themselves and their children.

The New Togetherness

If late modernity has ushered in a new individualism, it has also brought with it new forms of togetherness for a world in flux. The way worldschooling families respond to their children's homesickness, their teenagers' loneliness, and their own ambivalent desires for belonging is to experiment with new configurations of community, friendship, and togetherness on the move. In contrast to traditional notions of community centered on location-based proximity, face-to-face interactions, and long-term commitments, the communities worldschoolers create are flexible, dispersed, and mediated ones that hold their members together with a light touch. These are communities that coalesce loosely on the Internet, united by a shared vision of the good life. When worldschoolers do meet up face-to-face, they do so intermittently and briefly before going their separate ways again. From these encounters, children, especially, learn to navigate the temporary togetherness of come-and-go friendships. But these are not necessarily communities of happenstance. They are often carefully curated, and in some cases commodified, to appeal to kindred spirits who validate one another's decisions to take the path less traveled.[7] As we will see, it is through these kinds of fluid, intermittent, and deliberate social arrangements that worldschoolers thread the needle between the desire to be a "rebel" and the emotional need to be part of a "tribe."

Mediated Sociality

To the extent that we can say there is a worldschooling community, it is first and foremost an online community. As with education and work, the Internet has opened up a new world of possibilities for traveling families seeking a sense of community, serving as a hub where geographically dispersed families can find one another on their blogs or on a handful of private and public social media forums. As Mitch, a father of three from the United States, explains:

> [O]ne of the biggest blessings in my life over the past year has been the community of families on the move that we've become a part of through this blog. Initially we met other bloggers who shared goals similar to ours. Then we ended up in a private Facebook group full of families bucking the trend. [. . .] I think one of the most important components to achieving goals is to get connected with others who share similar goals.

For families who, by virtue of their lifestyle choices, are constantly on the move, the Internet is a relatively stable place where rebels who are "bucking the trend" of conventional life can find their tribe.

My experience engaging with the worldschooling community online was very similar to what Mitch describes. When I started the virtual fieldwork for this research in 2013, my initial online search brought me to a dozen or so blogs being published by traveling families. It was immediately obvious that these bloggers had all found one another, too. They were linking to one another's blogs, conducting and publishing interviews with one another, participating in group writing projects together, and filling one another's comments sections with questions, suggestions, and encouragement. As I began to correspond with these families, some of them invited me to join their private social media forums where parents exchanged advice about travel, education, and parenting.

The size of this online community of families ballooned over the course of my research. One of the forums in which I participated was founded in 2012 with a few dozen members; just five years later it had grown to more than 40,000 self-identified worldschoolers. That is not to say that all of those members were actively traveling. Many were in the planning phase or just dreaming, looking for inspiration from other parents with wanderlust. For aspiring worldschoolers, especially those who find little support among their existing circle of friends, extended family, or co-workers, the online community of world-schoolers offers the validation, encouragement, and guidance they need to launch a worldschooling lifestyle and pursue their dreams of self-fulfillment.

Pamela Smith, a white mother from the United States, explains how she turned to an online community of strangers when her own friends and family failed to support her worldschooling plans:

> I have received so much support and encouragement from my online community of family travelers, much more support than what most people in my "real" life have given us. My advice to other families who want to do long-term travel is to get involved on Twitter, Facebook, and forums and "meet" families who are already doing it. We really are a great community, willing to help, support and answer any questions you may have.

The fact that Pamela puts the word "meet" in quotation marks in her comment above illustrates the shifting nature of interactions among dispersed and mediated communities. In the absence of sustained, face-to-face interaction with friends and extended family members, these online relationships become a crucial touchstone.

Most of these forums are targeted at parents, but children also use mobile communication applications and social media platforms to connect with one another on the move. All of the children I met during my research, including my own son, used some combination of mobile communication technologies and social media platforms to stay in touch with old friends back home or with new friends they had met on the road. This involved exchanging texts, following one another on social media apps like Facebook or Instagram, or participating in on-line discussion forums. It often involved synchronous play via online video games. For example, when I visited with the Porter family while they were temporarily based in the United States, one of their sons was playing a video game with a friend in Germany. "That's how he stays connected to his friends," his mother explained. When I interviewed the Hoffmeyer family, they told me that their children regularly used texting and video apps to communicate with their cousins back in the United States.

In some cases, children used the Internet to interact with other kids they had never met in person. Some of these children and teenagers were enrolled in online learning communities and writing groups with a geographically dispersed set of students. Others were active in on-line discussion forums. If children were too young to create their own social media profiles, their parents would often set up and moderate discussion groups on their behalf. Parents of young children and even teenagers who were suffering from loneliness on the road also posted calls on the adult forums in the hopes of putting together a group of similarly aged children to chat with their kids online. When Vincent first admitted to Ella how lonely and isolated he was feeling, she immediately reached out to her online community of traveling families to see if any other unschooling and worldschooling teens felt the same way. They did, and she reported that Vincent added several new Facebook friends in a matter of days.

While research on teenagers' social media use is mixed in terms of the psychological harms and benefits, these stories suggest that many worldschooling kids develop meaningful and supportive friendships in online spaces.[8] Still, there is an impulse among worldschoolers to trans-late these mediated relationships into face-to-face encounters as well. It is common for parents to use their blogs and the social media forums to arrange in-person playdates and meet-ups with other families. When they do, these encounters tend to be intermittent and temporary, an-other feature of worldschoolers' mobile sociality.

Intermittent and Temporary Communities

"We're arriving in Sofia, Bulgaria next week; is anyone else there? Maybe we can get the kids together?" The destination varies—Chiang Mai, Paris, Melbourne, Buenos Aires, Vientiane—but posts like these regularly appear on the social media forums as parents tap into their online community to coordinate face-to-face playdates and get-togethers for their children.[9] This was so common, in fact, that when I reached out to families online to arrange an in-person interview, they usually interpreted my request as a proposal for a playdate. And in a way it was. Elliot played with the kids while I talked to the parents in what had, for many families, become a familiar mode of temporary sociality.[10]

Every time I participated in one of these playdates, I was reminded of a scene in *A Map for Saturday*, a documentary about long-term backpackers, where a young traveler from the United States talks about "five-hour friends."[11] Perched on a stone wall with Big Ben in the background, he explains that five-hour friends are the fellow travelers you meet in the hostel or train station and hang out with for a day or so before parting ways. Five-hour friends connect deeply and intensely, but briefly, fulfilling the human need for companionship in that moment without tying one another to long-term obligations. This was the case for worldschooling families who met up on the road, sometimes for an afternoon playdate, sometimes for a week-long meet-up.

Just as I was starting my fieldwork, for example, seven traveling families who had been following one another's blogs arranged to spend a week together in Penang, Malaysia, and they each posted about the meet-up on their own blogs. Since then, temporary worldschooling meet-ups have become more frequent and more formalized. A handful of entrepreneurially minded parents began organizing family summits in destinations that are already popular with worldschooling families, like Chiang Mai, Thailand or Mérida, Mexico. These conference-style get-togethers offer a week of sessions on long-term travel, family relationships, generating location-independent income, mobile learning and education, teen volunteering and leadership, creating community, and life fulfillment. It is no coincidence that the invitations for these events emphasize community. "Come one. Come all. Be Community," reads one announcement. "Come bring the kids and meet your tribe," beckons another.

In addition to these family summits are a series of temporary teen learning retreats that Ella and Vincent began hosting periodically when they recognized Vincent's need for peer interaction. They came up with the idea while attending a conference for unschooling families. Ella explains on her blog that back in his US elementary school, Vincent had nothing more in common with his friends than "being the same age and living within the same geographical area." Those friendships never blossomed into anything deep or lasting. And while traveling, Vincent had few opportunities to connect with other kids at all. At the unschooling conference, however, Vincent "came face to face with his peer group, an intelligent, quirky, liberal minded, self-directed group of teenage learners," according to Ella. Vincent's experience of finding "my people, my community," as he puts it, inspired both mother and son to organize learning retreats for other unschooling and worldschooling teenagers.

Their retreats bring small groups of teens together in a variety of destinations for three weeks of community-building exercises and firsthand learning about the local culture. Guided by the natural learning tenets of unschooling and the principles of intentional community, participants learn hands-on skills, for example, how to build grass houses in Wales, weave in Greece, or make chocolate in Peru. But Ella and Vincent distinguish these retreats from other study abroad programs because of the focus on community. The program is heavy on such lessons as developing leadership skills, storytelling, and trust-building. When asked about the enterprise he started with his mother, Vincent responded that one of the downsides of their mobile lifestyle is that "we can never really establish our roots [or] make a very desirable community," and so their community-building events "fill that void." The retreats cultivate a sense of bonding and, perhaps more important, show these "quirky" and "self-directed" teenagers that they are not alone in their unconventional lifestyle. As with the family summits, these learning retreats provide a much-needed dose of temporary co-presence that sustains worldschoolers' sense of community.[12] This is an apt metaphor for the way some worldschoolers think about community, not so much as a lifelong commitment to a particular group of people, but as a social pool that worldschoolers can dip into and out of to satisfy their thirst for companionship.

The key is to keep these communities light and loose. Among the worldschooling families at that first meet-up in Penang were Leah and Richard Reynolds and their three sons. They offer a cautionary tale about what can happen if you settle into a community for too long. When the Reynolds family left the United States, they headed first to a small village in Mexico, where they ended up staying for five years. They quickly established strong friendships with a group of expatriate families, but Leah and Richard, who had long dreamed of raising their boys while traveling the world, knew their time in Mexico was limited. They eventually came to the realization that:

> [T]here has been a bit of stagnation in our lives here over the past year or so. We both feel very strongly that for ourselves and for the kids' personal growth it is time to move on. One of the reasons we left the US to begin with was due to this feeling that our personal growth had severely slowed. [In Mexico], our growth as individuals and as a family has stagnated.

The decision to carry on with their travels was not an easy one, made even more difficult because, according to Richard and Leah, they had gotten a bit too comfortable in their new community. The family was sad to "leave the amazing community of friends that we have built up" in Mexico, and even after several months traveling through Southeast Asia, Leah wrote a long blog post about everything, and everyone, she missed in Mexico.

In that post, she observes that this move was hardest on her oldest son, who was twelve years old at the time. For him, she writes, "the connections to our community are quite strong and he is really feeling the tug at his heart when thinking about leaving." To alleviate their children's anxiety about leaving behind friends and pets in Mexico, Leah and her husband tell their boys:

> Learning to cope in a foreign situation is one of the best ways to overcome fears and insecurities. We explain that we will make new friends to add to our ever- growing list of people throughout the world that care about us. We also remind them (and ourselves) that if we had never taken the leap

to move to [Mexico], we would have never even met the terrific people that we are expecting to miss so much. Life is about the journey, we say!

Leah's comments capture worldschoolers' desires for support and solidarity, on the one hand, and, on the other, their anxiety over the potentially stifling monotony that threatens to derail one's personal growth. Keeping community ties light, intermittent, and temporary is one way to hedge against that stagnation while also enlarging one's circle of caring friends.

Instant Nomadic Friendships

Ella Tyree and Simona Knox seemed to be living parallel lives. They were both single mothers, Ella from the United States and Simona from the United Kingdom. They both abandoned their stable lives to travel the world. And their sons, Vincent and Leo, were both nine years old at the start of their respective worldschooling journeys. As I described earlier, Ella and Simona would find themselves in the same boat again a few years later, when their adolescent boys began suffering from loneliness and isolation on the road. Long before that, however, when Ella first discovered Simona's travel blog online, her initial instinct was that these two kindred families must eventually meet up somewhere along their travels. "I hope you and I will have the opportunity to meet," Ella wrote in a comment on Simona's blog. "I am certain the boys will become instant (nomadic) friends." With this turn of phrase—instant (nomadic) friends—Ella put her finger on the new mode of sociality that worldschooling children are expected to master: fast, mobile, intense.

In the mobile lifestyle of worldschooling, come-and-go sociality is the order of the day. New friends come together intermittently online and face-to-face, bond quickly over shared experiences and life philosophies, and then disperse just as suddenly. In addition to learning how to make friends quickly, therefore, perhaps one of the most important skills worldschooling children can learn is how to leave them just as effortlessly. Mobile togetherness is tinged by the constant specter of separation.

Thalia Lewis captures this sentiment on her blog. When Thalia was eight years old, her parents took her and her brother out of school. They traveled as a family for more than a decade. Now in her late teens, Thalia publishes her own worldschooling blog, where she posted the following reflection on mobile friendship:

> As a traveler, you make so many new connections and new friendships that sustain you for the small amount of time you usually have together. But they are all the very essence of bittersweet, because you have to say goodbye, and one by one you must walk out of each other's lives.

Thalia writes that she cherishes every moment she does get to spend with friends, in part because she knows these face-to-face encounters are fleeting, but also because they take place in some of the world's most famous cities:

> As a traveler, you do have to say goodbye to your friends, but first . . . you get to explore Merida, Paris, London, Kuala Lumpur, Rishikesh, Playa del Carmen, Cartagena, Portland, Cordoba, Beijing and a thousand other cities with them.

As each encounter comes to an end, Thalia is left wondering whether she will ever see her friends again. This question leaves her with "a hundred different emotions coursing through my body," and she goes on to explain how she holds her friends close, even when they are far away:

> It's a single smile suspended over time and space. It's the way [Olivia] sings her song and the way the faces I encounter stay sharp and clear in my mind long after they disappear from my sight. It's the unknown and the uncertainty, pooling out before us like an endless golden thread. [. . .] But if I begin to miss you too much, then I will take that golden thread in my hand and follow it across oceans to find you and just when I think I cannot go a single step further, there you will be, meeting me at the crossroads.

In this reflection, Thalia touches on the social skills she has acquired for making and maintaining meaningful relationships on the road. She has learned to savor the moments of co-presence she does have with friends, to weave those friendships into her life of travel and adventure, and to hold their memories close until they meet again.

Although she does not explicitly highlight it in this post, judging from the stories Thalia includes elsewhere on her blog, she makes extensive use of technology to stay in touch with her friends in the meantime. Perhaps the "golden thread" Thalia mentions is an allusion to these mediated connections, or perhaps it speaks to connections of a more spiritual nature. As she writes later in the post, "we come into contact with people we meet for a reason. We find each other against all odds at the ends of the world when the time is right." Despite this conviction, however, Thalia describes her dispersed friendships in terms of "the unknown and uncertainty." In this case, uncertainty—the fact that she doesn't really know whether she will see her friends' faces again—is not necessarily a problem, but an opportunity. The golden thread promises togetherness with the right people at the right time somewhere on the horizon.

Thalia is clearly taking some poetic license in describing love and loss on the move, but her reflection offers a poignant insight into the emotional terrain of worldschooling. Just as five-hour friends fit the fluid social needs of long-term backpackers, instant nomadic relationships suit the mobile lifestyle of worldschooling.

Intentional and Curated Communities

For worldschoolers, friendships and communities are not something to settle into like a habit, but rather something to be deliberately created. This points to another defining feature of worldschoolers' on-the-move communities: They tend to be carefully curated groups of like-minded travelers.[13] The very feeling that unites worldschoolers online and offline is their shared desire to defy convention and live an unorthodox lifestyle. As Leah explains, traveling the world can be lonely, but meeting other families along the way helps. "It takes a certain sense of adventure and willingness to live outside the mainstream paradigm to travel with kids," she writes. "For that, we feel immediate kinship with the brave families that attempt this lifestyle."

Worldschoolers often express a desire to take part in "intentional communities," a term that has several connotations. In one sense, worldschoolers use it to refer to the fact that they cannot take community for granted; that they have to be intentional about seeking and sustaining a sense of community on the road. "I love the community I have when we are out in the world traveling," Julia explains in a blog post. "But the fact of the matter is, I didn't just stumble upon community (although many serendipitous moments led me to it). Finding community is something I have had to work towards and it takes effort to build and maintain."

The term "intentional community" also refers in a more literal sense to residential communities of self-selected members who share resources and responsibilities in line with a common vision or set of principles, such as ecovillages designed to support sustainable lifestyles. Many parents dream of living for a while in this kind of an intentional community, especially one designed specifically for worldschooling families, and they share these dreams on their blogs and social media forums. One couple who had been worldschooling their kids for a few years floated the idea of creating an intentional community of traveling families aboard a schooner that would sail from port to port. And when a news story emerged that the mayor of a small village in Italy was offering cheap accommodation in an effort to restore the village's dwindling population, a group of worldschoolers began fantasizing about establishing a hub there for an intentional community. They even began outlining the principles for a community where free-spirited but likeminded people interested in natural learning, organic food and farming, and cooperative living could come and go, spending as much or as little time as they want in a ready-made community setting.

Nicola, a mother from the United Kingdom, weighed in on this forum thread: "We want to live in a community with like-minded (i.e. crunchy/granola) people who support homeschooling, appreciate natural approaches to healthcare, love gardening, and have ecofriendly attitudes. In short, we like quirky people!" The discussion about these particular intentional communities eventually petered out, but other experiments in intentional living have come to fruition. One couple converted an old farm in Italy into a co-working and co-living space that welcomes traveling families, and several communities and ecovillages have cropped up in Central America, South America, and Indonesia where worldschooling families are putting their shared utopian ideals into practice with fellow independent and quirky freethinkers.

The insistence that community should be thoughtful and intentional, not left to chance, frames community as yet another component—another choice—in the reflexive lifestyle project of worldschooling. As Ella took stock of Vincent's feelings of loneliness, she reflected on this notion of choice: "The beauty about our lifestyle is the ability to choose what we want to experience every day. We have the freedom to choose something else if it is not working," she writes on her blog. Ultimately, Ella frames Vincent's loneliness as a problem that can be solved, not by returning to their settled lives back home, but through the principles of free choice and lifestyle design. Loneliness becomes less a negative side effect of a mobile lifestyle than an aspect of Vincent's selfhood that requires management and improvement through ongoing lifestyle choices. Individual freedom and choice are both the cause of *and* the solution for his loneliness.

Commodified Community

If community can be a lifestyle choice, then it can also be commodified, and the cottage industry of secondary services I described in chapter 2 draws heavily on the discourse of community to package and sell experiences for traveling families. True to the entrepreneurial logic individuals are encouraged to apply to their lives, Ella and Vincent addressed Vincent's loneliness by launching a business organizing community-minded events. These experiences fed into Vincent's project of self-improvement not just by satisfying his need for social interaction with peers, but also by allowing him to develop his entrepreneurial skills.

Entrepreneurially minded families like Lauren and Edward Falk, whose blog I discussed in chapter 2, have also built their business on the concept of community. On the landing page of their website, they promise that subscribers will become part of a community "of truly unconventional and truly exceptional families" that support one another's aspirations to blend business with family travel. Their website offers paying members access to webinars, online business tools, productivity software, graphic design, marketing templates, and motivational resources—everything a budding digital nomad might need—packaged as a community of like-minded families. Like Ella and Vincent, Lauren and Edward are capitalizing on their own traveling lifestyles to create and facilitate community for other travelers who hope to learn how to buck the status quo in precisely the same way. Just as lifestyle becomes livelihood for these entrepreneurs, so too does community become an enterprise.

It is important to note that this commodification of community does not sit well with all worldschoolers, as an episode on one of the social media forums revealed. Participants of one of the fastest growing online forums logged on one day to find a "TM" superimposed above the group's name. The founder and moderator of the forum had apparently trademarked the group's name, but had done so without warning and without soliciting input from the members. When several members expressed their concern, the founder responded that she had trademarked the name to protect it from an unscrupulous opportunist who was trying to commercially exploit the community. Skeptical forum members questioned whether the founder was just trying to protect future profits for herself. The debate turned hostile, resulting in several members being removed from the forum and several others voluntarily leaving.

This was not the first sign of fracture in the community. As the forum's roster was growing over time, some members began to feel their voices were being drowned out by a normative discourse that tended to privilege the concerns of white, cisgendered, heterosexual, middle-class parents from the Global North. While the forum moderators continued to enforce an ethos of respect for each individual's perspective on the main forum, they also added subgroups for single parents, LGBTQIA+ parents, parents traveling with children with special needs, parents of teenagers, and parents of color and mixed-race families, all hosted under the umbrella of the main forum.

The controversy over the trademark issue could not be so easily contained. Some of the ousted members reconvened on another blog where they continued the debate. Meanwhile, on the trademarked forum, the moderator and her fellow administrators exercised their power to remove posts and close threads that took the conversation in a direction they didn't like. In this moment, it became very clear that what appeared to be an open and global community of worldschooling families was in fact subject to strict gatekeeping rules that governed who could speak and what they could say. Although this is a somewhat extreme example, it brings us back to the fundamental paradox of belonging to a "tribe of rebels." How is it possible for a community to be a source of together-ness and diversity? What does it mean to belong to a community of like-minded people when the very thing members have in common is their desire to defy convention and march to the beat of their own drum?

Community for the Individual

The invitation on Lauren and Edward's website implicitly filters the kind of people who are actually welcome in their community: "dreamers, doers, risk takers." Elsewhere on their website, they indicate that their online community is a place for people who "aren't content with the status quo," who have a "spark of rebellion in their soul," and who hold a "deep desire to live an extraordinary life." Likewise, Julia emphasizes the importance of freedom and difference in a blog post on the topic of community:

> Perhaps my favourite thing about life and community is diversity. Every-one is different, every single one. There [are] as many paths and lifestyles as there are humans on the planet and we are each entirely free to do it our own ways. I love that.

What Lauren and Edward are offering, and what Julia desires, is a com-munity for radical, freethinking individuals. But how can a community incorporate such extreme difference that everyone is "entirely free to do it our own ways"? How is it possible to be both "truly unconventional" and part of a group of like-minded others?

These are age-old questions, certainly not unique to worldschoolers or their particular configurations of community. As I thought about how worldschoolers aimed to make a community based on individualism and diversity, I was reminded of political theorist Iris Marion Young's classic work on community and difference among radical activists in the 1980s.[14] Much has been written about the opposition between liberal individualism and the ideal of community, but Young's work seemed especially pertinent. Observing the activists in her study, she noticed that they often turned to the ideal of community as an alternative to the exploitative and oppressive effects of a patriarchal capitalist soci-ety. Community, with its affective connotation as a warm and nurturing haven, was a far more appealing alternative to the cold reality of a society of strangers, Young admits, and she could see why the activists in her study were drawn to this "understandable dream."[15] The problem, Young cautioned, was that the desire for communal belonging easily slips into a desire for social wholeness, which in turn can be used to justify exclusion, racism, and the repression of social differences. In other words, a community's insistence on like-mindedness can become just as oppressive as the external social forces it promises to guard against. In the end, Young argues, community cannot fulfill its promise as an alternative to the oppression and exploitation of capitalism.

Like the social activists in Young's account, the families in my study place a similar kind of faith in community as an antidote to the social and emotional travails of late modernity. Because mobile and temporary encounters with other traveling families offer the sense of camaraderie that worldschooling parents and their teenagers crave, we might think of these communities as a remedy to the feelings of friendsickness, loneliness, and detachment brought on by the new individualism. A closer look reveals that these communities are not necessarily a challenge to individualism, but rather extensions of the individualistic pursuit of the good life. As much as these fluid communities offer a sense of fellowship and belonging, they are ultimately crafted to support worldschoolers' individual dreams and personal lifestyle aspirations without asking too much in return. They are, in effect, communities for the individual.

Unlike the social activists in Young's account, worldschoolers seek out community, not to address collective problems or pursue political solutions, but rather to realize their individual desires of self-fulfillment. This is not to suggest that worldschoolers' search for community is purely instrumental, or at least no more instrumental than most other forms of community in late modernity. In this sense, we might understand worldschoolers' search for community in terms of what Anthony Giddens calls "life politics."

For Giddens, life politics stands in contrast to emancipatory politics, which is concerned with the structural circumstances that lead to social division and oppression. Emancipatory politics is focused on communal issues like reducing exploitation and inequality, addressing the unequal distribution of power and resources, and promoting the ethics of justice, equality, and participation. Life politics, instead, is concerned with achieving a sense of individual liberation through reflexive self-reinvention. The way worldschoolers disrupt the doxa, as I described in chapter 2, is an example of life politics. In that case, worldschoolers' rejection of prescribed social norms and turn to entrepreneurialism was not part of a collective effort to overturn structural inequalities or expand economic opportunities to more people, but a strategy for pursuing their own lifestyle aspirations. Simply put, "emancipatory politics is a politics of life chances, life politics is a politics of lifestyle."[16]

As Giddens describes it, life politics refers to the exercise of power through market-based lifestyle choices rather than through traditional forms of civic or political action. Politically oriented consumer campaigns, fair trade initiatives, and even travel programs with an ostensible social justice agenda are all forms of life politics. Take voluntourism, for example, which is often promoted as a humanitarian and political intervention when, in fact, the primary change this kind of travel produces is the tourist's own self-transformation.[17] What is at stake in life politics, Giddens argues, is "the creation of morally justifiable forms of life that will promote self-actualization in the context of global interdependence."[18]

In the new forms of togetherness I described in the previous sections, worldschoolers create and consume community, and they do so as a morally justifiable lifestyle choice. What could be a more valid response to children's feelings of homesickness or loneliness than seeking out belonging and friendship? At the same time, however, parents hoping to prepare their children for the vicissitudes of a global future know that emotional independence is crucial. It is a message that has circulated since the late nineteenth century when, according to historian Susan J. Matt, psychologists, child-rearing experts, and American folklore began promoting the ideology of rugged individualism: Children must learn self-mastery, emotional control, and independence. It is telling in the story above, for example, that when Leo asks to settle down for a while, his mother Simona reframes his request not as a symptom of homesickness, necessarily, but rather as a need to assert his own independence and "become his own person."

In her historical analysis of homesickness, Susan Matt points out that these "painful lessons in individualism" coincided with the rise of industrial capitalism, an economic system that required a mobile and unfettered labor force able to move easily from farm to factory and from city to city.[19] Under these conditions, Matt explains, homesickness was not just a sign of immaturity, but a threat to individual and social progress.[20] To seize economic opportunity, individuals must be mobile, flexible, and unencumbered, not homesick. In the twenty-first century, that message has only intensified. As Elliott and Lemert observe, "Keep moving and don't commit yourself is the moral to be drawn from today's high-tech global economy."[21] Despite such powerful cultural messaging, however, homesickness persists, not just as an effect of a mobile lifestyle, but as a feature of a mobile world. Susan Matt even goes so far as to say that we live in a perpetually "homesick culture."

The kind of mobile communities that worldschoolers create for themselves are one strategy for reconciling these mixed messages of rugged individualism and perpetual homesickness. This may explain why worldschoolers are attracted to forms of community that are untethered to a particular geographical place, that coalesce intermittently and lightly, and that are intentionally composed of like-minded travelers who support rather than stifle one another's unconventional dreams of freedom. These communities are sources of useful information and much-needed emotional support for families taking an unconventional path. They provide a social outlet for lonely children as well as for parents seeking camaraderie on the road. In many ways, these communities make worldschoolers' personal lifestyle dreams possible. But participating in these communities serves another purpose as well: teaching children important life lessons about how to make and maintain social relationships in the fluid conditions of late modernity.

Conclusion

As the stories in this chapter suggest, worldschooling is not always as dreamy as it seems. Parents and children, and especially adolescents, experience homesickness, loneliness, and unrootedness on the road. Throughout this chapter, I have described how worldschooling families turn to the ideal of community for a sense of mooring in a churning world. Worldschoolers are masters of the intermittent and temporary meet-ups that sustain a community that is, by definition, in flux.

Through online discussion forums, global playdates, family summits, and learning retreats, worldschooling families cycle in and out of one another's lives. Under these conditions, worldschooling children, teenagers especially, learn how to forge and sustain nomadic friendships. To maintain these relationships, they deploy not only technical skills for communicating across oceans and time zones, but also the emotional skills required to develop distant friendships. These are life skills they can take with them into a mobile and global future.

The new global economy increasingly requires workers up and down the economic ladder to be constantly on the move, both digitally and physically. In their account of the "mobile lives" that many of us now live in the twenty-first century, Anthony Elliott and John Urry predict that the professional landscape will become networked to such a degree that most jobs will require significant social, digital, and physical mobility. Workers will gather intermittently in teams that assemble, dissemble, and reassemble around various projects in various locations.[22] Indeed, this is already true for freelance, contract, and remote workers, including digital nomads.

Come-and-go relationships are also emblematic of the type of social connections children are likely to have in their future personal and professional lives. Elliott and Urry suggest that our friends, acquaintances, and loved ones are more likely than ever to be geographically dispersed and on the move, a development that requires all kinds of technological, mobile, and emotional strategies to manage marriages, schedule family life, and sustain intimate relationships at a distance.[23] Sociologist Paula Bialski agrees, arguing that life in a mobile world requires us to know how to get close but avoid intimacy or to know how to become attached and then quickly detached as we circulate in and out of constellations of strangers. These are the skills, she observes, that "people have to acquire and adapt as they increasingly become mobile and come into contact with mobile others."[24] Or, as Beverly Yuen Thompson puts it in her study of the romantic lives of young digital nomads, they have to know how to get their "lovin' on the run."[25] Some theorists argue that these forms of sociality are shallow and fleeting, and they may be.[26] But if this is what the future of social life looks like, then it is important for children to become adept at bonding quickly but casually, at being flexible but friendly, at being collaborative but unattached.

Through worldschooling, children are learning all kinds of practical lessons about how to travel. They pick up roadworthy skills like converting currencies, taking public transportation, and navigating airports and train stations. Along the way, they also learn how to connect and how to say goodbye, how to do sociality in a light and loose way that fulfills their personal needs without making claims on their freedom, how to leverage technology to sustain relationships at-a-distance, and, if they're particularly savvy, how to commodify and consume community in line with their individual lifestyle aspirations. For worldschoolers, being part of a "tribe of rebels" means bending community to one's own life politics. These new configurations of togetherness and belonging are not about submitting to the obligations and constraints of communal life but about a larger lifestyle project aimed at self-fulfillment and self-actualization.

I have focused here primarily on the social skills an uncertain future may require of children, but I have also alluded to the complex emotional landscape of worldschooling. In effect, children are learning how to live mobile lives, both in terms of the practical matters of living life on the road and in matters of the heart. This is the thread I pick up in the next chapter, where I explore the way parents cultivate their children's global citizenship by encouraging them to "feel global."

GLOBAL AMERICAN DREAM

Meredith and Wes Armer had their lives all planned out. Wes was a rising star in the US Air Force. Meredith embraced her role as a military wife and mother to their three young girls. Moving from base to base as Wes climbed the career ladder was a small price to pay for a growing salary, secure benefits, and what the couple imagined would be an early retirement spent on a farm somewhere in North Carolina. However, that was still several years off, and Wes faced the very real possibility of multiple deployments in the meantime.

With a growing family—they were expecting their fourth daughter—neither Meredith nor Wes cherished the idea of long separations from the family. So they made the difficult decision for Wes to leave the military. After Wes received his honorable discharge, the couple started homeschooling their older daughters, launched a small marketing company, and eventually moved to Florida. By then, they had welcomed a fifth child to their family. After making the move to Florida, they realized they could maintain their marketing business online from anywhere in the world. Wes and Meredith decided to move again, this time to Costa Rica. From there, they decided to start traveling while homeschooling their five children along the way.

For Meredith, giving up life as a military family for an unconventional lifestyle as a worldschooler and location-independent entrepreneur prompted a fundamental shift in her idea of the American Dream. Originally, she equated the American Dream with her family's military identity, with their suburban lifestyle, and with their possessions. But they were growing increasingly dissatisfied with the "homes, fine furnishings, fat bank accounts," as she put it. These were just burdens, she explained, keeping them in places they didn't want to be.

In their new worldschooling life, they are still chasing the American Dream, but they define it in a very different way. "We're not so concerned about comfort like we used to be," Meredith observes. Her

American Dream now is to expose her children to a wealth of experiences. She writes on her blog: "We want our children to know what life is like outside of suburbia with all the pressures of having the best clothes, the most expensive toys and being involved in so many activities that you have to schedule family dinner time." She continues, "We also want our children to know that the world does not revolve around them, that life is hard at times with no easy way out or 'retail therapy' to cure the blues."

In addition to shifting their priorities away from consumption and comfort, Meredith and Wes express other hopes for their children:

> We want to expose them to REAL history by visiting places most American kids will only read about in books. [. . .] We want our children to be at ease talking to and being around people that are VERY different from themselves. [. . .] We want them to be able to communicate in more than one language, like most of the rest of the world does.

In this new version of the American Dream, Meredith dwells on what she wants her children to learn and the kind of people she wants them to be rather than on the material possessions she wants them to have.

The American Dream of financial success no longer rings true to Meredith, but another connotation of the American Dream certainly does: freedom. She concludes her blog post on precisely this point:

> Our new version of the American Dream does hold fast to a thread common to those who have immigrated to the US for years: having the freedom to pursue a better, more fulfilling life for our family. At this point in our lives, that includes a radically different life, full of cultural experiences only found in traveling in this amazing world we live in.

As Meredith describes it, this dream that drew millions of immigrants to the United States is now the dream that propels Meredith and her family beyond America's borders to roam the whole "amazing world."

Central to this dream of freedom is Meredith's desire to raise her children as global citizens. To this end, Meredith detaches the American Dream from America altogether, casting it instead in a global light:

I guess overall, our American Dream has shifted away from America. As our world becomes more connected through the internet, we are compelled to raise our children as more global citizens. [. . .] We feel its [*sic*] in the best interest of our children to grow up globally, with love and compassion for our fellow man [*sic*] around the world.

As they consider what the future holds in a technologically connected and culturally diverse world, Meredith and Wes come to the conclusion that it is in their children's best interest to grow up not just as American citizens, but as global citizens who feel connected to all of humanity through sentiments of love and compassion. Their American Dream has become a dream of global citizenship.

Meredith's story was published as part of a collective writing project organized by a group of family travel bloggers. Even though not all of the bloggers were from the United States, they decided to write on the common theme of the American Dream. Does it still exist? If so, what does it mean today? The contributions were written independently but published on the same day and linked across all of the participating blogs.[1] The authors each approached the topic from their own perspective, but they all referenced the original promise that hard work today will lead to material success tomorrow and for future generations. For these bloggers, however, the future does not look the way it once did. Their dream for their children is not the steady job, suburban home, or white picket fence that has long symbolized the American Dream. They expressed a desire for a new kind of future, one in which their children figure as culturally competent and compassionate global citizens with a world of opportunity at their fingertips. Like Meredith, almost all of the other bloggers in the project expressed a hope that through international travel, their children would learn to transcend their national citizenship and become citizens of the world.

"The 'American Dream' has taken on a completely different flavor for me," writes Mason Oberman, a single father who traveled for several years with his son Cal. "I didn't want his vision of the world to be a myopic nationalized one but instead to see himself more as a global citizen," he concludes. And another contributor, Jackie, who was traveling indefinitely with her husband and two children, explains how traveling redefined her American Dream from a life of possessions to a lifestyle of global experiences. "My American Dream extends beyond America," she writes. "We want our children to know something other than consumerism. The diversity we are experiencing on a day to day level cannot be taught in traditional schools. These experiences are going to shape and mold us into amazing global citizens." For parents like Meredith, Mason, and Jackie, travel promises to transform their children into global citizens in ways that their suburban lives and traditional schools could not.

Other contributors echoed the claim that the American Dream is more about freedom than about stuff, as Leah writes:

> [W]e are in control of ourselves and our path. We alone set the tempo for living out our dreams. We can live any illusion we choose, but we must dream it first. For us, the American Dream represents the freedom to choose how to spend our time. We choose simplicity, independence, and global exploration.

In these revised versions of the American Dream, the pursuit of happiness is not confined to material success or even to the borders of one's home country. In fact, the freedoms conferred by national citizenship—in this case US citizenship—allow families to chase their dreams at a global scale.

Joyce Vu, however, offers a somewhat different perspective in the story she contributed to the project. The daughter of immigrants who moved to the United States from Vietnam in a classic search for the American Dream, Joyce recognizes that her desire to leave America and travel the world with her child might be misinterpreted as a rejection of her hard-won American citizenship or a disregard for the risks her parents endured to bring her to the United States in the first place. Quite the opposite, Joyce argues: "I thank my immigrant parents for bringing me to the US, where I was able to grow up and think independently. I am grateful for my US passport. Right now, it is the key to my American Dream." Similar to the other contributors, Joyce reinterprets the American Dream as freedom—freedom to travel the world—a desire inspired by a culture that promoted her independent thinking and facilitated by a passport that smooths her international travel.

Like Joyce, many of the parents writing about the American Dream frame national citizenship not as an inherent identity, but as a launching pad for global mobility. Owning a passport from the United States, or from Australia or Canada or the United Kingdom, for that matter, is less a marker of one's national identity and more a promise of free and unfettered global mobility. These families may be leaving their American lifestyles behind, but they are certainly taking their US passports with them. Their stories frame the American Dream through a tension between national and global citizenship; of leaving a national home to make oneself—and one's children—at home in the world.

5

Home and World

Feeling Global in Uncertain Times

[We] have been able to be at home wherever we are together
in the world. We collect memories and build the bonds of
our family through the shared experiences of being in different countries, interacting with different people, speaking
different languages and eating different foods.
—Norman, blog post

Where do you call home?
Anywhere we are.
—Cal, blog post

Worldschooling parents are nearly unanimous in their desire to raise
their children as global citizens and in their conviction that travel is
the best way to do just that. This reflects an aspiration that is prevalent
among Global North middle-class families: to raise "global kids." Scholars have documented the extent to which white middle-class parents
try to encourage their children's global citizenship by signing them up
for foreign language classes, sending them to academic camps abroad,
bringing them along on international business trips, or enrolling them
in multicultural urban schools.[1] Anxious about their children's ability
to compete in a global economy, these parents invest in their children's
global citizenship. Worldschoolers, too, express the belief that children
who are raised with a global mind-set will be better positioned to thrive
in an uncertain future. Imparting a sense of global citizenship, then, is
yet another way a mobile lifestyle confers certain advantages to worldschooling children.

To hear worldschoolers describe it, global citizenship is not something that automatically happens but rather is an actively chosen and
deliberately practiced identity. From this perspective, worldschool-

ers frame global citizenship as an acquired worldview, a learned set of competencies, and a certain disposition that must be developed, ideally through international travel and exposure to a world of difference. The age of globalization may have made national citizenship feel more entrenched and consequential for some, but it has made it more loose and fluid for others. Anthropologist Aihwa Ong calls this "flexible citizenship." In her study of Chinese cosmopolitans, Ong discovered that Hong Kong's wealthy elite were engaging in new strategies of citizenship: working in one country, moving their families to another country, sending their children to school in a different country, and holidaying in yet another. According to Ong, her respondents leveraged the cultural and capital advantages of different countries in a carefully curated web of national, economic, and cultural allegiances that didn't necessarily align with one's national identity or with borders on a map.

The worldschoolers in my study tend to adopt a similarly flexible approach to citizenship. As the stories in the interlude suggest, they may embrace their national passports for the ease of mobility they afford, but many profess loose associations with their national identities and speak freely about their desire to transcend national borders altogether. In this chapter, I explore the various meanings worldschoolers attach to global citizenship and their efforts to make themselves at home in the world. The aim here is not to distill a fixed definition of global citizenship, but to show how parents play with the fluidity of the concept to justify their decision to worldschool their children.

Global citizenship is the culmination of the lessons parents most hope their children will learn from traveling and the kinds of people they want their children to become: globally minded kids equipped with the social, emotional, and entrepreneurial skills to thrive in the diverse and ever-changing world of tomorrow. To this end, parents lean toward definitions of global citizenship that emphasize its emotional aspects over its political or legal dimensions. In other words, they see global citizenship primarily as an emotional orientation. Throughout the chapter, I detail the various ways parents encourage their children to "feel global," focusing on the implicit feeling rules that govern the way children ought to feel about others and about themselves as members of the global community. What emerges is a profile of a global citizen who is equipped to thrive in the emotional landscape of a diverse and unequal world.

What Does Global Citizenship Mean to You?

Soon after leaving California to worldschool her son, Ella Tyree devoted a series of blog posts and podcasts to the topic of global citizenship. Ella could see that travel was clearly transforming Vincent into a global citizen, an unexpected but very welcome result of her decision to take him out of his public school to travel the world, and she was eager to explore the origins and meanings of the term. The series included several sole-authored posts documenting Ella's research and thoughts about global citizenship, but it also featured dozens of interviews she conducted with other worldschooling families. Almost to a person, the parents Ella interviewed said that the main reason they were traveling with their families was because they wanted their children to become global citizens.[2]

Global citizenship was, they claimed, the most important learning outcome of their worldschooling lifestyle. And yet they each approached the term from different angles. Their responses alternated from philosophical musings on being a member of the human family to appeals for social justice and human rights to a set of practical twenty-first-century skills to an emotional orientation to the world as a whole.

That Ella and her respondents should define global citizenship in such a range of ways is not surprising. Even if we intuitively know what global citizenship is, it is difficult to pinpoint a definition. Is it a political status, a collection of rights and responsibilities, a cultural aesthetic, a particular attitude?[3] In fact, global citizenship is one of those elastic terms that has been molded to fill any number of social, political, or economic needs at different points in time. The term is said to have originated in the fourth century BCE with the Greek philosopher Diogenes. When asked where he was from, Diogenes answered: "I am *kosmopolitês*" (a citizen of the world). In the centuries since Diogenes uttered those famous words, everyone from the Stoics of ancient Greece to the philosophers of the Enlightenment period, from the Romantic poets to twentieth-century presidents and postwar pacifists, and from study abroad promoters to corporate recruiters has wielded the term in service of their own moral, diplomatic, or capitalist aims. Global citizenship is not so much a phenomenon that can be defined as it is a screen onto which people project the hopes and worries of their time. This is certainly the case for worldschoolers whose wide-ranging interpretations of global citizenship reflect the aspirations of their mobile lifestyles and their concerns about preparing their children for the future.

When asked to define global citizenship, many worldschooling parents do so through the prism of an uncertain future. Ella explicitly claims that "having global experiences is one of the best ways to educate and prepare a child for the 21st century," and she goes on to explain:

> Our world is changing and exposure to global issues is the most valuable education you can provide. Travel can't help but to enrich and educate, and [. . .] create an empowered adult who thinks as a global citizen.

One of the fathers Ella interviewed concurred: "The perspective gained by becoming a global citizen is invaluable for the future of our children." For him this meant "learn[ing] to adapt to new environments, foods, and cultures." A mother from the United States responded that she and her husband decided to travel with their family because they wanted "to help our children become the people needed to lead in the future." She explained that "living in the suburbs is not the best way to prepare [our children] for the world they will live in, and that includes learning other languages, experiencing other cultures, and just knowing more about the world." These parents imagine a future of constant change and cultural diversity that will require their children to be global citizens if they are to become empowered leaders.

If global citizenship is a proxy for parents' concerns about an uncertain future, it is also a concept on which they pin their desires for their children's global belonging. Many of the worldschoolers' thoughts about global citizenship were informed by the idea that, despite our evident differences, we all share a common humanity. For example, another mother from the United States who cycled around the world with her husband and two sons, said that being a global citizen means:

> [U]nderstanding the unity of mankind [sic] and knowing that, if we strip the wrapper off, we are all the same. It doesn't matter what color your skin, what language you speak, what god you worship, or what currency you spend—underneath it all, we are all the same.

A single mother from the United States echoed this thought: "No one is separate, we are all just visitors here." Since we are all just visitors on the planet, she reasons, we can all be at home "wherever we happen to be." Other interviews touched on this same theme of common humanity, with one mother observing:

> Everyone seems to want the same things no matter where they live. They want to live peaceful, content lives and provide for their families. There is no better way to show a child that they are part of [a] bigger world [. . .] than by taking them out and experiencing what the world has to offer and showing them that they are welcome everywhere!

These responses suggest that being a global citizen means being welcome to make oneself at home anywhere and everywhere in the world, but a mother from the UK noted that global citizens must also be ready to give back:

> My son and I are global citizens because we learn constantly from others as we travel the world, although we never forget our roots, experiencing a myriad different ways of life and learning that our common humanity is the most important thing there is, and people have much more in common than they have in difference. We express our [global] citizenship not just by a mobile lifestyle. We make an effort to give back both financially and in terms of time to the communities we visit, most of which are much less wealthy than [the UK], where we come from.

Many of the parents Ella interviewed associated global citizenship with recognizing our similarities, but also the deep inequalities that exist in the world. And, like the mother cited above, most worldschoolers encounter these inequalities from a position of relative privilege, which carries with it particular responsibilities to "give back."

Despite all this talk about our common humanity, worldschoolers do not necessarily think of global citizenship as something children are born with as an inherent human trait. Global citizenship doesn't just happen. Instead, they describe it as something that must be coaxed into being through encounters with others and experiences in the world.

Norman articulates this belief on his blog when explaining why he and his wife travel abroad with their kids:

> We want our kids to be true global citizens, who are empathetic and curious about other people of other cultures. We, as parents, want to foster this sense of discovery both within ourselves, but more importantly for our children. We want to guide them along the way and give them the exposure and experiences to make good choices when they are older.

Anyone can be born into the global family of humanity, but to become a global citizen requires developing a certain temperament and a kind of emotional intelligence about one's place in the world. Children learn these lessons, but, as Norman's comments suggest, it is their attentive parents who create the experiences that bring about this learning and who prod children to be self-reflexive about the global disposition they are developing. Like middle-class parents more generally, worldschoolers see their children as projects to be developed.[4] The same impulse that prompts parents to cultivate their children's independence, which I described in chapter 3, can be seen in their desire to shape children's global subjectivities. Becoming a global citizen, like becoming independent, is an extension of late modernity's imperative to work on the self, to make good choices, as Norman puts it, and to craft a lifestyle that reflects the good life these families seek.

Being aware of one's place in our common humanity and attuned to the opportunities and responsibilities that come along with that requires self-reflexive work. As Ella explains, global citizenship requires "a shift in consciousness and a shift of attention." She argues that developing "concern, compassion and consideration for our fellow human beings" comes through "the inner change, the inner shift" that global citizens must cultivate in themselves.

The intercultural skills needed for the future; the recognition that we are all the same; the sense of obligation to others; and the ability to feel at home anywhere are all aspects of global citizenship that must be learned. And, as the worldschooling parents interviewed on Ella's blog repeatedly remind us, travel is the ideal teacher. Travel turns children "into smarter, happier and more well-rounded people: global citizens," says one mother. Another states matter-of-factly: "If you want to raise a globally minded child, you must travel outside your country and culture."

If global citizenship is learned, what exactly are parents teaching their children about becoming a global citizen? The statements above, with their language of compassion, concern, empathy, curiosity, happiness, and global-mindedness, offer a clue. Notably absent from these definitions are references to the legal, political, or bureaucratic aspects of global citizenship. Issues such as taxes, elections, birth certificates, social welfare entitlements, visas, and passports come up quite frequently in forums where worldschoolers offer one another practical advice about international travel, but these topics rarely appear in worldschoolers' conversations about global citizenship. For them, global citizenship is not a political or legal category, but an emotional orientation toward the world as a whole.

Ella says as much in one of her blog posts: "Our thoughts here are not of a political nature, nor do we wish to engage in a social, cultural, political or economic argument." Instead, she explains, what makes someone a global citizen is "an imaginative empathy that reaches beyond our immediate surrounding, and extends our hearts to those suffering in distant places." The implication, she argues, is that global citizens should not try to change the world "from the outside-in" through political activism, but "from the inside-out" by cultivating an inner emotional disposition of compassion.

While not all of the worldschoolers in my study would agree with Ella's rejection of political activism as an aspect of global citizenship, her framing of global citizenship almost exclusively as an existential and emotional orientation strikes a chord. When parents talk about teaching children to become global citizens, what they are really talking about is helping children develop a worldly self who knows how to "feel global."

Feeling Global: Life Lessons in Global Citizenship

Parents have high hopes for what their children will learn with the world as their classroom. What could be better than learning about world history while climbing Mayan ruins, learning math by converting currencies in Morocco, figuring out physics at the base of the Great Pyramids in Egypt, or engaging with environmental science while hiking glaciers in New Zealand? And yet, when parents are asked to distill what their children *really* learned from traveling the world, they are less likely to refer to these practical lessons and more likely to emphasize the life lessons travel imparts. Alongside math, history, and science, children learn how to cope with change, handle discomfort, express compassion, or feel gratitude. I call this the "emotional curriculum" of worldschooling, one that teaches children how to feel global.[5]

The concept of feeling global requires us to give some thought to what emotions are and where they come from. My understanding of emotion in this context is informed by a sociological perspective that sees emotions not merely as naturally occurring feelings that originate within individuals, but as external and socially constructed phenomena. As young children, we learn what and how to feel, what to do with our feelings, how to display them, and how to assess other people's emotional states. Sociologist Arlie Hochschild's research on emotion management has been pivotal for thinking about feelings in this way.[6] She highlights the extent to which our emotions are shaped by the "feeling rules" that govern social situations. Feeling rules are the implicitly or explicitly agreed parameters of how we *should* feel in a given social setting. As Hochschild describes it, feeling rules exist at that pinch point between how we feel and how we think we *should* feel about something or toward someone. In the context of such rules, then, we call up or suppress feelings to fit social expectations. Hochschild calls this "emotion work."

Emotion work occurs when we manage or regulate our feelings, or work to bring about a desired emotional state in others, in order to align with cultural norms. Hochschild argues that we all do this kind of work as we manage the emotional climate of family life and friendships in our private lives, but that this kind of emotional labor is increasingly expected as part of our paid work, especially in the service industry. For Hochschild, feeling rules come into play in the interpersonal exchanges we have at home or at work as we measure what emotional responses we owe one another in various situations. In the case of worldschooling, parents and children do all kinds of emotion work to manage family life on the road. In chapter 4, for example, I detailed the strategies parents use to regulate their children's feelings of homesickness or loneliness. In this chapter, I extend Hochschild's concept of feeling rules beyond interpersonal encounters to think about the broader set of feelings children are expected to learn and internalize in their role as global citizens.

The emotional curriculum of worldschooling includes a repertoire of feelings that children, especially children from the Global North, are encouraged to cultivate toward themselves, toward others, and toward their place in the world. For example, they learn to call up feelings of compassion and curiosity toward others, a sense of confidence toward themselves, and a sense of gratitude or responsibility in response to their relatively privileged position in the world. Feeling global also teaches children the emotional competencies they will need for competing in the global economy or navigating a world of difference, such as open-mindedness, adaptability, or flexibility. And it entails the emotion work children are expected to perform when confronted with uncomfortable experiences or disorienting encounters, for example by suppressing emotions like disgust or homesickness and calling up feelings of tolerance and adaptability. Knowing what to feel, how to express those feelings, and how to render those feelings into commodifiable skills are all part of the emotional labor children are learning to do as they feel their way through a fundamentally diverse, unequal, and uncertain world.

In the sections that follow, I offer a detailed analysis of four of the emotional lessons children are encouraged to learn on their way to becoming global citizens: coping with change, communicating across difference, feeling compassion toward those in need and gratitude for one's own good fortune, and venturing out of one's comfort zone. This is not meant to be an exhaustive account of the many emotional lessons children learn from traveling, but rather an illustration of how worldschoolers frame global citizenship as an emotional disposition that, ultimately, entitles their children to feel at home in an uncertain world.

Coping with Change

If children are to become global citizens, one of the first things they must learn is how to cope with change. This was a recurring theme in many of my interviews, including the one I conducted with Elsa and Byron Hart, a white couple from the United States. Elsa and I had met online months earlier, while her family was in Spain and I was still in the United States.

We kept in touch, and when we discovered that our paths would cross in Thailand, I asked Elsa if we could meet up for an interview. I knew from Elsa's blog that one of the main reasons the family decided to travel the world was because she and Byron were committed to raising their son and daughter as global citizens. I was curious to know more about how their approach to educating their kids on the road fit with their aspiration to foster their children's global citizenship. Plus, their children were around Elliot's age and I hoped the kids would enjoy hanging out for the afternoon. Elsa agreed and suggested we meet at a new café located in an upscale mall at the north end of the city.

The neighborhood where we were headed was not on Chiang Mai's tourist circuit, but it had become a popular hub for digital nomads enticed by cheap rents and reliable Internet connectivity. Elsa and Byron, who are themselves digital nomads with an active blog and e-book business, had rented an apartment nearby. After a long walk in the sweltering heat, Martin, Elliot, and I breathed a sigh of relief as we stepped into the air-conditioned mall. We found ourselves in an atrium filled with rows of tables piled with glossy brochures and posters displaying ivy-covered brick buildings on college campuses abroad. Three enormous balloons in the shape of the letters U, S, and A floated in the middle of the atrium. Young people milled around the tables, collecting brochures and chatting with representatives from English language programs in the United States and England. We had stumbled into a study abroad fair. We browsed alongside the Thai students for a few minutes before heading upstairs to meet the Harts.

The café Elsa had suggested was one of those cutting-edge co-working hubs that are cropping up to meet the needs of a mobile and digital workforce. The space had the high-design feel of a trendy tech startup, with soaring ceilings, sleek wooden platform seating, a bustling coffee bar, and power outlets everywhere. It was a popular spot for the international digital nomads who lived nearby, but on this day the café appeared to be filled with students in crisp blue and white uniforms, all glued to their screens. The drinks we ordered came with a tiny slip of paper on which was printed that day's wifi code. The Harts' son, Erik, grabbed the slip of paper, along with one of our digital tablets, and the three kids disappeared to a nook on the other side of the café while the adults gathered around one of the high-top tables.

Originally from the United States, the Harts had been living and traveling abroad with Erik, who was twelve years old, and Marisa, who was ten, for almost two years when we met. When Erik and Marisa were in the sixth and fourth grades, respectively, the Harts decided to leave their corporate jobs, pull the kids out of school, and sell their suburban home. They moved to a small coastal village in Spain for a year, and after an extended road trip through Europe, they were now traveling slowly through Southeast Asia, trying to figure out whether they should return to Spain or settle in some new destination for a while.

Elsa and Byron started by telling me how much their current life as digital nomads differs from the nine-to-five corporate jobs they had left behind in the United States. They had both worked for the same multinational company in the mid-Atlantic region of the country. Elsa, a self-described free spirit, had backpacked around Europe in her twenties, and when she and Byron were first married, they had lived in London for a few years. Even then, they knew they wanted to raise their children in an international setting. As Elsa told me: "Our kids were going to be global citizens from the get-go. Before we even knew we were having kids!"

At first, they harbored hopes that their company might give them an overseas posting. But that was before the 2008 economic crisis hit. Instead of handing out comfortable expat packages, the company started laying off employees. Elsa and Byron dodged the first few rounds of layoffs, but they could see the writing on the wall. Elsa recalled, "I was squirreling away money waiting for us to get laid off. One of us. I figured one of us would. The odds. I mean everybody in the neighborhood was."

By this time, Elsa had been reading blogs published by other traveling families and realized that if she and Byron could supplement their savings with online income, they could afford the lifestyle they wanted without being tied to a company. "I looked at our little nest egg and I was like, why don't we just lay ourselves off?" she explained. "Let's just go. The whole plan was to live internationally, and it wasn't coming to us. We had to make it happen." And so, as Elsa put it, they laid themselves off and moved the family to Spain.

They enrolled Erik and Marisa in a local school there, so they could become fluent in Spanish. When the school year ended, the family packed up and hit the road. At first, they registered the children in an online program to make sure they were reaching key benchmarks in the US public school curriculum. Marisa was missing third grade social studies and language arts. Would she know what verbs and adverbs are? What about the US presidents? Erik was missing advanced math and the seventh-grade social studies unit on the Civil War. Elsa and Byron signed them up for an online curriculum in math, language arts, and social studies to fill in the gaps. "Just in case," Elsa said.

However, like many of the accidental unschoolers I described in chapter 1, the family found it difficult to stay on track with the online program while traveling. At first, they tried to remain on a set schedule. As Elsa put it: "You're going to do that, except for today. Okay, you're going to do that, except for today. Well, there was always an 'except for today' a few times a week!" Travel days, special activities, spotty Internet connections; there was always an exception that pushed online school-work to the margins of the family's busy travel lifestyle. "So we decided to be a little bit more lax," Elsa said.

Now, Elsa continued, "the kids' creativity, it's almost out of control how curious they are. They're both full of ideas." To which Byron added, "We're letting them write whatever they want. And we're just flabber-gasted. Marisa read a little piece to us, was it about culture? She read two paragraphs to us and we were just speechless." Erik and Marisa may have been missing curricular units on US presidents, adverbs, the Civil War, and advanced math, but they were learning something else. "Life lessons," Byron said. "Like that adapting to change is important."

Both Byron and Elsa indicated that learning how to cope with change was an important lesson for global citizenship. Taking their own experience of weathering the economic recession as a case in point, they stressed how important it was to anticipate and adapt to changing conditions. This is a skill for which travel is an ideal teacher. While traveling, Elsa commented, "we all have to learn to adjust, because it's constant change." She contrasted long-term travel with a short-term vacation. "If you go on a week vacation and you don't like the food, you just return home and you go back to normal." But when you're on the road for months at a time, "you *have* to adjust." Elsa referred to these as the "deep, deep lessons" her children were learning. "It's because they've done it. They've lived through it," she said.

Elsa and Byron are not the only ones who see coping with change as a key attribute of global citizenship. Many worldschooling parents describe this lesson in terms of adaptability, flexibility, and resilience. Cora, a mother from the United States, writes on her blog that: "Perhaps one of the most important skills needed for the future 21st century global citizen is adaptability, flexibility and creativity and one learns that in spades on an extended world tour as a family!" Julia echoes this sentiment in a blog post on travel and education. "The world is changing," she writes, "and along with it the rules of the economic game and the job market." She continues:

> Very few corporations exist in a nationalistic bubble any more. The game has changed. The game is constantly changing. [. . .] Flexibility and creativity [. . .] are developed through doing hard things, through things going badly sometimes, through coping with the unexpected, through taking what you've got, which is perhaps not enough, and making the best of it, making it work, making something happen.

Travel is not the only way to develop a child's sense of flexibility or resilience, Julia acknowledges, but it is a "surefire" one.

As we talked at the café, Byron went on to point out that Erik and Marisa weren't just learning how to adjust to change, they were also learning how to monitor their own emotional responses to that adjustment. The Harts described the inevitable meltdowns each child had experienced while struggling to learn Spanish or dealing with culture shock in Thailand. In those moments, Byron encouraged Erik and Marisa to ask themselves: "How do [I] recognize that this change is upsetting me, and how do I channel or deal with that?" As evidence of what Erik and Marisa were learning, Elsa added that both kids are "writing books right now, e-books, on traveling and adjusting to change."

Not only were Erik and Marisa learning how to cope with change, they were also learning how to reflect on and monitor their own feelings about change, and to translate those feelings into a guide for others. Following in their parents' footsteps as digital entrepreneurs, Erik and Marisa were translating their feelings about constant change into commodified form: e-books. As Arlie Hochschild might say, they were learning how to do important emotional labor as global citizens.[7] In this case, knowing that change is inevitable, knowing how to cope with it, and perhaps even knowing how to capitalize on it, is a way of preparing children for the uncertainties they will face as twenty-first-century global citizens. So, too, is learning how to communicate across cultural differences.

Communicating across Difference

Worldschooling parents often point to their children's fluency in a second language or ability to talk with people who are different from them as markers of global citizenship. At first blush, communication may not seem like an emotional skill, but I was struck in my analysis by how often worldschooling parents conflated the ability to communicate with emotional competencies like confidence, open-mindedness, compassion, and connection to the global family of humanity. The story Julia tells about her fourteen-year-old son Drew is one example.

After traveling the world at a fairly steady pace for a few years with their four children, Julia and her husband Scott decided to slow down and rent a house in a small village in Central America for several months. While there, Drew, by this time a quiet, unassuming teenager, began volunteering at a local health clinic every day. After watching Drew disappear to the clinic each morning and return to the house each afternoon, Julia asked if she could tag along to see what he was doing every day. On the day she accompanied Drew, she was astounded to discover how much he was contributing to the busy clinic, helping serve meals, organizing activities, playing with the youngest children while they waited to see the doctor, and teaching the older children the English language. Overcome with pride in her son, Julia wrote:

> Today his kindness, his compassion, his dedication to a cause that touches his heart, his willingness to serve outside of his comfort zone, his willingness to make his own life uncomfortable and inconvenient in order to make someone else's a little bit better, his willingness to do the small things that no one sees, his effort to get beyond language barriers and over the immense cultural divide, and his day after day follow through brought me to my knees.

In this account of Drew's work at the clinic, Julia describes his contributions in terms of emotional qualities like heart, kindness, compassion, dedication, and discomfort, which she connects in the same breath to his ability to transcend language barriers and cultural divides.

For Julia, the scene she witnessed at the clinic was the culmination of her desire to raise all four of her children to be global citizens. She explains that when she and Scott first set out on their worldschooling journey, their intention was to help their children become global citizens by seeing "that everyone, everywhere is basically the same." They wanted their children "to get a firm grip on the privilege they enjoy as citizens of the first world and a sense of their responsibility within the larger world as a result." As Julia watched Drew exhibit those qualities in his work at the clinic, she concluded: "Travel did that. Mission accomplished."

We can infer from Julia's comments that the mission, in this case, was to encourage Drew to feel global: to overcome linguistic and cultural barriers, to feel kindness and compassion toward others, and to feel a sense of privilege and responsibility regarding his own comfortable position as a child of the Global North. I will pick up these two themes of compassion and comfort in a moment. Before I do, however, I want to examine how parents associate communication and self-confidence with their children's emerging global citizenship.

As I talked with Elsa and Byron that afternoon in the café, they confirmed that learning Spanish had been an enormous boost to Erik's and Marisa's self-confidence. "They can talk to anyone," Elsa said. To illustrate the point, Byron explained that the family had met some travelers from Argentina on the overnight train from Bangkok to Chiang Mai. Elsa picked up the story: "So for fourteen hours they were talking with these people from Argentina, no problem. And we met people from Puerto Rico, and there was that family from Chile." She nodded toward Byron, who explained that Spanish was proving almost as useful as English for communicating, with other travelers at least, and for getting around, even in Southeast Asia.

Like the Harts, many of the families in my study settled in a place for several months at a time so that their children could become fluent in a second or third language. Simona, for example, stayed in China for an extended period so that Leo could learn Mandarin. And Carolyn, a mother from the United States, scheduled five months in Central America into her family's itinerary so her children could learn to speak Spanish. Learning another language was at the top of Carolyn's list of desired learning outcomes, she writes, "partly because it's so good for brain development, partly because it's a great skill to have." Language acquisition through cultural immersion is, for many parents, the key to expanding their children's worldviews and making them more open-minded.

For the Harts, Erik's and Marisa's fluency in Spanish amounted to an emotional accomplishment as much as a linguistic one. By learning Spanish, they reasoned, the children were becoming more confident, broadening their worldviews, and gaining access to a larger world. As they recounted the many times Erik and Marisa had used their Spanish while traveling in Asia, I thought about the Thai students in the atrium downstairs, browsing English-language programs, perhaps in the hopes of staking their own claims to global citizenship. What kind of foothold did those students hope to gain by adding a summer in England to their résumés? As native English speakers, Erik and Marisa already had one global language in their pocket, but it was learning and speaking Spanish that made them feel cosmopolitan and connected to a wider global community.

Parents remark on their children's confidence talking with strangers, including adults, in another language. Just as often, though, they talk about the "universal language" of play or laughter. On their blogs and in interviews, parents recounted instances when their child played happily with other kids on the beach or at a local playground even though they did not share a common language. Holly, a mother from Canada who traveled with her husband and their three children, notes that her children have made friends "from all over the world, who speak different languages and play different games but that doesn't stop them from finding a way to play together."

Simona similarly believes that travel teaches children to communicate across deep cultural differences. She writes:

> Travel brings you into contact with people whose lives are vastly different from your own. If an urban, Western child can interact with nomadic hunter-gatherers, Buddhist monks, Asian politicians and the rural poor, sometimes without even a common language, they can understand and interact with *anyone*.

In some cases, parents appeal to this myth of a universal language to paper over the reality that, in many cases, their children and the people they are communicating with lead deeply unequal lives by virtue of their disparate material conditions.[8]

In other cases, however, recognizing the existence of such inequalities is precisely what attunes children to their role as good global citizens. For example, Holly explains that her children now realize "that they are lucky to have more than a lot of other kids, even though they are just travelling with a handful of toys." Like Julia, who was pleased to see that her son Drew was getting "a firm grip" on his first world privilege, Holly observes that as her children figure out how to play and communicate with new friends, they are exposed to a world of material disparities and cultural differences in which they occupy a relatively privileged position. For Holly, these experiences were profoundly edifying. She writes on her family's blog that "having the chance to play with children from other cultures has been the biggest educational advantage of this trip." In the end, she writes, her children are learning "huge lessons": "They are confident, will talk to anyone anywhere, form friends quickly and are more sharing than most kids their age."

According to these parents, the ability to communicate, whether with a newly acquired language or through the universal language of play, is evidence of children's growing cosmopolitan competence. Being able to talk to "anyone anywhere" is one sign that children are able to feel at home in the world. Communication across different cultures also exposes them to inequalities that call up two more emotional skills in the global citizen's tool kit: compassion and gratitude.

Compassion and Gratitude

Compassion is the emotion worldschoolers are most likely to mention when they talk about global citizenship. When the topic of global citizenship came up in one of the worldschooling forums, for example, commenters emphasized emotions like empathy, sympathy, and compassion. Daria and Ben, both parents from the United States, weighed in with the following thoughts:

> DARIA: Ultimately, I would really hope a strong sense of compassion and understanding of other cultures and beliefs will help [our children] become strong members of society the global community needs.

BEN: We really want our children to have empathy and sympathy with all global citizens human or otherwise. We truly believe traveling the world will help them find their place [and] make them better humans.

In these comments, parents frame compassion, empathy, and related sentiments like tolerance and acceptance, as the proper and desirable way for children to feel toward others as members of the global community. And while they acknowledge that children can learn compassion anywhere, even at home, they argue that travel is an exceptionally effective way to develop children's sympathetic side.

This is why Pamela advises families not to avoid hardships on the road, but to embrace them:

Dealing with issues while on the road and learning to problem solve are all things that will carry your child through life. Experiencing new cultures and places and learning compassion and understanding are key to developing world citizens. They will get to experience the diversity that our world has to offer. These are skills that cannot be taught in a classroom.

Leah makes a similar point on her blog. She explicitly states that one of the primary reasons her family is traveling is to foster her children's sense of empathy and compassion. She and her husband want their kids to experience different cultures, she explains, "not just for the sake of merely experiencing them, but also for empathetic reasons—so that they can relate to those from other cultures and have more compassion and understanding towards others."

Worldschoolers sometimes allude to an unspecified "other" toward whom children should feel a kind of free-floating compassion, but they also refer to specific encounters with people living in poverty as powerful catalysts for these emotions. For example, Leah's blog post is accompanied by a photograph of her boys in Nicaragua, where they were confronted with what Leah describes as "noticeable poverty" and "abundantly desperate" people. Below the photo, she offers this insight: "Compassion for others is a trait most easily gained through seeing firsthand the suffering and joy of people who are at first glance different than you."

Studies have found that encounters with poverty can increase tourists' sense of compassion, but critics warn that this can be problematic.[9] As Émilie Crossley observes in her research with volunteer tourists in poverty-stricken communities, coming face-to-face with poverty often sends tourists on a powerful "moral inner journey" through sadness, compassion, and appreciation. The problem, Crossley notes, is that the transformative effects of these emotions are often confined to the tourist herself and rarely result in the kinds of structural changes needed to actually alleviate poverty.[10] Instead, by looking to such encounters to produce a sense of compassion, tourists often end up rationalizing or romanticizing rather than remedying poverty.[11] I will say more about this in a moment.

If compassion is the right way for young global citizens to feel about others, then these children must also learn how to feel the right way about themselves in order to become "better humans" and the "strong members of society the global community needs," as Daria and Ben put it. This means turning to compassion's flip side: gratitude. As I mentioned earlier, worldschooling parents are anxious for their children to recognize and feel thankful for their privilege. For some parents, privilege refers to the suburban bubble of Western-style consumer abundance their children may have taken for granted in the past. Or it refers to the luxury of freedom and travel they are enjoying now. For others, it refers to the advantages their children possess by virtue of being white, middle-class, English speakers whose ease of travel is facilitated by owning Global North passports. Julia writes on her blog that it is important to her that her children are "acutely aware that our [North American] citizenships entitle us to privileges that many others would trade much of what they have for."

Privilege comes with its own set of appropriate feelings: gratitude, appreciation, and humility, but also responsibility. In a blog post reflecting on what she hopes her children will learn from travel, Maggie, a mother from South Africa whom we met in previous chapters, writes about precisely these emotional lessons: "I want my kids to understand and practice gratitude," she says, but "I want my children to be exposed to the harsh stuff too." What she wants them to understand, she writes, is that, "for many people, life is tough . . . and harsh . . . and many children do not have the luxuries (and the food and the toys) that our kids enjoy. I want my kids to appreciate what they have."

Maggie goes on to describe precisely the kind of global citizens she hopes her children will become through these experiences: "I want my children to be empathisers. And initiators . . . and problem-solvers . . . and solution-finders . . . and the types of people who QUESTION the Great Injustices of this planet—and who use their own brains to start imagining potential solutions." Beyond just recognizing their privilege, parents like Maggie encourage their children to *feel* a particular way about it. They want their kids to appreciate the advantages they enjoy, to be grateful for and humbled by their good fortune, and to feel responsible to pay it forward by becoming, as Maggie puts it, the planet's future "problem-solvers" and "solution-finders."

If this sounds vaguely like a guilt trip, it isn't. Guilt is not one of the emotions parents try to cultivate in relation to their children's privilege.[12] Worldschooling parents rarely prompt their children to see that the very advantages they enjoy contribute to the oppressive conditions of others, and rarely acknowledge this fact themselves. Instead, they focus on gratitude and responsibility, rather than guilt, as the appropriate ways for children to feel about their own privilege.

Lessons in privilege and gratitude were evident in the way parents responded to a particular phrase that cropped up frequently in the forums and on blogs: "Lucky kids!" Usually, this phrase appeared in the comments section of families' blogs where readers—some sympathetic, others more critical—would comment, for example, "What lucky kids";" "Your kids are lucky to have parents who are willing and able to show them the world"; or "You all are so lucky." Parents' responses to these kinds of comments were mixed, revealing a paradox about privilege. In some cases, parents agreed that they and their children were "lucky," lucky to have been born in a place that granted them the freedom and choices that made their journeys possible. However, many parents took offense at the phrase, like Uma, a mother from Australia, who writes, "I cannot tell you how annoyed I get when people tell me how lucky I am." Or Nichole, who remarks, "We get a bit annoyed hearing how 'lucky' we are, how others 'wish' they could do it, and how they simply 'can't afford' to travel as much as we do." Or Maggie, who admits to feeling irritated when people tell her how lucky she is. "Because *luck* infers [*sic*] that this way of life somehow . . . magically . . . luckily . . . dropped from the heavenlies and landed in my lap," she writes in frustration. Maggie goes on to tell a long story about the misfortunes she endured, the sacrifices she made in her professional and personal life, and the naysayers she bucked to get her online business launched and her family on the road.

And yet, these parents who chafe at the notion that their mobile lifestyles are a matter of luck—as opposed to their own hard work, gumption, and courage—are the same ones who urge their children to recognize their own privilege and to generate appropriate feelings of appreciation, gratitude, and responsibility in response to that privilege. Parents want their children to be conscious of their privilege, but they become irritated when their own privilege is called into question.

What can we make of this paradox? Perhaps these two reactions are not as contradictory as they appear. In fact, they serve a similar purpose. By insisting that they made their own luck through hard work and good choices, and by encouraging their children to feel gratitude and responsibility, but not guilt, in response to their privilege, these parents are justifying their own advantaged position in the world. In other words, they are making a case for their own privilege in an unequal world.

To explain how this entitlement gets produced, I want to return to the topic of volunteer tourism. One of the ways parents attempted to bring out their children's sense of compassion and responsibility was by enrolling their families in various volunteer programs. More than half of the families in my study volunteered while abroad, most while traveling in South and Southeast Asia, Africa, or Central America. Some families spent time at local daycare and community centers, often teaching English to young children, or working on wildlife and nature conservation projects. Through these volunteer programs, parents hoped to open their children's eyes to the inequalities that exist in the world and, at the same time, instill in them a sense of responsibility to make a difference in the world.

As I noted above, voluntourism comes with its own baggage that makes its emotional appeal problematic, to say the least. Volunteering abroad rocketed to popularity several years ago as tourists from the Global North sought to travel in more sustainable and responsible ways. Since then, however, critics have raised the alarm about unscrupulous programs, such as for-profit orphanages, that do more harm than good. By now, worldschooling parents are well-acquainted with these practical critiques, which they respond to by actively seeking out reputable programs and avoiding volunteering in orphanages. But scholars have critiqued voluntourism from a more theoretical angle as well. For one thing, they argue, these practices map onto what anthropologist Mary Mostafanezhad calls a "geography of compassion," a postcolonial legacy that positions the Global North as the source of altruistic "helpers" and the poor communities of the Global South as those who must be "helped."[13] Even when families from the Global North volunteer with the admirable intentions of fostering their children's feelings of compassion and responsibility toward others, they inevitably reproduce these uneven geographies and play into these postcolonial power hierarchies.

Furthermore, scholars contend, although voluntourism encounters are promoted as opportunities to "make a difference," they tend to result in the tourist's self-transformation rather than structural change for the local community.[14] One critique is that the emphasis on sentimentality shifts the spotlight away from social inequalities and histories of oppression and shines it instead on the relatively anodyne emotional experiences of individual volunteers.[15] In other words, when voluntourists feel compassion, gratitude, or responsibility, this may be less in direct response to someone else's life conditions and more a component of the volunteer's own emotional subjectivity as a global citizen. Feeling grateful for one's privilege in light of others' misfortune may be a morally justifiable response to inequality, but gratitude alone does not necessarily address the structural realities of that misfortune.

From this angle, critics might argue that the emotions of compassion and gratitude worldschooling children are encouraged to feel reinforce their privilege and help them internalize a sense of entitlement to that privilege in the first place. As long as children feel the right way about their own privilege—that is, they don't take it for granted and they recognize that with great privilege comes great responsibility—they are entitled to the "luck" they enjoy. These feelings of compassion, gratitude, or responsibility may not dismantle structures of power, but they justify one's position at the lucky end of an uneven scale. In other words, parents are not asking their kids to divest themselves of their privilege, or even to feel guilty about it, but rather to call up the appropriate emotional responses to it. Another way of prompting the "right" emotions of global citizenship is by pushing kids outside of their comfort zones.

Comfort Zones

As my interview with Elsa and Byron was wrapping up, I looked over at our kids, still engrossed in their video editing project on the other side of the café. From my vantage point, they appeared completely at home as they practiced their digital nomad skills in this sleek café. They exhibited a kind of savoir faire in this space, knowing how to order Thai snacks, how to access the free wifi, and how to work and play together with someone they had just met and to whom they would soon say goodbye. They did not strike me as children who were operating outside of their comfort zones. And yet, during our interview, Elsa and Byron spoke at length about the emotional discomfort Erik and Marisa had experienced while adapting to other cultures and to life on the road. I knew that periodic bouts of discomfort and culture shock were par for the course. Elsa made sense of these "meltdowns," as she called them, by framing them as learning opportunities. "Not that I want them to go through any pain," she said, "but through that, that's when you grow. That's when you figure things out."

In a blog post titled "What We Learned," Astrid, a mother from the United States who traveled around the world with her husband, Kevin, and their eleven-year-old twins, claims that many of the lessons her family gleaned from their years on the road were a result of difficulties and discomfort. "I am a firm believer that adversity makes for a better person," she writes. Echoing some of the themes I've already addressed here and in previous chapters, Astrid continues: "Before the trip, I felt the children wanted for naught and had no idea how lucky they were. Long-term travel drives adversity." To illustrate her point, Astrid details some of those adverse experiences and the lesson her children learned from them:

> The kids have slept outdoors on a hard bench during a typhoon, they have hiked through knee deep mud while picking leeches off their skin, they have had conversations with so many people of different cultures, they've seen kids their age working the fields instead of in school, they've bravely tried foods far outside their normal repertoire, they've seen that people live without heat, hot water, technology, new clothes. They have learned it's ok to be uncomfortable.

Another mother from the United States, Tracy Parsons, who traveled around the world with her husband, Gabe, and their nine children, four of whom have special needs, reaffirmed the widely held belief that getting kids out of their comfort zone is a crucial step toward raising a "globally minded child." "The longer you travel," she concludes, "the more your child learns, the deeper her understanding of the world will be."

Kamila Dhar, a mother of two from the United States, takes this logic one step further, suggesting that what children learn from moving outside their comfort zones is how to become "responsible and adaptable global citizens," as she explains at length in this blog post:

> We're not saying life on the road is perfect or that we never miss certain comforts of home. Sometimes things don't work. Other times we just can't get what we want—the only available diaper brand leaks, the coffee is not strong enough, no one speaks English, nothing on the menu is gluten-free—but we adjust as a family.

It is precisely through these challenges, however, that Kamila's children, and indeed the whole family, are becoming global citizens, as she explains:

> We spend every day now learning about our world with our children. We're more connected to each other but also realize how connected we are to the rest of mankind [sic] and our natural world. We knew this on a superficial level before our journey and live it every day now. We are learning what it means to be responsible and adaptable global citizens.

As these parents describe it, pain and discomfort may not be desired emotions in and of themselves, but they are a means to an end. Physical and social discomforts, including the lack of material amenities, encounters with strangers (especially in a different language), being confronted with unfamiliar foods or environments, or coming face-to-face with material poverty, are mechanisms for producing emotional competencies like adaptability, flexibility, or empathy. It is through *dis*comfort that children learn about the world and about themselves on their way to becoming "globally minded" kids.

These stories about children's physical and emotional discomfort may seem somewhat out of place in the overall emotional profile of global citizenship. When parents talk about the emotional learning outcomes of travel, they focus almost exclusively on "positive" feelings like compassion and adaptability.[16] As I discussed in chapter 4, however, feelings such as homesickness, frustration, meltdowns, fear, culture shock, and anxiety are also evident in worldschoolers' stories. What I want to point out here, however, is that when these feelings do appear, they are often framed not as a failure to feel the "right" way, but rather as a conduit toward feeling global. This is clear in the passages above where becoming a global citizen means making the most of discomfort and the opportunities it presents to learn about oneself and the world.

Perhaps even more important is that children learn to be comfortable outside of their comfort zones. Harris Jones, a father from Australia who traveled around the world with his wife and their seven-year-old daughter and nine-year-old son, told me a story that reflected this desire. I met Harris in the lobby of our Bangkok hotel, and as our kids played together, he told me about the week his family had spent volunteering at a community daycare center in a favela in Rio de Janeiro. Comments from worried friends and family members about how unsafe it would be to stay in a favela weighed on Harris's mind as the taxi from the airport wove its way deeper and deeper into the impoverished neighborhood where his family would be volunteering. Harris admitted that he and his wife were pretty nervous, but that they "put on brave faces" so the children wouldn't panic. When they arrived at the hostel where the volunteers stayed, "the kids just took it all in stride," Harris recalled. "There were all these other adults checking in, and they all looked a bit wide-eyed, wondering what they'd just gotten themselves into! But our kids didn't perceive anything. They just wanted to play with the children." Harris confided that he was proud of his children, precisely because they were so at ease outside of their comfort zones.

What Harris and other worldschooling parents really want isn't merely to get their children *out* of their comfort zones but to *expand* their comfort zones. They emphasize how comfortable their children are anywhere in the world, regardless of the deep cultural differences and stark material inequalities they encounter. They want them to be comfortable with strangers and oblivious to difference in ways that make them feel connected, as Kamila puts it, to all of humanity and the natural world. In other words, they want them to feel at home in the world.

In a post titled "Home is where our hearts are," Julia writes that her family is always at home no matter where they are. This is because, she explains, "our journey has taught us that home goes with us, and that the world, in the most generous, open-armed, hospitable sense, invites us to be truly at home wherever she finds us." Like the quotes at this chapter's opening, Julia's comments suggest that the ability to feel at home anywhere and everywhere—to experience the whole world itself as the child's comfort zone—is the ultimate outcome of a traveling lifestyle. In many ways, feeling at home in the world, and the sense of ease and entitlement this implies, is the culmination of what it means to "feel global."

At Home in Uncertainty

It is possible to know the past, even to have a confident idea as to what is going on in the present. But the future is beyond us in more ways than one. To the extent that we think about it we think about it with feelings. The future is a space of hopes and fears—thus the only human space that is filled less with facts and events than with our emotions.
—Anthony Elliott and Charles Lemert, *The New Individualism*, p. 22

The full extent of parents' hopes and fears for their children's futures is immeasurable, but these stories about coping with change, communicating across difference, feeling compassion and gratitude, and expanding one's comfort zone enlighten us to what worldschooling parents are dealing with. Like most middle-class parents, worldschoolers are living and parenting in anxious times fueled by very real possibilities of financial insecurity and downward social mobility. In a world of scarce resources and increasing economic inequality, middle-class families cannot assume that their children will enjoy a better quality of life than their parents.[17] Under these conditions, encouraging children to feel global is a way of tipping the scales away from the worries and toward the hopes parents harbor for their children's futures. In this context, feeling global sets children up to hold onto, and build on, the advantages conferred by class, race, and nationality, and it does this in two ways. First, it equips children with the kinds of emotional competencies that are likely to give them a leg up in future career endeavors. Second, feeling global is a way of internalizing and justifying children's sense of entitlement to their place of privilege in the world.

Worldschooling parents may pride themselves on having the courage to live an unconventional lifestyle, but this doesn't mean they are immune to the anxieties about a precarious job market and their children's chances for professional success. As I detailed in chapter 1, one of worldschoolers' main critiques of conventional schools is that they are operating according to an outdated model that prepares children for the factory jobs of yesterday, not the shifting technological and economic landscape of tomorrow. Like all parents, worldschoolers are concerned about their children's economic futures, and they are invested in developing the emotional and entrepreneurial skills their children will likely need to thrive in tomorrow's labor market.

Worldschooling parents don't know exactly what the future holds for their kids. What they do know is that the kinds of careers their children are likely to have probably haven't even been invented yet, and once they are, they will probably be in constant flux. The pundits tasked with forecasting the economic future can do little more than alert us to a few worrying trends: Tomorrow's job seekers will likely hold multiple jobs over the course of their careers, many of those jobs likely don't exist yet, and to get them, applicants will be competing with top students from all over the world, if not with the robots who threaten to replace us all.[18] Under these circumstances, parents can only guess at the kinds of academic knowledge or professional skills children might need to be financially successful.

The one thing that does seem clear is that to thrive in the uncertain economy of tomorrow, children will need to be emotionally flexible. Teaching children to calibrate, cultivate, and commodify their emotions in a constantly changing world seems like the best bet for an economic future that is up in the air. In this case, the pundits have also given us a handy aphorism to indicate where the future of work is going. In an article published in the *Harvard Business Review*, Dov Seidman, CEO of a leadership ethics company, argues that the future of work is shifting "from hands to heads to hearts."[19] He offers this image as a kind of abbreviated history of the technological and economic transformations of the past two hundred years. Seidman writes that if the manufacturing economy of the industrial revolution was about "hired hands" and the knowledge economy of the late twentieth century was about "hired heads," then the technology revolution of the twenty-first century is about "hired hearts." Seidman argues that even though machines have now learned to do the kinds of jobs humans did in the industrial economy and in the knowledge economy, they cannot replace what is most human about us: our feelings. This means that the jobs of tomorrow will be about creating value using "all the attributes that can't be programmed into software, like passion, character and collaborative spirit."[20] In other words, the work of the future will require emotional competencies and will entail massive amounts of emotional labor.

This is not an entirely new development. Arlie Hochshild alerted us decades ago to the commodification of emotion and the shift toward emotional labor. When she was writing about emotional labor, however, she was focusing primarily on the service economy, and especially on working women, with case studies of flight attendants, maids, and nannies having to manage and calibrate their own feelings and the feelings of others as part of the product being sold.[21] The commodification of emotion that she discovered in the gendered service economy is now becoming normalized across all sectors of the neoliberal labor market.[22] In this new "human economy," as Seidman puts it, the most desirable worker is one who is an "emotionally intelligent, competent, personable, confident and well-rounded individual."[23] Indeed, according to recent reports, employers are becoming increasingly interested in job candidates' emotional intelligence, such as deep cultural knowledge or skills in personal interaction.[24] As far as competitive advantages go, these emotional skills outweigh content knowledge.

That travel should be a conduit for this kind of learning is not a new idea either, nor is it confined to worldschooling. In earlier studies of backpacking and youth travel, sociologists Luke Desforges and Ian Munt observed that middle-class youth used international travel "to stoke up cultural capital," which they then used to accrue economic capital.[25] Today's travelers, worldschoolers included, might be said to be stoking up emotional capital for the same purpose. This has become especially evident among study abroad students, gap year travelers, and volunteer tourists.[26] Studies of volunteer tourism, for example, find that as much as voluntourists want to help people during their program abroad, they also hope to develop the "emotional capacities and entrepreneurial competencies" that will position them competitively in a labor market that values employees who can move fluidly across borders, are emotionally flexible, and adjust easily to rapid changes.[27]

Like worldschoolers, voluntourists display their global citizenship primarily through a repertoire of feelings. And perhaps the most important feeling of all is feeling at home in the world. As Wanda Vrasti argues in her study of voluntourism, this is the key emotional skill employers seek. "Being 'at home in the world' is no longer the mark of the cosmopolitan aristocracy," she argues, "but a requirement for all workers who wish to enter the ranks of the middle class." Vrasti explains that through a volunteer stint abroad, "individuals amass scarce social capital, demonstrate their cognitive and communicative skills, and become the transgressive, risk-taking subjectivities multinational capital thrives on."[28] For young people on the cusp of entering the labor market, success often hinges on their ability to sell these emotional competencies to employers.[29]

If this is the case, then worldschooling parents' attentiveness to cultivating their children's global selves, namely their ability to cope with constant change, to communicate with different people, and to broaden their comfort zones, begins to look like a significant advantage. As Vrasti suggests, being able to feel at home in the world is the price of admission to enter, or to stay in, the ranks of the middle class. The ability to feel at home in the world is not just a desirable characteristic of the neoliberal worker, however. It is also, as I argued earlier, an expression of entitlement. Learning to cope with change, transcend linguistic and cultural barriers, expand the edges of their comfort zones, and express compassion toward those who are less fortunate while feeling gratitude for their own privilege are all ways that worldschoolers lay claim to their place in the world.

In his study of privilege at elite boarding schools, Rubén Gaztambide-Fernández argues that students from wealthy backgrounds apply various ideological frames to justify their entitlement to their class privileges and elite education. They do this by drawing attention away from their privilege and focusing instead on accomplishments such as their commitment to learning, their hard work, their tolerance of difference, or their community service to make sense of their life advantages.[30] By focusing on their community service and charity work, in particular, these students present themselves in a positive light as caring, engaged, responsible, and generous citizens in order to rationalize and legitimize their otherwise unearned advantages.[31]

Of course, not all worldschooling families fall into the same elite socioeconomic category as the students in Gaztambide-Fernández's study, but they employ similar ideological frames to justify their privilege in the global scheme of things. When worldschooling parents say that they want their children to be aware of their privilege, what they really want is for their children to feel a particular way about that privilege. They expose their children to cultural differences, poverty, and economic inequality in order to generate the right kinds of feelings—adaptability, compassion, gratitude, responsibility—that in turn warrant that privilege. As children cultivate these global feelings, they not only learn the emotional skills they need to navigate in a world of difference, but they also internalize a sense that they are occupying their rightful place in a global and diverse world.[32] Meanwhile, these feelings mark them as empathetic and enlightened global citizens who are not the passive victims of uncertainty but the proactive leaders and problem solvers of tomorrow.

Conclusion

For worldschooling parents, watching their children blossom into young global citizens is evidence that their out-of-the-box life choices are on the right track. Global citizenship may be the desired learning outcome of travel, but it is also a component of the good life these families seek. The way worldschoolers define it, global citizenship is, itself, a lifestyle choice, and choosing to feel global aligns with their broader aspirations of individual freedom, personal choice, and self-reliance. In keeping with the new individualism I described in the previous chapter, worldschoolers frame global citizenship primarily as a matter of individual self-actualization.

By defining global citizenship as an emotional disposition, parents contain it within the realm of personal feelings. The world fades into a backdrop of cultural differences and material inequalities against which the protagonist—in this case, the young global citizen—can focus on developing a global self, one who properly calibrates his or her inner emotional states, is self-reflexive about those feelings, and who feels the right kinds of emotions toward others, toward him- or herself, and toward their place in the world. This is not to say that worldschoolers disregard the importance of connecting with others or participating in collective action against oppression, poverty, and injustice. As I mentioned earlier, many families volunteer their time and resources to local programs while they are on the road, and several of them have participated in organized protests or actively promote social justice causes.[33] However, as Ella described it, global citizenship is first and foremost about an inner shift, not outer actions. Learning to feel global is thus another module in the "pedagogy of the self." Similar to the way embracing risk is a form of identity work, as I described in chapter 3, feeling global is about developing children into particular kinds of selves who are emotionally ready to handle the profound instability of life in late modernity.

If global citizenship is a proxy for the future, it is evident from the stories presented in this chapter that worldschooling parents see the future as uncertain. In the previous chapter, I detailed the social skills children are likely to need as they navigate increasingly fluid constellations of friendship, intimate relationships, and professional networks. Here, I have focused on the emotional skillset parents hope their children will acquire as a result of their travels. I have explored how worldschooling parents frame global citizenship—and specifically the emotional disposition of feeling global—as a strategy for preparing their children to tackle whatever an unpredictable future brings their way. After all, in an uncertain world, these are the emotional skills they will need to handle *anything*, talk to *anyone*, and feel at home *anywhere*.

6

Privilege and Precarity

Raising Future-Proof Kids

The possibilities in life multiply when one accepts all of the
combinations and permutations presented to us in our cha-
otic existence rather than being focused on a well-worn and
predictable path with predictable rules. [. . .] The question
is not whether to trade stability for uncertainty, but whether
to accept that there is no stability and prepare ourselves for
the uncertainty in a more anti-fragile way.
—Ella, blog post

Worldschooling is at once a radical departure from the conventional
playbook for the "good life" and an utterly logical response to the anxieties, aspirations, and uncertainties of late modernity. At the beginning
of this project, I set out to understand what happens when middle-class
families mobilize the supposedly stable building blocks of their social
lives: school, work, parenting, community, and citizenship. I was curious
to know whether and how their self-identity, family life, social relationships, and sense of belonging shifted when recast in the light of mobility.
To that end, I explored how parents do work, family life, and education
on the road. I described how they navigate the modern epidemic of anxious parenting and their own doubts about the future from the vantage
point of mobility, and how they tap into the possibilities afforded by
new technologies to expand their children's social networks and cultivate their sense of global citizenship. What I found is that mobilizing
these various aspects of their lives was key to worldschoolers' dreams of
living a good life in turbulent times.

In this concluding chapter, I scrutinize that strategy a bit more carefully. In particular, I interrogate the extent to which the mobile lifestyle
of worldschooling entails personal solutions for coping with public so-

cial problems. I argue that, for many of the families in my study, these individualized strategies reflect and reinforce their privileged position in the world, enabling them to harness rather than suffer from precarity. At the same time, I trouble this dichotomy of privilege and precarity to illustrate the limits of a "winners and losers" approach to our shared mobility future. The chapter ends by asking how we might broaden our existing vision of the good life to encompass a more just and collective "good mobile life."

Throughout this book, I have detailed how parents simultaneously embrace and brace for uncertainty. The analysis offered here reveals the embodied practices and everyday strategies worldschoolers have devised to live, and live *well*, with risk and uncertainty. As they tell it, it is through mobility that they are able to lead fearless and joyful lives while also raising global kids who possess the skills and sensibilities to thrive in the uncertain world of tomorrow. Worldschoolers may not know what the future holds, but they do know that whatever it is will likely require the skills and self-enhancing resources that global travel teaches. The life lessons children learn from worldschooling—knowing how to convert currencies, try new things, read timetables, take risks, navigate airports, earn money online, pack light, go with the flow, make conversation in multiple languages, stay connected to distant friends—prepare children for a future that is up in the air. These children are developing global, mobile selves that have been "fundamentally recast in terms of capacities for movement," as Anthony Elliott and John Urry express it.[1] Regardless of whether worldschooling kids grow up to pursue a life of constant travel, their generation will need this kind of practical know-how and emotional savvy to live "mobile lives."[2] Taken together, then, the strategies worldschoolers deploy create and circulate new forms of capital that secure their children's relative privilege in an unequal world.[3]

The argument that parents seek to safeguard their children's social status by conveying economic and cultural advantages to them is hardly new. Throughout this book, I have referred to scholars like Annette Lareau, Margaret Nelson, Marianne Cooper and others who have detailed the way middle-class parents in the Global North use education, parenting techniques, and lifestyle as mechanisms for reproducing privilege across generations. Many of these studies draw on the work of French sociologist Pierre Bourdieu to identify how power and privilege are reproduced through various forms of cultural and social capital that position people up and down the social hierarchy.

This is the lens Annette Lareau uses to make sense of the persistent inequalities among poor, working-class, and middle-class school children.[4] In her study, Lareau finds that children's experiences and outcomes in school are determined not just by their parents' economic status, but by the kinds of cultural capital parents transmit to their children. Parents across the socioeconomic class spectrum convey cultural capital to their children, of course, disposing them to particular behaviors, tastes, competencies, preferences, and ways of being in the world, but not all cultural capital is equally valued in wider social and institutional settings. Lareau discovered that middle-class parents were more likely than poor and working-class parents to teach their children the kinds of cultural competencies that gave them an advantage in the institutional setting of the school. For example, they tended to teach their children how to negotiate with authority figures, how to marshal the right terminology in a given situation, and how to present and support arguments, and they enrolled them in extracurricular activities that enriched their academic learning. This form of concerted cultivation, Lareau argues, equipped the middle-class children in her study with the kind of cultural capital that was, in turn, valued and rewarded in the classroom. Marianne Cooper gives examples of upper-income parents, anxious about preparing their children to succeed in a turbulent economic future, who invested heavily in their children's cultural capital by exposing them to lifestyle experiences, such as international summer camps or specialized music lessons.[5] Margaret Nelson similarly found that the middle-and upper-class parents in her study enrolled their children in a "dazzling array" of extracurricular activities that might give them a competitive advantage in school, on standardized tests, in college admissions essays, and eventually in job interviews.[6]

My analysis of worldschooling reveals similar hopes about instilling cultural values, competencies, and mind-sets that are likely to be advantageous as children move into adulthood. There is, however, a key difference between worldschoolers and the parents Lareau, Cooper, and Nelson studied. In those studies, middle-class parents were concerned with teaching their children how to negotiate and leverage advantages in institutional settings, namely school. They defined success in institu-

tional terms—do well in school, go to a good college, get a good job—
and to this end, they sought to secure their children's future prospects
through institutional channels. Lareau, for example, describes how
middle-class parents intervened in institutional settings to attain advantages for their children, and Nelson and Cooper both describe how
parents work to get their children accepted into the "right" universities,
and later the "right" jobs.[7]

Worldschoolers see success unfolding along a radically different trajectory. They are not training their children to interact with authorities,
or advance themselves in institutional settings, but rather encouraging
them to become the authors of their own lives. Rather than teaching
children to subject themselves to institutions that cannot be trusted to
have their best interests at heart (like the government or the school system) or relied upon to offer a stable path to success (like corporate employment), they are preparing their children to forge their own path in a
precarious social and economic landscape. As I have described throughout the book, worldschoolers pursue the good life quite deliberately outside of—and, in some cases, in direct rebellion against—institutional
and collective forms of social life. In fact, their ideology of resistance is
central to the rebel identities worldschoolers hope to construct. What
this means is that worldschoolers tend to take a highly individualized
approach to their lifestyle projects.

The Good Life on *Our* Terms

I'm getting tired of the self-indulgence of travel and travel
blogging. Travel is incredibly rewarding, and finding personal happiness is something to savor. But is it more important than (or even separate from) collective happiness? Let's
be real, when people of privilege travel, it usually doesn't
help anyone but themselves.
—Elizabeth Aldrich, www.temporaryprovisions.com

After reading the account of worldschooling in this book, it may not
be surprising to learn that some of the parents in my study have been
accused of being selfish. Perhaps you were thinking it yourself. It is a critique worldschoolers confront frequently, and one for which they have

multiple answers. Some parents point to their efforts to help others and do good in the world along their journeys. As I mentioned in chapter 5, a majority of the families in my study participated in volunteer projects while traveling. And the family summits and learning retreats I discussed in chapter 4 often include some kind of community outreach or local service project, along with self-reflexive sessions on voluntourism's potential harm. A few use their travels more directly to benefit the classmates their children have left behind. They stay in touch with former teachers and share their experiences online or through video chats to engage students back in the classroom with the history, culture, and geography lessons their kids are learning on the road.

By far the most common response, though, is to reframe selfishness as an individual right, one that these parents feel compelled to exercise as good neoliberal subjects. We see this rationale in a comment Vera, a mother from the United States, posted on the social media forum:

> For us it boils down to what kind of individual we are hoping to raise. [. . .] We hope that [our son] will grow up to be aware of the larger world around him and his place in it. It's a choice and like any other choice, we're doing what we think is right for our family. No one else can remotely come close to making those decisions for us. And if that makes us selfish then we are guilty as charged.

And Dean appeals to the rights enshrined in the Declaration of Independence to justify his family's "selfish" pursuit of the good life:

> You may question our selfish act of leaving society to pursue our own happiness, but the founding fathers of the United States understood the importance of happiness. They understood it so well that they even wrote it into the Declaration of Independence: We hold these truths to be self-evident, that all men [sic] are created equal, that they are endowed by their Creator with certain unalienable Rights, that among these are Life, Liberty and the pursuit of Happiness.

If worldschooling is selfish, these parents reason, it is only because the choices they are making are deeply personal, tailored to their family's unique needs and individual dreams.

In chapter 4, I observed that worldschooling parents go to great lengths to establish that their lifestyle choices are not a template for anyone else. They are merely following *their* family's dreams. As Mitch writes on his blog, "Each family is different and has different personalities and skills, time and priorities, but for us this just seems so right." To which an anonymous reader comments: "We are all individuals not clones. This one size fits all world is monotonous and boring at best, dangerous to each individual on the planet at worst." Under these circumstances, where institutions like school and work, traditional scripts for parenting, and static forms of community and citizenship fail to add up to a good life, it is parents' obligation to do what is right for *their* children. Their choices may be selfish, but these parents see it as their responsibility to chase their own dreams.

From this perspective, worldschooling can be interpreted as an individualized escape from the collective projects of citizenship, community, work, and raising, educating, and caring for children. The life strategies I described in previous chapters are, in effect, personal solutions for coping with what parents perceive to be the wholesale failure of these institutions and the social epidemic of uncertainty that has followed in the wake of that failure. After all, what are middle-class parents supposed to do when cultural messages and government policies explicitly exhort them to take matters into their own hands, to empower themselves as consumers, choosers, and entrepreneurs, and to take responsibility for their own happiness?

According to Sam Binkley, they are doing precisely what modern subjects are supposed to do. Against the backdrop of neoliberal ideologies, he argues, "individuals are increasingly instructed in ways of acting (at work, in the family, among friends) that replicate the logics of the market," which requires them to "consider their careers in terms of the maximization of profit, to evaluate personal relationships in terms of emotional 'pay-offs,' to embrace life in terms of its experiential 'benefits,' etc."[8] Above all, Binkley stresses, "they are encouraged to approach these challenges alone, as solitary 'enterprises,' and to refuse any collectivist traditions previously fostered by the state."[9]

As I have described it, worldschooling is an enterprise in which desires, anxieties, successes, and failings are articulated around individual personhood, while attention is shifted away from common struggles, structural inequalities, and collective action. Encouraging children to feel global, crafting community in terms of a tribe of rebels, or adopting parenting techniques like cultivated independence are all strategies that seek to maximize individual capacities to thrive amidst mobility, flux, and uncertainty.

So, too, are the entrepreneurial subjectivities and managerial techniques that many parents apply to their mobile lifestyle projects. Studies suggest that people who embody an entrepreneurial subjectivity tend to overlook wider social structures or systemic inequalities, instead seeing the individual self as the locus of change.[10] As I explained in chapter 2, worldschooling parents responded to their previous unhappy working conditions not by joining a labor union or participating in workers' rights movements, but by launching themselves as entrepreneurial free agents and digital nomads. Entrepreneurs also interpret successes and setbacks in terms of individual character traits, which in turn positions work on the self as the solution to problems in the social sphere. For many of the worldschooling parents in my study, then, becoming an entrepreneur was a personal strategy for coping with change and insecurity in the labor landscape, while instilling an entrepreneurial mind-set in their children was a strategy for helping them develop the individual capacities for self-reliance and self-improvement that would serve them in the future.

Of the individualized strategies worldschoolers adopt in the face of collective problems, perhaps the most telling is their rejection of institutional schooling. As I have shown, worldschoolers frame their children's education not as a compulsory component of collective social life, but as an individual choice that reflects each family's personal values. In the educational choices they make for their children, worldschoolers tend to prioritize their individual desires for the good life over collective aspirations about the future.

In the industrialized nations of the Global North, compulsory education was designed to serve communal goals, whether that meant assimilating newly arrived immigrants, mitigating social and economic inequalities, preparing the next generation of workers to contribute to the national economy, or socializing a diverse citizenry into shared moral, political, and social norms. This is in part why some countries, such as Germany, prohibit homeschooling altogether and why others regulate it closely. And this, in turn, is why many parents choose to remove their children from what they see as institutions of state control. They argue that in a democratic society, parents have a fundamental right to educate their children as they see fit. In short, these parents see education as a private concern subject to individual choice rather than as a common good serving public and collective interests.

Besides, their rationale continues, even if they wanted to stay home, there is little they can do about the entrenched problems of an outdated public school system, the emptiness of suburban life, or an overscheduled existence that leaves little quality time with the kids. "Unfortunately, I can't change the system, and neither can you," Julia writes in a post explaining why she took her children out of conventional schooling. What Julia can do, however, and what she encourages other parents to do, is "to take responsibility for our own kids and their educations and make sure they get what they need." Whether this means long-term family travel or not, she says, it is up to parents to "make the most of the time and resources you have and get your kids into the world and give them the space and time they need to learn and grow beyond spelling lists and math facts." If parents feel unable to fix the system, as Julia puts it, then the next best choice is to abandon it altogether and invest their energies in the individual strategies over which they feel they have some control.

Critics argue that when parents exercise what they see as their individual right to remove their children from state-mandated education and follow a learning model of their choice—whether through unschooling, homeschooling, or worldschooling—they are undermining the progressive intentions of public schooling.[11] For example, in an article for *Slate* magazine, journalist Dana Goldstein admonishes liberal parents who homeschool and unschool their kids, arguing that these alternative forms of education violate progressive values. Although the demographic profile is changing now, these movements continue to be dominated by white, middle-class, two-parent families who can afford for one parent to stay home and dedicate a vast amount of labor and individualized attention to the children.

In the "go-it-alone ideology" of homeschooling, Goldstein sees several disturbing trends, such as a declining sense of trust in the public sphere, the reproduction of class privilege and patriarchal definitions of the nuclear family, and worse outcomes for the low-income students left behind. On this latter point, Goldstein cites research on "peer effects" that finds low-income students earn higher test scores when they attend school with middle-class kids, while the test scores of middle-class students are not influenced by less-privileged peers. In other words, the absence of middle-class students makes it harder for less-advantaged children to thrive.[12] What looks like a rightfully personal decision for middle-class parents actually has profound ramifications for the broader community. It is an example of what Richard Reeves calls "opportunity hoarding."[13]

This outcome bears out the findings of research conducted by Diane Reay and colleagues. Their study focused on middle-class parents in London who kept their children in conventional school settings but did so by having their kids attend inner-city comprehensive schools, where they would be exposed to a more diverse student body. Much like the worldschooling parents in my study, the parents Reay and her team interviewed were passionate about producing "well-rounded, tolerant individuals" who would be "socially fluent and adaptable," "resilient," and "global minded," all valuable skills to be learned through encounters with the racially, ethnically, and socioeconomically diverse composition of the comprehensive schools.[14] However, according to the researchers, the white, middle-class children were disproportionately enriched by this multicultural mixing, which gave them access to emotional competencies and cultural capital, in ways that did not necessarily benefit their non-middle-class and non-white classmates to the same extent. A choice that appeared to signal a civic commitment to a liberal ideal of multicultural solidarity on the part of middle-class parents effectively consolidated privilege to their already advantaged children. In their analysis, Reay and her co-authors see this as a case of "being trapped in privilege," where choices that are directed toward the common good actually accrue more value to the white middle classes than toward their class- and ethnic others.[15]

Worldschooling families are similarly trapped in a system that brings disproportionate value to them on the basis of their privileged race, class, and national identities regardless of their conscious efforts to cultivate empathetic and egalitarian sensibilities in their children. It is difficult to see how personal choices can lead parents out of this trap. As Reay and her co-authors observe, "ethical behavior is only partially achievable in a society which is structurally unethical in the way it distributes resources and opportunities."[16] This leaves parents in a quandary given that their individual efforts to behave ethically can do little to address structural inequalities.[17]

If parents are in a quandary, where does that leave scholars? Should we chide middle-class parents for the unintended consequences of their lifestyle strategies? Should we encourage worldschoolers to stay home and channel their energies into public school reform or workers' rights movement or other forms of social activism? I doubt this would get us very far. Many of the worldschoolers in my study are already acutely aware of their privilege and its effects, and some of them have engaged in social activism both at home and on the road. In response to this dilemma, then, Reay and her co-authors pose two challenges to scholars.

First, they encourage us to "develop critiques which, while recognizing how people negotiate inequitable situations, also constantly keep in play the structural injustices within which they are situated."[18] To this end, I have tried to understand how this particular moment in late modernity, one characterized by new freedoms and new obligations, requires certain kinds of responses and makes certain moves possible for these families. Second, they call on scholars to "recognize the complexities of whiteness," to document the way it is lived and experienced, and to account for the fact that not everyone who is white is "equally white."[19] I read this as a call to trouble our understandings of how race and privilege intersect, with whiteness often serving as a metaphor for privilege,[20] and to dismantle the entrenched dichotomies and assumed associations of power, race, and class.

The families in my study, most of whom are white, enjoy considerable advantages as they take their lives out on the road, but this does not mean that they all experience privilege in an unequivocal or uniform way. I have interrogated the complex and nuanced ways in which families alternately lean on, surrender, and amplify their privilege through travel. What looks like a privileged escape from the problems of communal life from one angle can look like a dangerously precarious situation from another. To understand the mobile lifestyle of worldschooling in all its complexity, then, we need to understand how these families balance privilege and precarity.

Privilege in Precarious Times

The unprecedented level of freedom that late modernity has bestowed on individuals can be truly exhilarating, but the flip side of that freedom is precarity. The term precarity is often used to describe the economic uncertainties, social anxieties, and wealth inequalities that have followed in the wake of casualized work and hollowed-out social welfare programs. It has become a shorthand for the prevailing atmosphere of insecurity in late modern life.

Sociologist Arlie Russell Hochschild describes this atmosphere of precarity in terms of the strategies people use to "edge out the pressures" of uncertainty.[21] She explains that individuals have to become comfortable with anxiety, competition, and change beyond their control, a point she illustrates with the example of "acid rainproof fish." She explains that in the lakes and rivers of New England, where the waters have been contaminated by acid rain blown in from as far away as the Midwest, the fish have developed into a new breed that can survive in the polluted waters. Like the acid rainproof fish, she says, a new kind of neoliberal subject is emerging, one that is adapted to the conditions of precarity.

The ideal worker she describes is one who dives in despite the anxiety, "who makes him- or herself apparently impervious to this new insecurity." She describes this worker as someone who "is tough, but personable," who is able to "confront raw capitalism head on," and who knows how to "make do without job security." The people who will weather the acid climate of neoliberalism, she says, are the ones who "understand that it is uncertain, but get out there anyway." Hochschild's metaphor of the acid rainproof fish resonates with my argument that worldschoolers are trying to raise "future-proof kids." The kind of life lessons and cultural capital parents hope to convey to their children—for example, learning how to become adaptable, self-reliant, independent, creative, resourceful, comfortable with change, and at home in difference—are precisely the kinds of sensibilities and subjectivities that precarity calls for.

What we must acknowledge, however, is that although we are all living in precarious times, we are not all oriented toward the ups and downs of uncertainty in the same way. Our socioeconomic standing places us in different "risk climates," as Marianne Cooper puts it.[22] For one thing, not everyone is equally able to reinvent themselves from scratch. Physical and social identities are in many ways more fluid than ever before, but systemic inequalities based on race, class, sexuality, and gender have proved stubbornly durable. And although many entrepreneurial world-schoolers subscribe to a story of bootstrap heroism in which anyone with the desire and the self-discipline can find a way to escape the status quo, there are very real physical, financial, geographical, political, and social constraints that make such a life choice much more difficult for some people. The freedom to refashion one's self and craft one's lifestyle is a limited resource. And it comes at a cost.

Privilege in Precarity

Worldschoolers don't want their children to be at the whim of uncertainty, but they also don't want them to merely cope with it. Instead, they want their children to be able to leverage precarity for their own fulfillment. The key to thriving in precarity is the ability to frame flexibility as autonomy, responsibility as self-empowerment, uncertainty as an opportunity, and mobility as a choice. And this ability is a function of privilege.

It is tempting to think of privilege and precarity as occupying opposite ends of a scale, but my analysis suggests that the reality is far more complicated. We need to understand them as two sides of the same coin, intersecting in ways that produce new kinds of vulnerability and new kinds of value. Consider, for example, the concept of the "precariat." When we think about the precariat, we often think of the dispossessed and marginalized underclass of neoliberal capitalism. According to British economist Guy Standing, this new working underclass is defined by the conditions of their labor, which is increasingly insecure, unstable, informal, and part-time.[23] The precariat, lacking any kind of job security or labor-related protections, is the face of staggering wealth inequalities, a class victimized by a transforming labor landscape. But this profile of the precariat underclass does not tell a complete story. The labor conditions Standing describes are now commonplace, not just at the bottom rungs of the retail and manufacturing industries or in the pseudo-entrepreneurial gig economy, but throughout professional fields such as health care and teaching, as well as in the creative, digital, and knowledge industries. Across the board, today's workers are likely to move from job to job and even more likely to take on freelance employment.[24]

Against the image of the precariat as the victimized working class, some scholars have projected a more positive image of a "romantic free spirit," as Standing puts it, a rebel who "rejects norms of the old working class steeped in stable labour, as well as the bourgeois materialism of those in salaried 'white collar' jobs."[25] Members of this segment of the precariat are defined not by their subjugation to market logics, but by their "free-spirited defiance and nonconformity [...] against the dictates of subordinated labour."[26] They even welcome the idea of precarious labor. As Hochschild explains in her interview, advice books tell private sector workers to think of themselves not as employees of a company, but "as a stand-alone company, a 'brand called me.'"[27] These advice books also tell us that flexible, project-based, freelance work promises to usher in a more vibrant and equal society in which each of us will be empowered to craft our own networks, invest in our own skills, and capitalize on our unique talents.[28]

Clearly, life in the precariat is a better deal for some people than for others. Depending on where you land on the social hierarchy, the shifts in work conditions can be either exciting or terrifying. For example, the current generation of digital nomads seems to have figured out how to play these changes to their advantage, as journalist Beth Altringer observes:

> Young people in particular are placing a higher priority on flexible professional lifestyles and personally meaningful work. What's clear is that if pursuing a meaningful career while traveling the world is viable, who would not choose it? If, all else equal, you could do just as well professionally but with more autonomy, flexibility, and excitement outside of work, then surely nomads have cracked the code on work-life balance.[29]

And it is not just young people. For many worldschoolers, the emergence of new kinds of work and more flexible ways of working is an exciting development that grants new freedom in the pursuit of their lifestyle aspirations.

The previous chapters revealed many stories of this kind of embrace of precarity. Throughout this book, we have heard stories of worldschoolers' "leap of faith" into an unpredictable life of unschooling, entrepreneurialism, and constant travel. We have seen the way they teach their children to leverage risk as a learning opportunity, see uncertainty as value waiting to be created, harness change and discomfort as avenues to global selfhood, and commodify their mobile lifestyles. These are the people who are able to marshal the financial, cultural, and mobility capital needed to ride out waves of success and failure. In these scenarios, worldschoolers are the heroes, not the victims, of precarity.

This more nuanced definition of the precariat gives us a foothold for understanding how worldschoolers negotiate privilege and precarity. On the one hand, some worldschoolers might land in the precariat based on the conditions of their work, much of which is relatively low-paid, freelance, flexible, and temporary with few benefits or protections. On the other hand, however, worldschoolers have not had job insecurity thrust upon them. Many of them voluntarily quit salaried jobs and chose to enter the insecure world of entrepreneurial, flexible, part-time work as part of a lifestyle trade-off. They very much identify themselves with the "free-spirited defiance and nonconformity" that Standing describes. But their privilege derives from more than just an attitude. It also rests on their ability to exercise their privilege in a world of systemic inequalities.[30]

Even accounting for the socioeconomic range among worldschoolers, these families are relatively privileged by global standards. This privilege travels well, in no small part due to their whiteness and to the Global North passports these travelers tend to carry. Being from an industrialized nation with a strong currency means that global political and economic conditions usually work in their favor. The freedom of mobility they enjoy is also predicated on the literal and figurative immobility of people and places in the Global South. For example, the past fifty years of postcolonial geopolitics and neoliberal economic policies have ensured that the cost of living has remained low in places that are now desirable hubs where lifestyle migrants, digital nomads, and worldschoolers can stretch their dollars, pounds, and euros to afford their mobile lifestyles. In this sense, worldschoolers can capitalize on this kind of "geoarbitrage," as I described it in chapter 2, but only because these places occupy the most precarious position in the global economy.

Worldschoolers possess another powerful form of cultural capital: the technical and discursive know-how to frame their lifestyle choice as a success story. They are skilled at using social media platforms to define their experiences as edifying, brave, and enviable, and they benefit enormously from the ability to portray their family's mobility as a moral lifestyle choice. In contrast to parents and children farther down the power hierarchy, who often have little control over the negative lens through which their mobility is perceived, worldschoolers are able to present their rejection of the status quo and their pursuit of family travel in positive terms like living the good life, learning from travel, taking entrepreneurial risks, investing in their children's future, and becoming global citizens. They are the authors of their own narratives.

As we know, however, behind the highlight reels that people publish on social media, there is often another reality. In fact, Julia Porter wrote a scathing blog post aimed at her fellow worldschoolers, lifestyle travelers, and digital nomads, calling them out for filtering their images and sugarcoating their travel stories. She implores her counterparts, the "shiny-happy digital nomad gods of the world, masters of our destinies and livers of life on our own terms," to stop pretending that their dreamy lifestyle doesn't come with difficulties and struggles, illness, and bad smells. She admonishes them to stop pretending that they can actually work from the beach or a hammock, or get an Internet connection in a rice paddy, or earn enough money to live while working just four hours a week. And to readers, she warns, don't be fooled by that "badass travel chick" who seems to be living the lifestyle you crave, "but who actually lives below the poverty line and is secretly so homesick she cries about it."

Precarity in Privilege

As much as worldschoolers exercise their privilege to make the most of the freedoms late modernity offers, they are not immune to the hazards of precarity. In previous chapters, for example, I described the fears, worries, and emotional consequences that are part of a mobile lifestyle. The entrepreneurial digital nomads in my study, in particular, write at length about the difficulties they face as freelance workers. They describe working insane hours to launch and maintain their businesses, the sense of panic when income sources evaporate, and the anxiety they feel as they watch blog traffic peak and plateau. They suffer the pressures of having to stay one step ahead to rustle up the next paying project or waking up at 4 a.m. to video conference with someone on the other side of the world. Freelance work and self-employment may be flexible, but the work and income are still insecure.

In a blog post detailing her path to digital nomadism, Leah writes that many of her friends and readers are jealous of her family's mobile lifestyle because "the freedom we have to travel or live anywhere seems exotic and exciting to most suburbanites." And she admits that "it is pretty awesome." Nevertheless, she concedes, "it's not without challenges and sacrifices." She goes on to describe the years of work and planning that preceded her family's departure, the late nights she and her husband spent creating their online business, the self-doubt, the early stumbles, and the financial challenges they endured during the transition and continue to experience now that they are on the road.

It is worth noting that Leah's story about the strains and insecurities of digital nomadism is told as part of a post in which she urges other families to swallow their fears and take a similar leap into a mobile lifestyle. Leah encourages wary readers with tips for leaving behind friends and family, what to do with their house, or getting the right gear. Worried about the children's education, about covering your monthly bills, or affording health care when you get sick on the road? According to Leah, none of these things are guaranteed at home, anyway, so why not pursue the independent lifestyle of your dreams? The message Leah sends her readers is that the life of a digital nomad family is unpredictable and insecure, but that's okay. This is what they signed up for. And at least on the road, they can determine their own path. Leah has made herself "impervious to insecurity," as Hochschild puts it, and urges her readers to do the same.

The insecurities Leah describes, those associated with education, income, illness, and health care, for example, are everyday realities for most of the worldschoolers in my study. But even within this group, there is considerable variability in how families are positioned vis-à-vis precarity and privilege. Some have more financial resources, or the right kinds of credentials and experience to land online work, or fewer obligations to extended family, or varying levels of physical and mental health that make it more or less feasible to seize the opportunities of a precarious economy. As I have noted, most of the families I interviewed and followed online came from middle-class backgrounds, having held stable professional jobs before hitting the road. Leah's story is quite typical of the worldschoolers who adopted an entrepreneurial strategy for affording their mobile lifestyles. For these parents, the unpredictable costs of travel and the financial precarity of self-employment are reasonable trade-offs for the freedom and autonomy they enjoy.

A few of the families I interviewed were much better off financially. They had either saved plenty of money for their trips or were independently wealthy and therefore had no need to earn an income while traveling. Though many of them did publish blogs during their journeys, they were not under pressure to monetize them. If these families found themselves in a compromising situation, they could afford to get themselves out of it. Precarity was not as threatening to them or their lifestyle as it was to other families.

A few of the families I met were barely scraping by, traveling on shoestring budgets that left little room for error. This was the case for Monique, a single mother from France, who was traveling with her ten-year-old son, Axel, when I met her at a campground in Australia. Axel and Elliot had met earlier in the day on the beach, and later Monique and I chatted as we prepared our meals in the camp's shared kitchen. Monique shared with me her deep mistrust of government institutions like the state school system and her plans to take Axel to visit her family in France once they were done traveling around Australia. Her frustrations and aspirations sounded very much like those of the other worldschooling parents I'd met online and in person.

As we talked, Monique revealed that she was divorced from Axel's father, an Australian citizen, from whom she received a meager child support stipend. Their custody agreement also meant that she could not leave the country with Axel, which put the plans to visit France on indefinite hold. I eventually realized that Monique and Axel were staying at our campground not because they wanted to be camping, necessarily, but because they could not afford other accommodations. Nevertheless, she presented her lifestyle as a carefree choice and described Axel's days spent camping and surfing as part of her larger pedagogical plan for him. The precarity Monique faced, and her efforts to mobilize resources to deal with it, were quite different from my own experience and from

Leah's experience, which in turn differed from the experiences of the independently wealthy families I had met.

* * *

It is clear that we require a more nuanced account of how privilege, precarity, and power are mutually constituted through mobility. A handful of scholars have begun to push our understanding in this direction. Anthropologist Vered Amit, for example, reminds us that mobility, even among the professional classes, is not necessarily a sign of privilege. The highly mobile freelance workers profiled in her study lead quite comfortable lives abroad, but these workers occupy what Amit calls a "middling" position, a far cry from the elite status of mobile executives. They may be hypermobile, Amit acknowledges, but they are not necessarily "free to roam around the world at will" since the terms of their employment often determine when and where they move, nor is their current and future financial security guaranteed.[31]

Kate Botterill's study of British retirees living in Thailand similarly challenges the notion that a mobile lifestyle equates to privilege.[32] She argues that her respondents' privileged status as White Western expatriates and their relative affluence in relation to Thai residents often masks the precarious aspects of aging abroad. Despite the many advantages these retirees enjoy, they face financial insecurity caused by currency value fluctuations and dual pricing, uneven access to medical care, and state-imposed limitations on social services.

These scholars point to a similar paradox in their findings: The significant material comforts and social status many lifestyle migrants, expatriate families, and mobile professionals enjoy abroad are juxtaposed with uncertainty and a loss of control.[33] These mobile individuals are certainly not at the destitute or dispossessed end of the precariat, but the conditions of their work keep them in an insecure social and economic position. As Kate Botterill describes it, their privilege is "discordant."[34]

This call for a more nuanced understanding of privilege and precarity is not meant to diminish the material and emotional hardships faced by forced migrants, refugees, or asylum seekers nor to deny the large-scale inequalities evident in the global scope of family mobilities.[35] On the whole, worldschoolers occupy an undoubtedly privileged position, especially compared to other migrant and refugee families who have no choice but to take their children and their lives on the road in search of a better life. At the same time, however, maintaining binary distinctions that pit a mobile elite in stark contrast to a vulnerable precariat risks missing the world of complexity in people's lived experiences. And it does little to reveal the specific mechanisms through which new configurations of global inequality are produced.

Understanding how mobility is intertwined with the reproduction of social inequalities requires us to pay careful attention to the way certain people's privilege is both amplified and tempered by precarity. The mobilities and lifestyles I've described in this book parlay existing privilege into new kinds of capital, but also new kinds of vulnerability. If we are to grasp the way mobility reproduces power hierarchies and account for the range of strategies individuals use to live with uncertainty, we must move away from dichotomous thinking and toward a more finely calibrated framework that sees privilege and precarity as multifaceted, relational, performed, and interwoven.

This is not a question just for worldschoolers, or even just for long-term travelers, lifestyle migrants, or digital nomads, but for all of us who live in this age of extreme mobilities.[36] As Elliott and Urry remind us, we are all living mobile lives now, whether we are the ones doing the traveling or the ones bearing the brunt of its impact. We may think of worldschooling as an alternative lifestyle, but worldschoolers' effort to "future-proof" their kids actually heralds the new normal Elliott and Urry describe. If more and more of us are living mobile lives, whether by choice or by circumstance, then we need a better understanding of how these ways of life produce new forms of capital, new kinds of vulnerability, and new modes of social distinction. And we need a better understanding of the limits and opportunities mobility poses for reimagining a "good mobile life" in uncertain times.

Epilogue

The Good Mobile Life

We are dreaming all wrong.
—Toni Morrison, *The Foreigner's Home*

The good life worldschoolers dream of is one that hinges on freedom, autonomy, joy, personal choice, rebellion, and self-actualization. In the face of uncertainty, their impulse is not to root down or to look for stable ground, but to go with the flow. To follow their individual desires. To become mobile selves who can ride out the turbulence and even have fun along the way.

As the stories I have recounted throughout the book suggest, worldschooling parents mobilize a range of strategies to prepare their children to thrive in tumultuous times. Travel teaches the important lessons of embracing risk, asserting one's independence, managing nomadic friendships, and feeling global. These skills place worldschooling children at the forefront of a transforming world. Global kids, the ones who travel light in both the material and the social sense, are the ones who are best positioned to embrace uncertainty as an opportunity rather than a threat.

I have argued that these strategies are highly individualized, tailored to equip children with a personal set of tools to weather a climate of social and economic uncertainty rather than aimed at building a collective response to the destabilizing conditions of late modernity. In other words, the good life these families imagine is one that individuals must carve out amidst the anxieties, uncertainties, and inequalities that swirl around them, not one that redresses the tragedies of late modern life at their core. This individual version of the good life may feel fun and free and future-proof, but it is also a limited resource reserved for a privileged few.

But the story does not end there. I want to conclude on a more hopeful note by revisiting some of the paradoxes of worldschooling as potential openings for a more collective and equitable version of the good life. Among these are the competing desires for communal belonging and individual freedom captured in the notion of a "tribe of rebels"; the complex interplay between freedom and compulsion; and the contradictory discourses of indeterminacy and design that are implicit in the way worldschoolers perceive the future and frame uncertainty as opportunity. In these tensions, I see glimmers of hope for an alternative kind of good life, one that I refer to as the "good mobile life."

The concept of the good mobile life is inspired by recent scholarship on mobility justice.[1] The field of mobilities studies has long been concerned with understanding how mobility reproduces power hierarchies and shapes unequal social relations. In her book, *Mobility Justice*, Mimi Sheller pairs the politics of mobility with social justice theory to sketch out an agenda for researching, designing, and advocating for alternative mobility futures that channel the power of mobility toward more collective, just, and sustainable outcomes. Following this line of thinking, scholars, activists, and policy makers have begun to imagine scenarios for reclaiming equitable access to mobility and shared infrastructures of mobility beyond the scope of the state or the market, a set of public goods that Sheller refers to as the "mobile commons."

Sheller explains that the mobile commons is not just about protecting the individual right to freedom of movement or even about maximizing mobility—whether that means access to everyday forms of local transportation or to the luxuries of world travel—but rather, extending the capacity for "shared mobilities and free spaces for movement."[2] The good mobile life, then, is one in which individual mobility is not prioritized over all else, but rather embedded in—and indeed, reliant upon—collective, equitable, and sustainable movement that constitutes the mobile commons. It is in the interstices between wanting to be alone and together, between freedom and compulsion, and between uncertainty and design that worldschooling unlocks the potential for pursuing these aims.

To address the first of these paradoxes, worldschoolers may define the good life in the image of their own individual dreams, but theirs is hardly a solitary pursuit. Worldschooling defies the myth of the lone traveler wandering the globe in search of knowledge.[3] On the contrary, family travel is, by definition, a social affair. Some of the families in my study were traveling the world with as many as nine children. There is nothing solitary about that! In her research on location-independent families, Fabiola Mancinelli describes family travel explicitly as a "practice of togetherness," and most of the families I spoke with reveled in the joys and messiness of family bonding on the road.[4]

As I described in chapter 4, the parents, young children, and teenagers in these families often harbored very different kinds of fears and desires, which required family members to compromise, collaborate, and make uncomfortable commitments to cope with the emotional fallout of their lifestyle. The painful feelings of isolation and loneliness that parents and children experienced on the road also reveal the limitations of this do-it-yourself, go-it-alone lifestyle. Recognizing that the good life is not so good alone, many worldschoolers reached out to other families, created communities, and forged friendships on the move. In previous chapters, I critiqued how easily some of these efforts fell into a form of commodifying community for the individual, but I also see here the promise of a collective project.

Put differently, the good life does not have to be *either* an individual pursuit *or* a collective project, but rather must be both. In fact, some theorists argue, individual freedom and communality are in a symbiotic relationship. In their analysis of mutual hospitality, for example, Anthony Ince and Helen Bryant draw on the anarchist theories of Peter Kropotkin to suggest that individual freedom is not possible without collective cooperation. Whereas we often think of collective arrangements, like communities or governments, as external structures designed to curtail our individual freedoms, Kropotkin argues that the two are co-constitutive in the sense that "collective mutual support safeguards individuals' capacity to exercise liberty and vice versa."[5] According to this perspective, genuine liberty requires the sharing of mutual aid among individuals who are "co-responsible" for one another.[6] Worldschoolers may imagine their good lives in individualistic, rebellious terms, but their desire to be together as a family and in community signals the fundamental human need for sociality.

The question of individual agency is also at stake in a second paradox: the interplay between freedom and compulsion. In this case, autonomy is the name of the game. The ability to exercise choice over whether, where, and under what conditions to move determines where one falls on the power spectrum. The lived reality is rarely so simple. Immigrants and refugees who have little control in the matter of their own movements or agency over the immobilities that are imposed on them in camps or detention centers are clearly at the precarious end of that spectrum. However, even the apparently privileged classes of hypermobile professionals and lifestyle migrants often feel they have no choice but to be mobile. Where is the line between autonomy and compulsion in worldschooling?

Worldschoolers are largely free to move, and they celebrate autonomy as a guiding principle of their mobile lifestyles, but autonomy is a complicated matter in late modernity. As I explained in the introduction to the book, the freedom to choose and craft our own lives often hardens into the obligation to do so. In chapter 2, for example, I cited Amy, who wrote on her blog: "We can't afford to do this. We couldn't afford not to." Her comment was posted in response to a question about her family's travel budget, but it also captures a sense of coercion. However exciting the prospect of world travel, Amy feels as though she couldn't *not* choose to pursue this lifestyle dream. What passes for privilege may actually be something like compulsory autonomy.

This is especially true in neoliberal societies where self-reliance becomes mandatory for entry into the upper and middle classes. In critiques of neoliberal governance, however, theorists frame this in a slightly different way, arguing that what looks like autonomy is actually acquiescence to the ideologies of the state. Neoliberalism, both as an economic theory and as a mode of governance, is predicated on notions of freedom. This includes the tenets of the free market, or course, but also principles of individual liberty, which is defined as both freedom *from* the protectionist welfare state and the freedom *to* chart one's own best future. Political theorist Lois McNay observes that neoliberalism does not govern by curtailing individual autonomy, but by shaping autonomy in the image of the market.[7] "Individual autonomy is not the opposite of or limit to neoliberal governance," she argues, "but rather lies at the heart of disciplinary control through responsible self-management."[8] Neoliberal governmentality sets individuals free, but free to monitor, improve, and govern themselves in a market economy.[9] In other words, what looks like autonomy—launching an online business to fund a carefree mobile lifestyle, for example—is actually a form of adherence to neoliberal rationality.

To push the point even further, in a neoliberal society, the good life is firmly associated with mobility. The ideal neoliberal subject is one who is untethered. In fact, as Noel Cass and Katherina Manderscheid argue, "the *need* for mobility" has become, without question, "a fixed requirement of the good life."[10] This version of the good life is cemented in the cultural imaginary as a mobile life, whether that means the global mobilities of a traveling lifestyle, as with worldschooling, or the various forms of automobility that make a respectable middle-class urban or suburban lifestyle possible.

Cass and Manderscheid find this coupling of mobility and the good life deeply problematic. The compulsion to be mobile not only levies considerable economic, environmental, and justice costs, they argue, but it actually limits human autonomy. What they propose, instead, is the concept of "autonomobility," a principle that acknowledges that "freedom from compulsion (to stay or to move) is the value required to equitably ensure mobility justice under scarcity."[11] Autonomobility is not about protecting the individual right to freedom of movement, but rather about ensuring the right not to move.[12]

Anthropologist Ghassan Hage gives us another way of thinking about the rights and requirements of mobility. He defines the good life as the feeling that our life is "going somewhere," which he contrasts with the feeling of "stuckedness." Stuckedness is that situation in which a person has no choice and no alternative to his or her current situation, but also lacks the ability "to grab such alternatives even if they present themselves."[13] The opposite of stuckedness is not movement, as such, but rather what Hage refers to as "existential mobility," a sense that one's life is being propelled in the right direction.

Autonomobility and existential mobility are both crucial features of the good mobile life. This is neither to say that all families and all children should move, or should even desire to move, to the extent worldschoolers do, nor that worldschoolers should stay home. It is not a question of expanding access to resources and infrastructures of movement. In fact, the good mobile life may be one that is not all that mobile. Instead, it is about creating equitable societies in which freedom, autonomy, and a sense of purpose in life can take many forms. In this context, existential mobility presumes that people have a future story to live into, which brings me to the third and final paradox.

The future figures in worldschoolers' life strategies in two ways: looming on the horizon both as a specter of uncertainty and as an object of deliberate design. In one sense, worldschoolers frame the future as a set of unknowable and unstoppable forces. Because we are at the mercy of the future and its uncertainties, all we can do is brace ourselves for the chaos, the thinking goes. At the same time, however, worldschoolers take destiny into their own hands. Through techniques of lifestyle design, disruption, and deliberate choice, they set about carving a different path than the one given to them in order to create a better future for themselves and their children.

As my analysis has suggested, worldschoolers are simultaneously oriented to both of these versions of the future. In fact, their lifestyle design endeavors can be interpreted as a way of imposing certainty onto an indeterminate future. While I have suggested that these efforts toward lifestyle design are symptomatic of the "new individualism" of late modernity, there is a promising opening in this ontological orientation toward the future. What if we were able to direct this fervor for creating a better life for one's family toward the collective project of creating a more just mobility future?

Of course, we don't know what the future will bring, and our very best guesses are hardly encouraging. The unrelenting pace of global capitalism, resource extraction, and technological change, the acceleration of climate change and irreversible biodiversity loss, the global spread of viruses, the unraveling of liberal democracy, and the resurgence of a malicious strain of xenophobia all pose seemingly insurmountable challenges. And, incidentally, these are all scenarios that our current attachment to unsustainable and inequitable mobilities has put into motion. Under these conditions, worldschooling parents are not wrong to prepare their children for a daunting future. But these problems are only insurmountable if we continue to confront them alone, armed only with individualized strategies aimed at safeguarding our own corner of privilege. In the documentary film, *The Foreigner's Home*, Toni Morrison forewarns that "the destiny of the twenty-first century will be shaped by the possibility or collapse of a shareable world."[14] The question can no longer be, how do I equip *my* child to face these challenges, but how can we equip *all* children to create a better world out of the mess they are inheriting? Even better, how can we adults start the process?

A first step is to question the pervasive logic of risk through which we are now living into the future. As I have suggested in my analysis, world-schoolers are already doing this in some ways by encouraging children to welcome risk and refusing to let fear dictate their life choices. Life in the risk society compels us to brace for, avoid, and mitigate hazards. It requires of us a reactive stance that justifies and normalizes individual survival tactics over collective strategy. But this approach signals our acquiescence to living in a risk society.[15] It doesn't encourage us to question the political and economic policies that have created this age of insecurity in the first place. Perhaps the most rebellious thing we can do is remember that there are other ways of being in the present and anticipating the future than through the prism of risk.

In his book, *The Future as Cultural Fact*, anthropologist Arjun Appadurai rejects the numerical logic of the risk society, one in which everything is calculated in terms of an "ethics of probability." Instead, he proposes an "ethics of possibility," one that offers "a more inclusive platform for improving the planetary quality of life and can accommodate a plurality of visions of the good life."[16] Rather than focusing on protecting ourselves from future harms, an ethics of possibility enables us to proactively envision what is desirable and what is good. He calls this ability to imagine and construct a good future the "capacity to aspire." Aspiration, and the capacity to aspire, are prerequisites for the kind of collective will and political action needed to bring such desirable futures into being.

Appadurai is quick to remind us, however, that the capacity to aspire, much like existential mobility, is not equally distributed. The ability to hope for and pursue the good life remains largely in the hands of a wealthy and privileged few, but our collective fortunes rest on our ability to expand the capacity to aspire to all people. The mutual dreaming, community organizing, political advocacy, and practical designing that must go into creating the good mobile life requires both the capacity to aspire and existential mobility, resources in which worldschoolers are already rich. In this sense, they are well positioned to do the imaginative and hands-on work that mobility justice requires. This work of troubling existing systems and designing more just futures cannot be done alone, however.

What would it look like to work together to build a more just and sustainable future, not just for our own kids, but for all of us? In other words, what if, instead of orienting ourselves toward future-proofing our children, we oriented ourselves toward human-proofing the future? This would be a future in which, to cite Sheller, we might learn how to "move over the Earth—lightly, carefully, with concern for others, and especially through difficult efforts of translation and accompaniment across differ-ence."[17] This future requires us to imagine the good life not as a personal project but as a collective one. After spending the last several years in the company of worldschoolers, I am confident that these families have much to contribute to the collective project of bringing such an alterna-tive mobility future to life.

ACKNOWLEDGMENTS

I have been thinking and talking about this project since 2009 and working on it in earnest since 2014, which has given me plenty of time to chalk up a large number of debts to the many people and organizations that have supported this work. First, I would like to express my profound gratitude to the intrepid traveling families who made their stories available in interviews and online. I cannot overstate the degree of generosity with which people responded to my requests for meet-ups and interviews. Despite the critical scrutiny to which I have subjected these families' choices and practices, I have an abiding respect for the courage and imagination it takes to live one's life *otherwise*, and I hope that I have done your stories justice in my retelling and interpretation of them.

This project benefited enormously from the support I received from the College of the Holy Cross and the community of scholars there. Thanks to generous financial support from the College in the form of an Arthur J. O'Leary award and a Holy Cross Faculty Fellowship, I was able to conduct extensive fieldwork, hire research assistants, and take the time needed to write this book. I would like to thank my department colleagues for their intellectual support throughout the research, with special thanks to Ara Francis and Melissa Weiner for sharing their respective expertise with me when this project was little more than an inkling of an idea, and to Ann Marie Leshkowich, Renée Beard, and Kendy Hess for providing ample doses of advice, perspective, and friendship just when they were needed most. Many thanks to Amanda Luyster and Min Kyung Lee for launching and coordinating the *Shut Up and Write!* sessions in which many of these chapters took form, and to the colleagues who labored alongside me, for providing the time and accountability for writing.

For their incomparable administrative support, I would like to thank Margaret Post and Paula Hall. Meg Taing and Kyle Carr provided skilled and creative research assistance at various points in the project. I am also grateful to the brilliant students in my Development of Social Theory, Sociology of Emotion, Sociology of Travel and Tourism, and Global Sense of Home classes who kept me on my toes with their curiosity and insightful questions about my research.

Throughout the course of this project, I received helpful feedback from a number of academic and public audiences. I would like to thank Garth Lean for inviting me to present a very early version of the research at Western Sydney University, and to the seminar participants there, among them Gordon Waitt, Aimee Matthews, and Christiane Kühling, who helped shape my thinking at a critical point in the project. Thank you to Zsuzsa Millei for collaborating with me to organize the session on Mobile Geographies of Learning at the Association of American Geographers conference and to all of the contributors on that panel who inspired me with their own research and with their comments on my project. I had the opportunity to return to the University of Lapland for a long visit, where I presented this work to an encouraging audience. A very warm thank you is due to Soile Veijola for her generous mentorship, thoughtful questions, and enthusiasm for the project. I am also grateful to Johan Edelheim, Emily Höckert, and Outi Rantala for talking things through with me during that visit. Heartfelt thanks are due to Dorina-Maria Buda, who hosted me as a visiting scholar at Leeds Beckett University, where I was able to receive feedback from a vibrant community of researchers.

For giving me the opportunity to present this work to an even wider audience, I owe thanks to Ellen Mahoney of Sea Change Mentoring and Ann Marie Gleeson of Primary Source. Ellen invited me to present at a Families in Global Transition conference, where I was able to meet corporate relocation experts, counselors, international school educators, and parents who expanded my perspective on children's global mobilities. Ann Marie invited me to present the Summer Institute on Teaching for Global Understanding where a lively audience of K-12 classroom teachers provided invaluable feedback on my research. Both Ellen and Ann Marie also dedicated several hours to brainstorming with me about how to frame my study for a broader readership.

This project is indebted to my teachers and mentors, the late John Urry, whose influence is visible throughout this book, and Mimi Sheller, whose creative and groundbreaking research constantly challenges and inspires me. And to the entire community of mobilities scholars, thank you for providing such a generous intellectual home for my interdisciplinary work. Thank you to Paul Lynch, Alison McIntosh, and Peter Lugosi, my co-editors at *Hospitality & Society*, for their support during this project and for their patience with my occasional absences from my editorial duties as I attended to fieldwork and writing.

I can think of nothing more generous than to read and comment on the messy early drafts of a project, and so I am particularly indebted to Lydia Brauer, Inge Hermann, and the anonymous reviewers who provided candid and constructive feedback on various chapters of the book. I am grateful to Ilene Kalish at New York University Press for seeing the potential in this book and to the editorial and production teams for bringing it to fruition.

To the colleagues I've cornered at various receptions, to my friends and family members, and to all the fellow parents on the sidelines at soccer games who endured far longer than necessary summaries of my book in response to innocent questions about how the writing was going, thank you for your patience. In particular, I would like to thank my neighbors, Bob and Linda Flinton, who have kept my life and my spirits afloat on many occasions. I am beyond grateful to my trail running partners, Michele Potter and Laura Younkman, both brilliant athletes and gifted writers who helped me work through my ideas mile by mile. And Lydia Brauer deserves thanks here, as well, not only for her keen scholarly insights on this project, but for being a wickedly funny and stalwart friend under every conceivable condition. Thank you, also, to my gifted yoga teachers, Liz Fox, Hollie Laudel, Kari Malen, and Leta Roy, for helping me stay grounded and live a semblance of a balanced life while writing.

My sincerest thanks go to my family, the ones who pay the invisible costs of creating a book like this. Thank you to my parents for being my first and most fervent cheerleaders and for always keeping copies of my books on the coffee table. And to my husband Martin Molz and my son Elliot, this book only exists because of you. In the preface, I acknowledged the significant contributions you made to the design and implementation of this research, but we all know that your efforts didn't end when we landed back home. That's just when the hard work started. Thank you for your patience with all the ways this book took over our lives, from my early-morning and late-night writing sessions to my notes scattered all over the kitchen. Elliot, thank you for bringing so much laughter and wonder to my life. Your sense of humor lights up my world like nothing else. I am astounded daily by your drive, intellect, and kindness. And to Martin, words fail to express how much I love you and how grateful I am for all the ways you challenge and sustain me.

APPENDIX A

Methodology: Mobile Virtual Ethnography

Studying a mobile phenomenon like worldschooling, a lifestyle practiced by a dispersed group of families, across multiple geographical locations, and in a range of mediated sites, poses significant methodological challenges. To meet these challenges, I applied a multi-method approach I call "mobile virtual ethnography."[1] Mobile virtual ethnography combines methodological innovations in virtual ethnography online with techniques for moving with and following travelers in person.[2]

The online component of this project involved following and studying the blogs that traveling families published online and participating in two social media forums where worldschooling communities congregated to share advice and inspiration. Conducting research on blogs and social media sites raises important methodological questions about what kind of data these online sites entail.[3] Echoing the traditions of travel writing and diary keeping out of which blogging evolved, travel blogs usually feature chronological posts documenting the travelers' experiences in various destinations. But travel blogs are more than online archives; they are interactive stories and sites of social interaction. In keeping with the tone of self-disclosure common in diaries, blogs are also carefully staged forms of self-presentation.

For this reason, we cannot assume that travel blogs offer a neutral account, but rather must consider them to be "performative acts" of self-constitution and social interaction. Citing Erving Goffman's concepts of impression management and presentation of self, Nicholas Hookway explains that blogs capture the "ongoing 'drama' of everyday interactions, selves, and situations," not least of all because blogs are written for an audience that, in most cases, can write back.[4] In other words, blogs are performative sites where texts, meanings, selves, and socialities are co-produced with an online audience.

In my analysis, I approached travel blogs not merely as sources of documentary evidence, but as a vital component of the lifestyle project to which worldschoolers aspire. When writing about lifestyle, Anthony Giddens argues that "we are, not what we are, but what we make of ourselves."[5] The way we make ourselves, he adds, is not just through consumer choices, but through reflexive techniques, like self-therapy or self-improvement programs, that enable individuals to sustain a "coherent, yet continuously revised, biographical narrative."[6] For worldschoolers, blogs largely serve this function as a site where travelers can process and make sense of their new, unconventional life paths, not least of all with an audience of like-minded mobile families who validate these choices.

As I have shown throughout the book, travel blogs and social media sites are integral to worldschoolers' pursuit of the good life. They are places where worldschoolers preserve and share travel memories, but also exchange educational resources, circulate advice, and offer emotional support. In many cases, families' blogs were also income-generating enterprises that funded the very lifestyle that fueled them, as I discussed in chapter 2. And, as I described in chapter 4, they often served as online hubs around which worldschoolers' fluid and mediated forms of community coalesced. Through their blogs, worldschoolers also performed a number of interrelated roles, most visibly as travelers and parents, but also as self-branded entrepreneurs, rebels, and global citizens. My analysis thus focused on travel blogs and social media forums as online performances that aligned with worldschoolers' larger projects of self-presentation and lifestyle design.

To compile the blog sample, I started with a broad online search for traveling families and used a "virtual snowballing" technique to generate a list of more than two hundred relevant blogs.[7] I then used purposive sampling to narrow down to a database of fifty blogs being published by families who were currently traveling while educating their children.[8] For twelve months, I followed these blogs, essentially "hanging out online" with mobile families.[9] I subscribed to their updates, checked in weekly to read new blog posts and browse through photos, and combed through the comments and responses posted by readers, keeping extensive field notes of my impressions and interactions with these online texts. I eventually downloaded all of the content from the blog sample for coding and analysis. Part of that content included guest posts and interviews with other worldschoolers, links to other families' travel blogs, and links to relevant online resources such as related articles, books, videos, and podcasts that bloggers posted to illustrate, explain, justify, or prompt debate about the worldschooling lifestyle. I added these external materials, including several TED talks, newspaper articles, and magazine articles, to the larger database I analyzed.

For seven of the twelve months during which I was conducting this online fieldwork, I traveled the world with my husband, Martin, and our son, Elliot, who was ten years old at the time. We designed our itinerary to include many of the hubs and destinations popular among these traveling families in the hopes of improving our chances of meeting up with other families during our travels. The plan worked. We met, traveled with, and interviewed a dozen worldschooling families in person in Argentina, Australia, Thailand, Singapore, and the United States. Some of these were members of the social media forums I frequented or authors of blogs I was following; others were families we happened to meet in restaurants, hostels, playgrounds, or campgrounds.

In both my online and in-person interactions, I made my role as a sociologist clear to respondents, forum moderators, and participants. But it was my status as a fellow worldschooling parent, not to mention as a white, middle-class professional, that positioned me as a member of the community and facilitated my access to these families. My field notes document my interactions with these families, but they also reflect my own experiences and struggles as a worldschooling parent during this time. In this sense, my research included an analytical autoethnographic component that yielded deeper insights into the emotional and logistical aspects of worldschooling that didn't always appear on blogs or in interviews.[10]

Informed by Leon Anderson's formulation of "analytic autoethnography," I became a temporary but full participant in a worldschooling lifestyle with the intention of developing a deeper theoretical understanding of this emerging phenomenon.[11] As productive as I found this autoethnographic approach, it also posed a difficult dilemma for me. On the one hand, conducting this fieldwork fulfilled a dream Martin and I had long before Elliot joined our family. Like many of the parents I interviewed, we had spent much of our twenties living, working, and backpacking around the world, and once our son was born, we wanted to share those experiences with him as well. On the other hand, by the time I launched this project, my research on tourism and backpacking had made me aware of the way these leisure mobilities rely on and reproduce global inequalities. I understood that our ability to travel as a family was a function of our middle-class status and my professional identity, not to mention a generous research grant and paid sabbatical from my institution. The fact that nearly every person I told about my plan to take my son out of formal schooling and travel the world for a year responded by saying, "What a wonderful opportunity for him!" rather than reporting me to the authorities was further evidence of the advantages I enjoy as a white, middle-class professional woman from the Global North. I worried then, and worry still, about the ways this fieldwork makes me complicit in the kind of "dream hoarding" that Richard Reeves describes in his critique of the American middle class.[12] I knew that the journey would only reinforce our privilege, but this is also what I wanted to better understand. How were these middle-class families using a mobile lifestyle to shore up their status in a shifting economic landscape? What new kinds of cultural capital were these enterprising parents accruing for themselves and their children?

Although I have made my experiences visible in the analysis above, as Anderson advocates, the account I have provided in this book is not an explicitly autobiographical one. Instead, I aimed to foreground the personal narratives of the worldschooling families I traveled with and followed online. My family's story is just one of many that comprise the complex, and sometimes contradictory, phenomenon of worldschooling. Nevertheless, taking an autoethnographic approach during the fieldwork shaped my engagements with other families and made me acutely aware of some of the subtle dilemmas and unexpected challenges and joys that shape the worldschooling experience. For example, as I mentioned in the preface, while we were on the road, my husband and son would often accompany me and participate in research interviews with other worldschooling families. In these face-to-face research encounters, as well as in the online ones, I was always positioned as both a researcher and a mother, to the extent that my motherhood became a central component of the method.[13] The insights I was able to draw from my role as a worldschooling parent, in turn, informed the kinds of questions I asked in interviews and sensitized me to the key analytical themes that are at the heart of this book.

I conducted interviews with families who were on the road, as well as a few families who had returned home from their worldschooling journeys. Some of these interviews lasted a few hours, but others lasted an entire day and continued in ongoing email or social media interactions. In keeping with mobile virtual ethnography, my intention was to move with families and to live their mobile lifestyle with them. This meant that many of the interview encounters involved activities such as camping, sitting by the pool, or sightseeing. It is not uncommon for worldschooling families to contact one another online to arrange to meet up with each other along the way, often for the purpose of a playdate for the children, and so my interlocuters were not surprised when I reached out to them. Indeed, these research interviews often took place in the context of playdates or day trips in various destinations.

I used a qualitative analysis software program to code and analyze the transcripts from these interviews, along with my field notes and the digital data I collected. I applied pseudonyms during the coding process, and all of the names and other identifying features associated with data from families' blogs, social media forums, and interviews have been changed. In some cases, I have merged or altered stories to protect the privacy of respondents. While scholars agree that travel blogs constitute a largely untapped source of rich data, the ethical standards governing research on blog content are far from settled. Many scholars argue that publicly available online content is subject to the standards of fair use and does not require informed consent from authors. Others argue that certain kinds of content should be treated as private or personal data.[14]

In navigating this distinction, scholars often describe a continuum between non-intrusive and engaged web-based research. At one end, researchers collect and analyze existing data without communicating with its producers. At the other end, researchers interact with the bloggers they are studying.[15] My research approach spanned this continuum, including both in-person interviews and engaged online interaction with travelers, for which I gained informed consent, as well as non-intrusive collection of publicly available online blog content. In many cases, these different forms of data involved the same person, which meant there was no straightforward way to anonymize a traveler's interview data *and* credit the blog source, or to anonymize some narratives and not others.

The matter was further complicated by the fact that some world-schoolers would interview or quote one another on their own blogs, which made it difficult to trace original authorship. To address this dilemma, I opted to use pseudonyms for all of the travelers in my study, including those I interviewed and interacted with as well as those whose blogs I analyzed as existing public content. Exceptions include TED talk presenters, families profiled in mainstream media outlets, or blogs used as secondary data, in which case I used actual names. This decision was informed by the guidelines proposed by Hailey Stainton and Elitza Iordanova, who recommend anonymizing primary data (in this case, interview data, travel blogs, and social media content), and crediting secondary data (in this case, TED talks and newspaper and magazine articles).[16] Although some of my respondents claimed not to care whether I used their real names or a pseudonym, I deemed it more ethical to anonymize primary data extracts across the board.

In coding the data, I used grounded, qualitative, and inductive techniques to identify recurring themes and discern patterns in and across the data. By triangulating these various sources of online, in-person, and autoethnographic data, I was able to gain a nuanced understanding not only of the varied practices that make up the phenomenon of worldschooling, but also the personal meanings parents attach to traveling and learning, to parenting and family life, and to preparing their children for the future.

Study Sample: Who Are Worldschoolers?

This appendix offers a portrait of the worldschooling families included in the study's sample and represented throughout the book. The majority of parents in my blog sample and those I interviewed in person are white, middle-class professionals in their thirties and forties. In this sense, worldschoolers reflect what scholars have found in other studies of voluntary long-term travel and lifestyle migration, which is that these practices tend to be pursued by an overwhelmingly white and affluent population with passports from the wealthy nations of North America and Western Europe.[1]

This is not to say that all worldschoolers are white. A few of the families in my larger sample self-identified as black, Asian, or multiracial. And in the time since I conducted the fieldwork for this book, a greater number of parents of color have been publishing blogs and participating in the social media forums for worldschooling families.[2] One of the social media forums I followed hosts a group specifically for travelers of color. On a related note, although the homeschooling community remains overwhelmingly white, researchers have reported a recent rise in the number of black families opting to homeschool and unschool their children, which I expect will be paralleled by a rise in worldschooling among families of color.[3] Nevertheless, the experiences reflected in my data sample represent a predominantly white and middle-class perspective, one that provides insight into the reproduction of privilege through the intersection of race and class.

As I explained in the introduction, my designation of middle class is debatable, given that many of the parents in my sample left salaried jobs and downsized their possessions. As I have shown throughout this book, however, their social networks, their tastes and preferences, their ways of parenting their children, their desire to travel, and their assumption that the world is theirs to explore all reflect and reproduce a thoroughly middle-class worldview, especially from the vantage point of the Global North. This situates these families in a category scholars call "middling migrants," those lifestyle migrants who are neither among the jet-set elite nor the most destitute travelers.[4] The worldschooling families in my study may not be the power movers or the victims of a shifting global economy; nevertheless, it is here among a relatively affluent middle class that we see the nuanced ways in which new kinds of cultural value are produced and circulated to the next generation.

The children in the families I studied ranged in age from infants born on the road to teenagers entering university, though most of the children were elementary and middle-school age. The terms of my institutional human subject research approval meant that I only interviewed parents and children above the age of eighteen, though kids were present during my interviews and I had access to the views they expressed in the publicly available blog content. The perspectives I have offered throughout this book, however, primarily represent parents' accounts of, and aspirations for, their lifestyles and their children's futures. Table B.1 offers a pseudonymous list of the parents whose interview, blog, or social media extracts are cited throughout the book, along with available demographic details.

This focus on parents' narratives is not meant to discount the views and experiences of the children themselves, who make massive investments in their families' worldschooling projects. In other contexts, scholars have foregrounded children's perspectives of family tourism, migration, expatriate lifestyles, or third culture upbringings.[5] In worldschooling, too, there is a rich vein of children's narratives that I hope future research will mine, though for the purposes of this book, my analysis focuses on their parents' narratives.

TABLE B.1. Parents Cited

Parents/Children	Nationality/ Country of Origin	Race	Source
Ruth and Adam Abbott 7 children	United States	White/ Black	Blog
Meredith and Wes Armer 5 children	United States	White	Blog
Kyle and Cheryl Baronetti 2 children	United States	White	Blog
Rose Barrett 1 child (Kairo)	Australia	White/ Asian	Blog
Angela and Samuel Carter 3 children	United States	White	Blog
Jackie and Paul Chapman 2 children	United States	White	Blog
Katya and Michael Christensen 2 children	United States	White	Blog/Social Media Forum
Kevin and Astrid Clark 2 children	United States	White	Blog
Maggie Coates and Trevor Hastings 2 children (Lola; Isaiah)	South Africa	White	Blog
Holly and Stan Cormier 3 children	Canada	White	Blog
Uma and Trey Crawley 2 children	Australia	White	Blog
Amy Devon Sharp and Mac Sharp 2 children	Canada	Black	Blog
Kamila and Avi Dhar 2 children	United States	Asian	Blog
Elaine and Rob Emerson 2 children	United States	White	Blog
Edward and Lauren Falk 5 children	Canada	White	Blog
Marie and Charles Franco 5 children	United States	White	Featured on a fellow world-schooler's blog
Sari and Ben Frisch 3 children	Israel	—	Featured on a fellow world-schooler's blog
Jay and Mia Hardwick 3 children	United States	White	Blog
Elsa and Byron Hart 2 children (Erik; Marisa)	United States	White	Interview/Blog
Hallie and Arthur Henderson 3 children (Michaela; Dani; Nikolas)	Eastern Europe	White	Blog
Kim and Matt Hoffmeyer 2 children (Dylan; Caleb)	United States	White	Interview/Blog/Social Media Forum
Norman and Helen Huang 2 children	United States	Asian	Blog
Harris Jones 2 children	Australia	White	Interview

TABLE B.1. *(cont.)*

Parents/Children	Nationality/ Country of Origin	Race	Source
Johanna and Reed Keogh 1 child (Ethan)	United States	White	Blog
Simona Knox 1 child (Leo)	United Kingdom	White	Blog
Monique LaSalle 1 child (Axel)	France	White	Interview
Iris and John Lewis 2 children (Thalia; Alistair)	United Kingdom	White	Blog
Bryce and Randy McHugh 2 children	United States	White	Featured on a fellow world-schooler's blog
Mitch and Carolyn Meijer 3 children	United States	White	Blog
Sarah and David Milken 1 child (Colin)	United States	White	Interview/Blog
Mason Oberman 1 child (Cal)	United States	White	Blog
Tracy and Gabe Parsons 9 children	United States	White/ Asian	Blog
Nichole and Anson Peters 4 children	United States	White	Blog
Scott and Julia Porter 4 children (Annie; Sam; Alex; Drew)	Canada/United States	White	Interview/Blog/Social Media Forum
Leah and Richard Reynolds 3 children	United States	White	Blog
Jan Baker and Stuart Richmond 2 children	Australia	White	Blog
Cathryn and Mike Silva 3 children (Isabella; Callie; William)	United States	White	Blog
Pamela and Gary Smith 2 children	United States	White	Blog
Ella Tyree 1 child (Vincent)	United States	White	Blog
Joyce Vu 1 child	United States	Asian	Blog
Judy and Dean Willis 1 child (Addie)	United States	White	Blog
Mark and Anna Woodward 2 children	United States	White	Blog
Vera	United States	—	Social Media Forum
Daria	United States	—	Social Media Forum
Ben	United States	—	Social Media Forum
Nicola	United Kingdom	—	Social Media Forum

Notes: 1. Parents are listed by the pseudonyms used throughout the book. Relevant demographic data are not always discernible from travelers' blogs or social media posts.

2. Table cells listing "—" indicate that this information was not available.

The term "family" means different things to different people, and I have applied it here to a range of familial configurations. While most of the families in the sample fit the heteronormative definition of a nuclear family, there were several single-parent and same-sex parent families, blended and adoptive families, as well as several families traveling with children who have special needs. In my analysis, I considered family from a sociological perspective that is more concerned with the way people "do" and "display" family, for example through practices like traveling together or publishing photos and narratives online, than with particular kinship structures.[6] Throughout this book, I have sometimes referred to respondents generally as "parents" or as "families," and at other times as "mothers" and "fathers." It is worth noting that parenting among worldschoolers, as in other forms of alternative education, involves gendered forms of emotional labor, with mothers often shouldering the burden of anxiety and responsibility for their children's educational achievements.[7] Nevertheless, I do not make an explicit gender analysis here, focusing instead on the hopes and worries about their children's educational experiences, general well-being, and future chances that both fathers and mothers expressed.

For the most part, these families' original countries of residence are in the Global North, namely North America, Europe, and Australia. Of the twelve families I interviewed, four were originally from the United States; four from Australia; two from France; one from Japan; and one family had dual citizenship in both the United States and Canada. Some of these families were also represented in the study sample of fifty blogs. Roughly thirty-three of the families in the blog sample had their primary original residence in the United States; seven in Canada; six in Australia; two in the United Kingdom; and one each in Bulgaria, Italy, the Netherlands, and South Africa. The total exceeds fifty because several of the families represent more than one nationality (for example, one parent may be from the United States and the other from Canada, or a parent was born elsewhere and later became a citizen of another country). Furthermore, some families are multiracial, including families with parents or adopted children from different races. This, along with the fact that blog authors do not necessarily self-disclose identifying information, makes it difficult to generalize the demographic details by family. Although national, racial, and ethnic identities are not always discernible from the travel blogs, the available information suggests that the vast majority of the families in the study sample are or appear to be white, with a handful of families self-identifying as Asian, black, or multiracial. What is evident, however, is that most of these families come from positions of cultural, national, racial, and/or class privilege, which helps to explain the hopes and anxieties that drive worldschoolers' quest for the good life.

NOTES

INTRODUCTION

1 Raquel Cool, "The Rise of 'World Schooling': Families Who Home School with World Travel," *Gogo*, September 13, 2016, http://concourse.gogoair.com/.

2 Puar, "Writing My Way 'Home.'"

3 Cooper, *Cut Adrift*, 38.

4 Sheller and Urry, "New Mobilities Paradigm."

5 Urry, *Sociology beyond Societies*; *Mobilities*.

6 Elliott and Urry, *Mobile Lives*, preface.

7 Ibid., 4.

8 Eli Gerzon, "Worldschooling," (2007), http://eligerzon.com.

9 A number of news articles have covered worldschooling, including: Isabel Choat, "The Rise of Travelling Families and World-Schooling," *Guardian*, January 29, 2016, www.theguardian.com; Réka Kaponay, "I Go to School But It Doesn't Have Four Walls: My School Is the World," *Guardian*, May 11, 2016, www.theguardian. com; Hannah Barbey, "Our Children Aren't Ready for Class, So We Are 'World-schooling' Them Instead," *Telegraph*, September 6, 2016, www.telegraph.co.uk; Valerie Strauss, "Parents to 'World School' Their Two Daughters for a Year—With a Flexible Travel Schedule and a Broad Curriculum," *Washington Post*, March 27, 2017, www.washingtonpost.com; Adam Harteau and Emily Harteau, "This Family's Road Trip Never Ends," *New York Times*, August 28, 2017, www.nytimes.com; and Shannon Galpin, "Our Worldschooling Adventure," *Outside*, March 5, 2018, www.outsideonline.com.

10 Hage, "Waiting," chapter 8.

11 Mclachlan, "Global Nomads"; Eidse and Sichel, *Unrooted Childhoods*; Pollock and Van Reken, *Third Culture Kids*; Korpela, *More Vibes in India*.

12 For examples of research on children's urban commuting practices, see Barker et al., "Road Less Travelled"; on family tourism practices, see Haldrup and Larsen, "Family Gaze"; Carr, *Children's and Families' Holiday Experience*; Obrador, "Place of the Family"; and Schänzel, Yeoman, and Backer, *Family Tourism*; on children's experiences of migration, see Skelton, "Children's Geographies"; on family mobilities, see Holdsworth, *Family and Intimate Mobilities*; and Murray and Cortés-Morales, *Children's Mobilities*. See Olwig, "Privileged Travelers?"; Kunz, "Privileged Mobilities"; and Coles and Fechter, *Transnational Professionals* on expatriate families. On military families, see Park, "Military Children and Families"; and Atwood, "Families' Emotion Work."

13 See Cohen, "Lifestyle Travellers"; Kannisto, *Global Nomads*; Hannam and Diekmann, *Beyond Backpacker Tourism*, for research on backpackers' mobile lives.

14 Williams, *The Pursuit of Happiness*.

15 For examples of this literature, see Duncan, Cohen, and Thulemark, *Lifestyle Mobilities*; Kalčić, "Going Nomad"; Benson and O'Reilly, *Lifestyle Migration*; and Korpela, *More Vibes in India*.

16 This term was coined in the late 1990s by Tsugio Makimoto and David Manners in their book *Digital Nomad* and has been revived in recent scholarship. See, for example, Thompson, "Digital Nomad Lifestyle"; and Reichenberger, "Digital Nomads."

17 Cohen, "Nomads from Affluence"; and see Vogt, "Wandering."

18 Cohen, "Lifestyle Travellers," 1543.

19 Åkerlund and Sandberg, "Stories of Lifestyle Mobility," 353.

20 And see Duncan et al., *Lifestyle Mobilities*, 4; O'Reilly and Benson, "Lifestyle Migration," 2; Cohen, "Lifestyle Travellers," 1545; Reichenberger, "Digital Nomads," 364.

21 Åkerlund and Sandberg, "Stories of Lifestyle Mobility," 355.

22 Williams and McIntyre, "Place Affinities," 210.

23 Cooper, *Cut Adrift*; Amit, *First Class*; Conradson and Latham, "Transnational Urbanism."

24 Cooper, *Cut Adrift*, 125.

25 See also Giddens, *Modernity and Self-Identity*; Beck, *Risk Society*; Lash and Urry, *Economies of Signs and Space*; Jameson, *Postmodernism*; Bauman, *Liquid Modernity*; Harvey, *Neoliberalism*; and Elliott and Urry, *Mobile Lives*.

26 Giddens, *Modernity and Self-Identity*, 5.

27 Ibid., 82.

28 Ibid., 81.

29 Elliott and Lemert, *New Individualism*.

30 Beck, *Risk Society*.

31 Brown, "End of Liberal Democracy"; Harvey, *Neoliberalism*.

32 Cichelli and Octobre, "*Youth and Globalization*."

33 Cooper, *Cut Adrift*, 14.

34 McNay, "Self as Enterprise."

35 Vrasti, *Volunteer Tourism*, 21.

36 Binkley, *Happiness*, 4.

37 See John Urry, *Mobilities*.

38 Jensen, Sheller, and Wind, "Together and Apart."

39 Hall and Holdsworth, "Family Practices"; Schänzel and Lynch, "Family Perspectives."

40 Skelton, "Children's Geographies"; Schneider and Limmer, "Job Mobility."

41 Cf. Mancinelli, "A Practice of Togetherness"; Korpela, "Lifestyle of Freedom?."

42 Pollock and Van Reken, *Third Culture Kids*; and see Mclachlan, "Global Nomads."

43 Hays, *Cultural Contradictions of Motherhood*.

44 In fact, according to historian Paula J. Fass, *The End of American Childhood*, in the face of pervasive risks and uncertainties, asserting some sense of control has

become the guiding principle of good parenting today. And see Mose, *The Playdate*; Valentine, *Culture of Childhood*.

45 Cooper, *Cut Adrift*, 117.
46 See Lee et al., *Parenting Culture Studies*; Giles, *Mothering*.
47 Jennifer Lois found this to be the case in her study of homeschooling mothers who served the dual roles of parent and teacher, which required them to expend an enormous amount of physical and emotional labor.
48 Sheller, *Mobility Justice*.
49 Urry, *Mobilities*, 6.
50 Ahmed, *Cultural Politics*; Sheller, *Mobility Justice*.
51 See Ehrenreich and Hochschild, *Global Woman*; Parreñas, *Children of Global Migration*; Mose, *Raising Brooklyn*.
52 Amit and Salazar, *Pacing Mobilities*.
53 Bourdieu, *Distinction*.
54 Binkley, *Happiness*, 117.

CHAPTER 1. SPARK AND FIDGET

1 Lareau, *Unequal Childhoods*; Reay, *Class Work*; Reeves, *Dream Hoarders*.
2 Cooper, *Cut Adrift*, 100.
3 Ibid., 109.
4 Reese, *America's Public Schools*, 28.
5 Ibid.
6 Reese, *Promise of School Reform*, 13.
7 Bowles and Gintis, *Schooling in Capitalist America*, 9. Also see Freire, *Pedagogy of the Oppressed*; Illich, *Deschooling Society*.
8 Bowles and Gintis, *Schooling in Capitalist America*, 128.
9 See Rose, "Christian Fundamentalism"; Stevens, *Kingdom of Children*.
10 See Kapitulik, "Homeschooling"; Lois, *Home Is Where the School Is*; Bhopal and Myers, *Home Schooling*.
11 Van Galen, "Ideology, Curriculum, and Pedagogy." Scholars have since argued that Van Galen's typology is overly simplified and have sought to bring a more complex analysis to homeschoolers' motivations; see Lois, *Home Is Where the School Is*.
12 Holt, *How Children Fail*; *How Children Learn*; Illich, *Deschooling Society*; Smith, Barr, and Burke, *Alternatives*.
13 For Illich, schools were beyond needing reform as the provision of universal education could never be effectively provided through institutional schooling. He saw schools as inherently structured to reproduce social inequalities.
14 Baltodano, "Neoliberalism."
15 A comprehensive history of NCLB and its aftermath is beyond the scope of my discussion here, but a useful account can be found in Reese, *America's Public Schools*.
16 Baltodano, "Neoliberalism," 495; Torres and Schugurensky, "Political Economy."

17 Goldstein, "Liberals."

18 Tanz, "The Techies."

19 Cited in Smith et al., *Alternatives*, 11.

20 For examples of these counterarguments, see Audrey Watters, "The Invented History of the 'Factory Model of Education,'" hackeducation, April 25, 2015, http://hackeducation.com; and Jack Schneider, "American Schools."

21 Cooper, *Cut Adrift*, 111.

22 Robinson, "Do Schools Kills Creativity?"

23 Ibid.

24 Adler, "Travel as Performed Art."

25 Locke, *Essay Concerning Human Understanding*; Rousseau, *Émile*. Historian Edward Gibbon, a beneficiary of the Grand Tour himself, wrote at the time that, "according to the law of custom, and perhaps of reason, foreign travel completes the education of an English gentleman," cited in Zuelow, *History of Modern Tourism*, 15.

26 According to the Institute for International Education, the US nonprofit organization that administers the Fulbright exchange program, more than 325,000 American college and university students studied abroad during the 2017–2018 academic year, up 3.8 percent from the previous year, but representing a staggering 541 percent increase over the past thirty years (www.iie.org/). The number of international students coming to the United States also rose at remarkable rates, from about 350,000 in 1987 to well over a million in 2017. The Erasmus program for student exchanges within Europe had 244 student placements in international institutions in 1987; by 2013 that number had grown to 272,000. The program has facilitated more than 3 million student exchanges since its inception in 1987 (http://ec.europa.eu/).

27 For definitions and analyses of gap year travel, see Snee, *A Cosmopolitan Journey*; Heath, "Widening the Gap"; and Simpson, "Doing Development."

28 Caton and Santos, "Images of the Other"; Gindlesparger, "Awesome Time."

29 Holt outlines his unschooling philosophy in *How Children Fail* (1964) and subsequent books such as *How Children Learn* (1967), *Freedom and Beyond* (1972), and *Escape from Childhood: The Needs and Rights of Children* (1974).

30 Given that the homeschooling movement in the United States grew from about 850,000, or 1.7 percent of all school-aged children, in 1999 to more than two million in 2011, or 4 percent of all school-aged children, it follows that unschooling has become significantly more widespread as well.

31 Illich, *Deschooling Society*; Gatto, *Dumbing Us Down*; Kohn, *Punished by Rewards*; *Unconditional Parenting*.

32 The quote appears to come from John Holt's book *Teach Your Own*.

33 Aurini and Davies, "Choice without Markets," 469.

34 Ibid.

35 See Allison, *Without Consensus*. Writing in 1973, education historian Clinton Allison described this tension as a struggle between consolidation and centraliza-

tion across the nation's schools, on the one hand, and the belief that education must "reflect the pluralistic nature of our society" and provide "possibilities for experimentation with ways of teaching, learning, and living" on the other.

36 Lareau, *Unequal Childhoods*.

HACKSCHOOLING

1 LaPlante, "Hackschooling."
2 Tanz, "The Techies."
3 LaPlante, "Hackschooling."
4 Guttentag, "Airbnb."

CHAPTER 2. HACK AND DISRUPT

1 Cooper, *Cut Adrift*, 38.
2 According to Altringer, "Globetrotting," the most common occupations among digital nomads are consulting, service provision in technology, media, online sales, finance, or life coaching.
3 Makimoto and Manners, *Digital Nomad*, 15.
4 Ibid., 16. However, Makimoto and Manners did foresee the rise of electronic teaching and the emergence of "virtual" classrooms at the university level.
5 Reichenberger, "Digital Nomads."
6 Cooper, *Cut Adrift*, 9.
7 Mancinelli, "Practice of Togetherness," 314.
8 Ibid.
9 This story is also quite common among lifestyle migrants, long-term travelers, and digital nomads. In her research with long-term RVers, Celia Forgét calls this a "wake-up call."
10 MacCannell, *The Tourist*; Urry, *Tourist Gaze*.
11 Bourdieu, *Distinction*, 167, italics in original.
12 Wajcman, *Pressed for Time*.
13 Giddens, *Modernity and Self-Identity*.
14 Bourdieu, *Distinction*, 166.
15 Ibid., 169.
16 Ferriss, *4-Hour Work Week*, 113.
17 Altringer, "Globetrotting."
18 Occasionally, this topic crops up on various social media forums where members discuss the legacy of systemic privilege left by colonialism. Some question the tactic of moving to a lower cost country as a way of affording a mobile lifestyle, and debates get quite heated about whether lifestyle migrants are helping or hurting local economies in former colonies.
19 Tullis, "7 Skills."
20 Feiler, *Happy Families*.
21 See Scharff, "Psychic Life."
22 Covey, *7 Habits*; Ferriss, *4-Hour Work Week*.

23 Eleff and Trethewey, "Enterprising Parent," 243.
24 Altringer, "Globetrotting." For example, see Elaine Pofeldt, "Digital Nomadism Goes Mainstream," *Forbes Magazine*, August 30, 2018, www.forbes.com/.
25 Thompson, "Digital Nomad Lifestyle."
26 See Freeman, *Entrepreneurial Selves*; Hess, "Metaphors Matter."
27 According to Peter Miller and Nikolas Rose, in a neoliberal society, the imperative to become entrepreneurial extends to the spheres of consumption and lifestyle as individuals are compelled to act as "entrepreneurs of themselves, seeking to maximize their 'quality of life' through the artful assembly of a 'life-style' put together through the world of goods." Miller and Rose, "Governing Economic Life," 25; and see Freeman, *Entrepreneurial Selves*.
28 Miller and Rose, "Governing Economic Life," 25.
29 Foucault, *Biopolitics*, 226.
30 Vrasti, *Volunteer Tourism*, 32.
31 Cooper, *Cut Adrift*, 38.
32 Vrasti, *Volunteer Tourism*, 37.
33 Ibid., 21.
34 See Eleff and Trethewey, "Enterprising Parent."
35 For a critical analysis of the productive potential of disruption, see Veijola et al., "Disruptive Tourism."
36 Cooper, *Cut Adrift*; Nelson, *Parenting Out of Control*.

ARCADE

1 Skenazy, *Free-Range Kids*; Hanna Rosin, "The Overprotected Kid," *The Atlantic*, April 2014. www.theatlantic.com/.
2 Bruce Kirkby, "A 13,000-Mile Experiment in Extreme Parenting," *Outside*, June 22, 2014, www.outsideonline.com/.
3 Ibid.

CHAPTER 3. FEAR AND JOY

1 Sharon Hays coined the term "intensive mothering" in her 1998 book, *The Cultural Contradictions of Motherhood*. The term "helicopter parenting" emerged in the popular press and was critiqued by Julie Lythcott-Haims in her 2015 book, *How to Raise an Adult*. These forms of intensive parenting are also referred to as "snowplow," "lawnmower," and "bulldozer" parenting to describe parents who clear the way for their children.
2 Senior, *All Joy*.
3 Ibid., 189.
4 Zelizer, *Priceless Child*.
5 See Millian Kang's work on parenting among second-generation Korean American women for a more nuanced account of the heterogeneous ways mothers negotiate these cultural forms of parenting.
6 Lee et al., *Parenting Culture Studies*, 11.

7 Ibid.; and see Murray and Cortés-Morales, *Children's Mobilities*.

8 Furedi's insistence that children are safer today needs to be qualified in terms of race, class, and gender. As Rachel Pain points out in her article "Paranoid Parenting?," socioeconomically disadvantaged children do actually face more dangers in their daily lives than affluent middle-class children.

9 Gill Valentine's analysis also foregrounds the way gender shapes both parents' and children's experiences of risk, showing how mothers and fathers adopt different roles in assessing risk and enforce different standards of safety for sons and daughters. Indeed, it is worth pointing out that mothers often shoulder a greater share of the emotional labor involved in managing risk on behalf of their children than fathers do, though both mothers and fathers perform their parenting roles in a context of risk.

10 Murray and Cortés-Morales, *Children's Mobilities*; Gill Valentine also points out that society tends to see children as "angels" or "devils" and both are fraught for parents. On the one hand, they fear danger will befall their angels, while on the other hand, they fear that their devils may perpetrate harm. In either case, parents are to blame for failing to protect their angels or control their devils.

11 Holdsworth, *Family and Intimate Mobilities*.

12 Cited in Boyne, "Cosmopolis and Risk," 57.

13 And see Cooper, *Cut Adrift*.

14 Nelson, *Parenting Out of Control*, 8.

15 Cooper, *Cut Adrift*, 97.

16 Fass, *End of American Childhood*. Bristow, "Double Bind."

17 Beck and Beck-Gernsheim, *Normal Chaos of Love*, 119.

18 Ibid.

19 Valentine, *Culture of Childhood*, 20–21; and see Francis, *Family Trouble*.

20 See Cater, "Playing with Risk?," and Matthews, "Journeys into Authenticity."

21 See Germann Molz, *Travel Connections*, chapter 5; and "Eating Difference."

22 See Elsrud, "Risk Creation," and Yar and Tzanelli, "Kidnapping for Fun."

23 Matthews, "Journeys into Authenticity," 83.

24 Yar and Tzanelli, "Kidnapping for Fun."

25 Sandseter and Kennair, "Children's Risky Play," 266.

26 Ibid., 269.

27 Ibid., 270.

28 Hochschild, *Managed Heart*.

29 Yar and Tzanelli, "Kidnapping for Fun."

30 Ibid., 109.

31 Ibid., 113.

32 Ibid., 120.

33 Valentine, *Culture of Childhood*, 15.

34 For example, in her study of middle-class families in New York, Tamara Mose explains the rise of the supervised playdate as an effect of this kind of fear-based discourse.

35 Fass, *End of American Childhood*, 237.

36 Yar and Tzanelli, "Kidnapping for Fun."

37 Lareau, *Unequal Childhoods*.

38 As we will see in the next chapter, both younger and adolescent children also express mixed emotions about all this family togetherness. I raise the issue here to illustrate how the desire for family togetherness—which parents often frame as the reward for taking that risky leap of faith—can conceal the diversity of emotions that adults and children feel.

39 In their study of families holidaying in caravan parks, Marie Mikkelson and Bodil Blichfeldt found that good, quality family time was often premised on not seeing the kids for hours. The parks allowed for wider independence since children could play outside, unsupervised, which contributed to a happier family vacation.

40 Hochschild, *Outsourced Self*.

41 Hunt, "Risk and Moralization," cited in Lee, "Introduction," 13–14.

42 Lee, "Introduction," 2.

HOMESICK-ISH

1 Williams, *Pursuit of Happiness*, 117.

2 Germann Molz, "Global Abode."

CHAPTER 4. REBEL AND TRIBE

1 As I mentioned in the introduction to this book, research on expat, military, and missionary families suggests that "third culture kids" develop a unique emotional profile, one marked by chronic grief, rootlessness and restlessness, isolation, difficulties with trust and safety, and loss of personal identity and a sense of belonging. At the same time, however, researchers point out that these negative emotions are interwoven with other emotional capacities, such as an enhanced sense of empathy and adaptability. See, for example, Gilbert, "Loss and Grief"; Pollock and Van Reken, *Third Culture Kids*; and Cockburn, "Changing Worlds."

2 Elliott and Lemert, *New Individualism*, 3.

3 Ibid.

4 Ibid., 9; and see Scharff, "Psychic Life."

5 Iyer, *Global Soul*.

6 See Matt, *Homesickness*, for a historical analysis of this sentiment.

7 Thompson, "Digital Nomad Lifestyle."

8 Weinstein, "Social Media See-Saw."

9 As I explained in the introduction, this is how I managed to connect with several of the families I interviewed for this research.

10 In all of my correspondence with other worldschooling families, I was very clear about my position as a sociologist and about the research intentions of our meetings.

11 Silva-Braga, *A Map for Saturday*.

12 In this sense, worldschooling sociality mirrors what researchers find in studies of mobile sociality more generally, that it tends to involve periodic physical travel for intermittent face-to-face encounters that sustain the social relation at a distance later. See, for example, Elliot and Urry, *Mobile Lives*, and Urry, *Sociology beyond Societies*.

13 Although the online forums, family meet-ups, and teen learning retreats I've described so far aim to be broadly inclusive in terms of race, ethnicity, nationality, physical ability, sexual orientation, or socioeconomic background, judging from the photos posted online, the reality is more homogeneous. The participants may be an international bunch, but in the photos they appear to be predominantly white, they hail primarily from the industrialized nations of the Global North, and it is clear from the published programs and promotional materials that English is the common language of these gatherings. This is not to say that vast differences do not exist among people who share similar racial, national, linguistic, or socioeconomic backgrounds, but rather to highlight the tension between uniformity and individual freedom.

14 Young, "Ideal of Community."

15 Ibid., 300.

16 Giddens, *Modernity and Self-Identity*, 214.

17 Jakubiak, "Ambiguous Aims"; Mostafanezhad, *Volunteer Tourism*; and see Lean, *Transformative Travel*.

18 Giddens, *Modernity and Self-Identity*, 215–16.

19 Matt, *Homesickness*, 36.

20 Ibid., 252.

21 Elliott and Lemert, *New Individualism*, 7.

22 See Elliott and Urry, *Mobile Lives*; Wittel, "Network Sociality"; Bauman, *Liquid Love*.

23 See Wajcman, *Pressed for Time*, chapter 6.

24 Bialski, *Intimately Mobile*, 127.

25 Thompson, "I Get My Lovin.'"

26 See Bauman, *Liquid Love*.

GLOBAL AMERICAN DREAM

1 My focus here is on the use of the American Dream as a cultural imaginary through which families make sense of past disappointments and future aspirations, but it is worth commenting on the structure of this writing project in relation to the discussion in chapter 2. By adopting a common theme and linking to one another's websites, the bloggers generated rich content and employed a strategy for boosting views and possibly subscribers across their websites, so it was also a savvy move from a blogging-as-business, lifestyle-as-livelihood standpoint.

CHAPTER 5. HOME AND WORLD

1 See Cooper, *Cut Adrift*; Reay et al., "Darker Shade."

2 Yi-Ping Eva Shih, "Redefining Cosmopolitanism."

3 Hannerz, *Two Faces*; Urry, "Globalization and Citizenship"; Dower and Williams, *Global Citizenship*.

4 Lareau, *Unequal Childhoods*.

5 I first developed this concept in Germann Molz, "Learning to Feel Global."

6 Hochschild, *Managed Heart*.

7 Ibid.; and see chapter 3.

8 Zeddies and Millei, "Global Village."

9 Zahra and McIntosh, "Cathartic"; cf. Mostafanezhad, *Volunteer Tourism*.

10 Crossley, "Affect," 8.

11 See Crossley, "Poor but Happy."

12 When the parents in my study mentioned guilt, it was most often in relation to a sense of guilt about the materialistic and consumerist lifestyles they had led previously. Recent scholarship has examined travelers' guilt in the context of volunteer tourism. Some scholars attribute the rise of voluntourism to an ever-increasing "guilt-conscious society." See Callanan and Thomas, "Volunteer Tourism," 183. Critics argue that through volunteer work, tourists merely buy out the guilt associated with their affluence and privilege. See Lyons et al., "Gap Year," 372. On the other hand, some voluntourists desire to feel—rather than assuage—the guilt. For example, Émilie Crossley's respondents narrated guilt as "an unpleasant yet necessary experience" that ultimately "facilitate[d] the positive change in the self," such as an enhanced sense of responsibility to the world's poor. See Crossley, "Affect," 9; Sin, "Responsible."

13 Mostafanezhad, "Geography of Compassion"; Sin, "Responsible"; Zeddies and Millei, "Global Village."

14 I have summarized these critiques elsewhere. See Germann Molz, "Giving Back"; "Making a Difference."

15 Mostafanezhad, *Volunteer Tourism*; Allon and Koleth, "Doing Good."

16 Buda, *Affective Tourism*.

17 Nelson, *Parenting Out of Control*.

18 Ibid.; Senior, *All Joy*.

19 Dov Seidman, "From the Knowledge Economy to the Human Economy," *Harvard Business Review*, November 12, 2014, https://hbr.org.

20 Ibid.

21 Hochschild, *Managed Heart*; Ehrenreich and Hochschild, *Global Woman*.

22 And see Veijola and Jokinen, "Hostessing Society."

23 Allon and Koleth, "Doing Good," 63.

24 Jeff Colvin, "Humans Are Underrated," *Fortune Magazine*, July 23, 2015, 100–13; Eliza Gray, "How High Is Your XQ?" *Time Magazine*, June 22, 2015, 40–46.

25 Munt, "The 'Other,'" 109; Desforges, "Travelling."

26 Courtois, "Study Abroad as Governmentality"; Snee, *A Cosmopolitan Journey*.

27 Lyons et al., "Gap Year," 370; and see Simpson, "Dropping Out"; and Jones, "International Youth Volunteering."

28 Vrasti, *Volunteer Tourism*, 130.

29 Allon and Koleth, "Doing Good," 63.

30 Gaztambide-Fernández et al., "Entitlement"; and see Gaztambide-Fernández, *Best of the Best*.

31 Gaztambide-Fernández and Howard, "Why Study Up?," 2.

32 Gaztambide-Fernández et al., "Entitlement."

33 Although not included in my original sample, a debate recently broke out on a worldschooling social media forum concerning taking children to protest sites. The cause in question was the ongoing protests at Standing Rock and parents debated the safety concerns about potentially exposing their children to violent protests.

CHAPTER 6. PRIVILEGE AND PRECARITY

1 Elliott and Urry, *Mobile Lives*, 4.

2 Ibid.

3 See Oliver and O'Reilly, "Bourdieusian Analysis," on the new expressions of class distinction among lifestyle migrants.

4 Lareau, *Unequal Childhoods*.

5 Cooper, *Cut Adrift*, 98.

6 Nelson, *Parenting Out of Control*, 8.

7 For his part, Bourdieu distinguishes a particular kind of institutional cultural capital that comes in the form of degrees, credentials, and titles.

8 Binkley, *Happiness*, 119.

9 Ibid.

10 Scharff, "Psychic Life."

11 Kapitulik, "Resisting Schools," 125. In his research on homeschooling, Kapitulik compares the predominantly white, middle-class homeschooling parents in his sample with the low-income Latina and African American women Nancy Naples profiled in *Grassroots Warriors*, her renowned 1998 book on "activist mothering." While both sets of parents vocally criticized their children's schools as deeply flawed institutions racked by social problems, they addressed their concerns in different ways. The activist mothers in Naples's study sought to change the conditions in their children's neighborhoods and school by taking jobs in social service agencies, participating in community-based activism, joining community groups, and raising awareness about local issues. The white, middle-class parents in Kapitulik's study left school altogether, retraining their focus on their individual homes and families.

12 Goldstein, "Liberals."

13 Reeves, *Dream Hoarders*.

14 Reay et al., "Darker Shade," 1046.

15 Ibid., 1055.

16 Ibid.

17 Ibid., 1054.

18 Ibid., 1055.

19 Ibid., 1054–55.

20 Oke, Sonn, and Baker, *Places of Privilege*, 5.

21 Hochschild, "Sociology of Emotions."
22 Cooper, *Cut Adrift*, 14.
23 Standing, *Precariat*, 3. And see Standing, *Work after Globalization*. Standing identifies seven classes: the elite (plutocracy); the salariat; the proficians; the manual laborers, old working class and working poor; the precariat; the unemployed; the detached (lumpen proletariat).
24 Altringer, "Globetrotting."
25 Standing, *Precariat*, 9.
26 Ibid.
27 Hochschild, "Sociology of Emotions," 184.
28 Hoffman and Casnocha, *Start Up*.
29 Altringer, "Globetrotting."
30 Åkerlund and Sandberg, "Stories of Lifestyle Mobility."
31 Amit, "Couple of Years"; Amit, *First Class*; and see Oke et al., *Places of Privilege*.
32 Botterill, "Discordant Lifestyle Mobilities."
33 See, for example, Suter, "European Corporate," and Kunz, "Privileged Mobilities."
34 Botterill, "Discordant Lifestyle Mobilities," 9.
35 This is a point Botterill and Amit emphasize as well.
36 Sheller, *Mobility Justice*; Kannisto, *Global Nomads*.

EPILOGUE

1 Cook and Butz, "Moving."
2 Sheller, *Mobility Justice*, 169.
3 For a critique of this myth of the solitary traveler, see Kaplan's analysis of Said's "Reflections on Exile" in *Questions of Travel*.
4 Mancinelli, "A Practice of Togetherness."
5 Ince and Bryant, "Reading Hospitality," 220.
6 Ibid.
7 McNay, "Self as Enterprise," 56, 64.
8 Ibid., 56.
9 Binkley, *Happiness*, 4.
10 Cass and Manderscheid, "Autonomobility."
11 Ibid.
12 Ibid.
13 Hage, *Waiting*, 10.
14 Morrison, *The Foreigner's Home*.
15 See Cooper, *Cut Adrift*, 213.
16 Appadurai, *Future*, 299–300.
17 Sheller, *Mobility Justice*, 170.

APPENDIX A

1 Germann Molz, *Travel Connections*, chapter 2.
2 Büscher, Urry, and Witchger, *Mobile Methods*.

3 Azariah, "Traveler as Author"; Germann Molz, *Travel Connections*.
4 Hookway, "Enter the Blogosphere," 94; Goffman, *Presentation of Self.*
5 Giddens, *Modernity and Self-Identity*, 75.
6 Ibid., 5.
7 Baltar and Brunet, "Social Research 2.0."
8 See Noy, "Sampling Knowledge."
9 Kendall, *Hanging Out.*
10 For a detailed discussion of analytical autoethnography, see Anderson, "Analytic Autoethnography."
11 Ibid., 373.
12 Reeves, *Dream Hoarders.*
13 See Brown and Casanova, "Mothers in the Field," 42; and Frohlick, "You Brought Your Baby."
14 For a helpful summary of these debates, see Stainton and Iordanova, "An Ethical Perspective."
15 Ibid.
16 Ibid.

APPENDIX B

1 See O'Reilly, "From Drifter to Gap Year"; Benson, *British in Rural France*; Benson and O'Reilly, *Lifestyle Migration*; Thompson, "Digital Nomad Lifestyle."
2 Bianca Williams, personal communication.
3 National Center for Education Statistics (NCES), "Homeschooling in the United States: Results from the 2012 and 2016 Parent and Family Involvement Survey," December 2019, https://nces.ed.gov. The NCES report indicates that in 2016, 59 percent of homeschoolers in the United States were white, 26 percent were Hispanic, 8 percent were black, 3 percent were Asian or Pacific Islander, and 4 percent were Other, non-Hispanic. Several mainstream news articles have also reported on the rise of black families homeschooling and worldschooling their children. See, for example, Keshia McEntire, "More Black Families Choosing Homeschooling," *Indianapolis Recorder*, July 6, 2017, www.indianapolisrecorder.com/; Je'don Holloway, "Why Home Schooling Is an Increasing Option for Black Families," *Philadelphia Tribune*, December 5, 2017, www.phillytrib.com; Anthonia Akitunde, "Unschooling: Why More Black Families Are Joining This Radical Education Movement," *MUTHA Magazine*, March 6, 2018, http://muthamagazine.com; Sam Weber and Connie Kargbo, "Black Families Increasingly Choose to Homeschool Kids," *PBS News Hour*, April 22, 2018, www.pbs.org; Melinda D. Anderson, "The Radical Self-Reliance of Black Homeschooling," *The Atlantic*, May 17, 2018, www.theatlantic.com. And the following article documents the emergence of worldschooling in Hong Kong: See Yupin Ng, "Hong Kong Children Learn Life Lessons with the World as Their Classroom," *South China Morning Post*, April 21, 2018, www.scmp.com/news.

4 Conradson and Latham, "Transnational Urbanism."

5 See Eidse and Sichel, *Unrooted Childhoods*; Nette and Hayden, "Globally Mobile Children"; Laoire et al., "Childhood and Migration"; Lijadi and van Schalkwyk, "Narratives of Third Culture Kids"; and Hay, "Missing Voices."

6 Finch, "Displaying Families"; Haldrup and Larsen, "Family Gaze"; Morgan, *Family Connections*; and Holdsworth, *Family and Intimate Mobilities*.

7 Lois, *Home Is Where the School Is*.

BIBLIOGRAPHY

Acosta, Rina. *The Happiest Kids in the World: How Dutch Parents Help Their Kids (and Themselves) by Doing Less*. New York: The Experiment, 2017.

Adler, Judith. "Travel as Performed Art." *American Journal of Sociology* 94, no. 6 (1989): 1366–91.

Ahmed, Sara. *The Cultural Politics of Emotion*. Edinburgh: University of Edinburgh Press, 2004.

Åkerlund Ulrika and Linda Sandberg. "Stories of Lifestyle Mobility: Representing Self and Place in the Search for the 'Good Life.'" *Social & Cultural Geography* 16, no. 3 (2015): 351–70. http://dx.doi.org/10.1080/14649365.2014.987806.

Alexander, Jessica. *The Danish Way of Parenting: What the Happiest People in the World Know About Raising Confident, Capable Kids*. New York: TarcherPerigee, 2016.

Allison, Clinton B., ed. *Without Consensus: Issues in American Education*. Boston: Allyn and Bacon, 1973.

Allon, Fiona and Maria Koleth. "Doing Good: Transforming the Self by Transforming the World." In *Travel and Transformation*, edited by Garth Lean, Russell Staiff, and Emma Waterton, 57–72. Farnham, UK: Ashgate, 2014.

Altringer, Beth. "Globetrotting Digital Nomads: The Future of Work or Too Good to Be True?" *Forbes Leadership Forum*, December 22, 2015. www.forbes.com/.

A Map for Saturday. Directed by Brook Silva-Braga. Passion River. 2007.

Amit, Vered, ed. *Going First Class?: New Approaches towards Privileged Travel and Movement*. New York and Oxford: Berghahn Press, 2007.

Amit, Vered. "'In a Couple of Years (or Three or Four), I'll Stop Travelling So Much': The Challenges of Modulating Skilled Work Mobility." In *Pacing Mobilities: Timing, Intensity, Tempo and Duration of Human Movements*, edited by Vered Amit and Noel B. Salazar, 163–80. Oxford and New York: Berghahn, 2020.

Amit, Vered and Noel B. Salazar. "Why and How the Pacing of Mobilities Matters." In *Pacing Mobilities: Timing, Intensity, Tempo and Duration of Human Movements*, edited by Vered Amit and Noel B. Salazar, 1–18. Oxford and New York: Berghahn, 2020.

Anderson, Leon. "Analytic Autoethnography." *Journal of Contemporary Ethnography* 35 (2006): 373–95.

Andreotti, Vanessa and Lynn Mario de Souza, eds. *Postcolonial Perspectives on Global Citizenship Education*. London and New York: Routledge, 2014.

Appadurai, Arjun. *The Future as Cultural Fact: Essays on the Global Condition*. New York: Verso, 2013.

Arum, Richard and Josipa Roksa. *Academically Adrift: Limited Learning on College Campuses*. Chicago: University of Chicago Press, 2011.

Atwood, Kristin. "Families' Emotion Work in Transnational Settings: The Case of Military Families." *New Global Studies* 7, no. 3 (2013): 1–22.

Aurini, Janice and Scott Davies. "Choice Without Markets: Homeschooling in the Context of Private Education." *British Journal of Sociology of Education* 26, no. 4 (2005): 461–74.

Azariah, Deepti Ruth. "The Traveler as Author: Examining Self-Presentation and Discourse in the (Self) Published Travel Blog." *Media, Culture & Society* 38, no. 6 (2016): 934–45. https://doi.org/10.1177/0163443716664483.

Baltar, Fabiola and Ignasi Brunet. "Social Research 2.0: Virtual Snowball Sampling Method Using Facebook." *Internet Research* 22 (2012): 57–74.

Baltodano, Marta. "Neoliberalism and the Demise of Public Education: The Corporatization of Schools of Education." *International Qualitative Studies in Education* 25, no. 4 (2012): 487–507.

Barker, John, Peter Kraftl, John Horton, and Faith Tucker. "The Road Less Travelled—New Directions in Children's and Young People's Mobility." *Mobilities* 4, no. 1 (2009): 1–10.

Bauman, Zygmunt. *Liquid Modernity*. Cambridge: Polity, 2000.

Bauman, Zygmunt. *Liquid Love: On the Frailty of Human Bonds*. Cambridge: Polity, 2003.

Baumrind, Diana. "Effects of Authoritative Parental Control on Child Behavior." *Child Development* 37, no. 4 (1966): 887–907.

Baumrind, Diana. "Child Care Practices Anteceding Three Patterns of Preschool Behavior." *Genetic Psychology Monographs* 75, no. 1 (1967): 43–88.

Beck, Ulrich. *Risk Society: Towards a New Modernity*. London: Sage, 1992.

Beck, Ulrich and Elisabeth Beck-Gernsheim. *The Normal Chaos of Love*. Translated by Mark Ritter and Jane Wiebel. Cambridge: Polity, 1995.

Benson, Michaela. *The British in Rural France: Lifestyle Migration and the Ongoing Quest for a Better Way of Life*. Manchester, UK: Manchester University Press, 2013.

Benson, Michaela and Karen O'Reilly, eds. *Lifestyle Migration: Expectations, Aspirations and Experiences*. London: Routledge, 2016.

Benson, Michaela and Nick Osbaldiston, eds. *Understanding Lifestyle Migration: Theoretical Approaches to Migration and the Quest for a Better Way of Life*. London: Palgrave Macmillan, 2014.

Berlin, Isaiah. "Two Concepts of Liberty." In *Four Essays on Liberty*, 118–72. Oxford: Oxford University Press, 1969.

Bhopal, Kalwant and Martin Myers. *Home Schooling and Home Education: Race, Class and Inequality*. London: Routledge, 2018.

Bialski, Paula. *Becoming Intimately Mobile*. New York: Peter Lang, 2012a.

Bialski, Paula. "Technologies of Hospitality: How Planned Encounters Develop Between Strangers." *Hospitality & Society* 1, no. 3 (2012b): 245–60.

Binkley, Sam. *Happiness as Enterprise: An Essay on Neoliberal Life*. Albany: SUNY Press, 2017.

Botterill, Kate. "Discordant Lifestyle Mobilities in East Asia: Privilege and Precarity of British Retirement in Thailand." *Population, Space and Place* 23 (2017): 1–11. https://doi.org/10.1002/psp.2011.

Bourdieu, Pierre. *Distinction: A Social Critique of the Judgement of Taste*. London: Routledge, 1984.

Bowles, Samuel and Herbert Gintis. *Schooling in Capitalist America: Educational Reform and the Contradictions of Economic Life*. Chicago: Haymarket Books, 2011 [1976].

Boyne, Roy. "Cosmopolis and Risk: A Conversation with Ulrich Beck." *Theory, Culture & Society* 13, no. 4 (2001): 47–63.

Brantlinger, Ellen. *Dividing Classes: How the Middle Class Negotiates and Rationalizes School Advantage*. New York and London: Routledge, 2003.

Bristow, Jennie. "The Double Bind of Parenting Culture: Helicopter Parents and Cotton Wool Kids." In *Parenting Culture Studies*, edited by Ellie Lee, Jennie Bristow, Charlotte Faircloth, and Jan Macvarish, 200–15. London and New York: Palgrave Macmillan, 2014.

Brown, Tamara Mose and Erynn Masi De Casanova. "Mothers in the Field: How Motherhood Shapes Fieldwork and Research-Subject Relations." *Women's Studies Quarterly* 37, nos. 3–4 (2009): 42–57.

Brown, Wendy. "Neoliberalism and the End of Liberal Democracy." *Theory & Event* 7, no. 1 (2003). http://muse.jhu.edu/.

Buda, Dorina Maria. *Affective Tourism: Dark Routes in Conflict*. London: Routledge, 2015.

Büscher, Monika, John Urry, and Katian Witchger, eds. *Mobile Methods*. London: Routledge, 2010.

Callanan, Michelle and Sarah Thomas. "Volunteer Tourism: Deconstructing Volunteer Activities Within a Dynamic Environment." In *Niche Tourism: Contemporary Issues, Trends and Cases*, edited by Marina Novelli, 183–200. Oxford: ButterworthHeinemann, 2005.

Carr, Neil. *Children's and Families' Holiday Experience*. London: Routledge, 2011.

Cass, Noel and Katharina Manderscheid. "The Autonomobility System: Mobility Justice and Freedom Under Sustainability." In *Mobilities, Mobility Justice and Social Justice*, edited by Nancy Cook and David Butz, chapter 7. Oxon and New York: Routledge, 2019.

Cater, Carl I. "Playing with Risk? Participant Perceptions of Risk and Management Implications in Adventure Tourism." *Tourism Management* 27, no. 2 (2006): 317–25.

Caton, Kellee and Carla Almeida Santos. "Images of the Other: Selling Study Abroad in a Postcolonial World." *Journal of Travel Research* 48, no. 2 (2009): 191–204.

Chaney, Edward. *The Evolution of the Grand Tour*. London: Routledge, 2000.

Chua, Amy. *Battle Hymn of the Tiger Mother*. New York: Penguin, 2011.

Cichelli, Vincenzo and Sylvie Octobre. "Introducing *Youth and Globalization* and the Special Issue: *The Rise and Fall of Cosmopolitanism, Youth and Globalization*." *Youth and Globalization* 1, no. 1 (2019): 1–18.

Cockburn, Laura. "Children and Young People Living in Changing Worlds: The Process of Assessing and Understanding the 'Third Culture Kid.'" *School Psychology International* 23, no. 4 (2002): 475–85.

Cockerham, William C. *Society of Risk-Takers: Living Life on the Edge*. New York: Worth, 2005.

Cohen, Erik. "Nomads from Affluence: Notes on the Phenomenon of Drifter-Tourism." *International Journal of Comparative Sociology* 14, nos. 1–2 (1973): 89–103. https://doi.org/10.1163/156854273X00153.

Cohen, Scott. "Lifestyle Travellers: Backpacking as a Way of Life." *Annals of Tourism Research* 38, no. 4 (2011): 1535–55.

Coles, Anne and Anne-Meike Fechter, eds. *Gender and Family Among Transnational Professionals*. London and New York: Routledge, 2008.

Conradson, David and Alan Latham. "Transnational Urbanism: Attending to Everyday Practices and Mobilities." *Journal of Ethnic and Migration Studies* 31, no. 2 (2005): 227–33.

Cook, Nancy and David Butz, eds. *Mobilities, Mobility Justice and Social Justice*. Oxon and New York: Routledge, 2019a.

Cook, Nancy and David Butz. "Moving Toward Mobility Justice." In *Mobilities, Mobility Justice and Social Justice*, edited by Nancy Cook and David Butz, ch. 1. Oxon and New York: Routledge, 2019b.

Cooper, Marianne. *Cut Adrift: Families in Insecure Times*. Berkeley: University of California Press, 2014.

Courtois, Aline. "Study Abroad as Governmentality: The Construction of Hypermobile Subjectivities in Higher Education." *Journal of Education Policy* (October 2018): 1–21.

Covey, Stephen R. *7 Habits of Highly Effective People*. Salt Lake City, UT: Franklin Covey, 2015.

Cremin, Lawrence. *The Transformation of the School: Progressivism in American Education, 1876–1957*. New York: Knopf, 1961.

Crossley, Émilie. "Affect and Moral Transformations in Young Volunteer Tourists." In *Emotion in Motion: Tourism, Affect and Transformation*, edited by David Picard and Mike Robinson, 85–98. Farnham, UK: Ashgate, 2012a.

Crossley, Émilie. "Poor but Happy: Volunteer Tourists' Encounters with Poverty." *Tourism Geographies* 14, no. 2 (2012b): 235–53.

Davies, Bronwyn and Peter Bansel. "Neoliberalism and Education." *International Journal of Qualitative Studies in Education* 20, no. 3 (2007): 247–59.

Deresiewicz, William. *Excellent Sheep: The Miseducation of the American Elite and the Way to a Meaningful Life*. New York: Simon & Schuster, 2014.

Desforges, Luke. "Travelling the World: Identity and Travel Biography." *Annals of Tourism Research* 27 (2000): 926–45.

Dewey, John. *Democracy and Education: An Introduction to the Philosophy of Education*. New York: Macmillan, 1916.

Dower, Nigel and John Williams, eds. *Global Citizenship: A Critical Introduction*. London: Routledge, 2016.

Druckerman, Pamela. *Bringing Up Bebé: One American Mother Discovers the Wisdom of French Parenting*. New York: Penguin, 2014.

Duncan, Tara, Scott Cohen, and Maria Thulemark, eds. *Lifestyle Mobilities: Intersections of Travel, Leisure and Migration*. London: Routledge, 2016.

Ehrenreich, Barbara and Arlie Russell Hochschild. *Global Woman: Nannies, Maids, and Sex Workers in the New Economy*. New York: Henry Holt, 2004.

Eidse, Faith and Nina Sichel. *Unrooted Childhoods: Memoirs of Growing Up Global*. London: Nicholas Brealey, 2004.

Eleff, Leanne Ralya and Angela Christine Trethewey. "The Enterprising Parent: A Critical Examination of Parenting, Consumption and Identity." *Journal of the Association for Research on Mothering* 8, nos. 1–2 (2006): 242–52.

Elliott, Anthony and Charles Lemert. *The New Individualism: The Emotional Costs of Globalization*. London and New York: Routledge, 2006.

Elliott, Anthony and John Urry. *Mobile Lives*. London and New York: Routledge, 2010.

Elsrud, Torun. "Risk Creation in Traveling: Backpacker Adventure Narration." *Annals of Tourism Research*, 28, no. 3 (2001): 597–617.

Fass, Paula S. *The End of American Childhood: A History of Parenting from Life on the Frontier to the Managed Child*. Princeton, NJ: Princeton University Press, 2016.

Feiler, Bruce. *The Secrets of Happy Families*. New York: Harper Collins, 2013.

Ferraro, Aimee. "Evaluation of a Temporary, Immersive Learning Community Based on Worldschooling." *Journal of Unschooling and Alternative Learning* 10, no. 20 (2016): 16–27.

Ferriss, Timothy. *The 4-Hour Work Week: Escape 9–5, Live Anywhere, and Join the New Rich*. New York: Crown, 2007.

Finch, Janet. "Displaying Families." *Sociology* 41, no. 1 (2007): 65–81.

Forget, Célia. "'Time to Hit the Road': Understanding Living on the Road Through Shifts in Thinking about Time." In *Pacing Mobilities: Timing, Intensity, Tempo and Duration of Human Movements*, edited by Vered Amit and Noel B. Salazar, 79–99. Oxford and New York: Berghahn, 2020.

Foucault, Michel. *The Birth of Biopolitics: Lectures at the Collége de France, 1978–1979*. London: Palgrave Macmillan, 2008.

Francis, Ara. *Family Trouble: Middle-Class Parents, Children's Problems, and the Disruption of Everyday Life*. New Brunswick, NJ: Rutgers University Press, 2015.

Freeman, Carla. *Entrepreneurial Selves: Neoliberal Respectability and the Making of a Caribbean Middle Class*. Durham, NC: Duke University Press, 2014.

Freire, Paulo. *Pedagogy of the Oppressed*, 30th Anniversary Edition. New York: Bloomsbury, 2000 (1970).

Frohlick, Susan E. "You Brought Your Baby to Base Camp? Families and Field Sites." *Great Lakes Geographer* 9, no. 1 (2002): 49–58.

Furedi, Frank. *Paranoid Parenting: Why Ignoring the Experts May Be Best for Your Child*. Chicago: Chicago Review Press, 2002.

Gatto, John Taylor. *Dumbing Us Down: The Hidden Curriculum of Compulsory Schooling*. Gabriola Island, BC: New Society, 1992.

Gaztambide-Fernández, Rubén A. *The Best of the Best: Becoming Elite at an American Boarding School*. Cambridge, MA: Harvard University Press, 2009.

Gaztambide-Fernández, Rubén, Kate Cairns, and Chandni Desai. "The Sense of Entitlement." In *Privilege, Agency and Affect*, edited by Claire Maxwell and Peter Aggleton, 32–49. London: Palgrave Macmillan, 2013.

Gaztambide-Fernández, Rubén and Adam Howard. "Introduction: Why Study Up?" In *Educating Elites: Class Privilege and Educational Advantage in the US*, edited by Adam Howard and Rubén Gaztambide-Fernández, 1–12. Boulder, CO: Rowman & Littlefield, 2010.

Germann Molz, Jennie. "Eating Difference: The Cosmopolitan Mobilities of Culinary Tourism." *Space and Culture* 10, no. 2 (2007): 77–93.

Germann Molz, Jennie. "Global Abode: Home and Mobility in Narratives of Round-the-World Travel." *Space and Culture* 11, no. 4 (2008): 325–42.

Germann Molz, Jennie. *Travel Connections: Tourism, Technology and Togetherness in a Mobile World*. London and New York: Routledge, 2012.

Germann Molz, Jennie. "Giving Back, Doing Good, Feeling Global: The Affective Flows of Family Voluntourism." *Journal of Contemporary Ethnography* 46, no. 3 (2015): 334–60.

Germann Molz, Jennie. "Making a Difference Together: Discourses of Transformation in Family Voluntourism." *Journal of Sustainable Tourism* 24, no. 3 (2016): 805–23.

Germann Molz, Jennie. "Learning to Feel Global: Exploring the Emotional Geographies of Worldschooling." *Emotion, Space and Society* 23 (May 2017): 16–25.

Giddens, Anthony. *Modernity and Self-Identity: Self and Society in the Late Modern Age*. Cambridge: Polity, 1991.

Gilbert, Kathleen R. "Loss and Grief Between and Among Cultures: The Experience of Third Culture Kids." *Illness, Crisis and Loss* 16, no. 2 (2008): 93–109.

Giles, Melinda Vandenbeld, ed. *Mothering in the Age of Neoliberalism*. Bradford, ON: Demeter Press, 2014.

Gindlesparger, Kathryn Johnson. "'Share Your Awesome Time with Others': Interrogating Privilege and Identification in the Study-Abroad Blog." *College English* 81, no. 1 (2018): 7–26.

Goffman, Erving. *The Presentation of Self in Everyday Life*. New York: Doubleday, 1956.

Goldstein, Dana. "Liberals, Don't Homeschool Your Kids." *Slate Magazine*. February 16, 2012. www.slate.com/.

Guttentag, Daniel. "Airbnb: Disruptive Innovation and the Rise of an Informal Tourism Accommodation Sector." *Current Issues in Tourism* (2013). https://doi.org/10.1080/13683500.2013.827159.

Hage, Ghassan. "Waiting Out the Crisis: On Stuckedness and Governmentality." In *Waiting*, edited by Ghassan Hage, chapter 8. Melbourne: Melbourne University Publishing, 2009.

Hage, Ghassan. *White Nation: Fantasies of White Supremacy in a Multicultural Society*. London: Routledge, 2012.

Haldrup, Michael and Jonas Larsen. "The Family Gaze." *Tourist Studies* 3, no. 1 (2003): 23–46.

Hall, Sarah Marie and Clare Holdsworth. "Family Practices, Holiday and the Everyday." *Mobilities* 11, no. 2 (2016): 284–302.

Hannam, Kevin and Anya Diekmann, eds. *Beyond Backpacker Tourism: Mobilities and Experiences*. Bristol: Channel View, 2010.

Hannam, Kevin, Mimi Sheller, and John Urry. "Mobilities, Immobilities and Moorings." *Mobilities* 1, no. 1 (2006): 1–22.

Hannerz, Ulf. *Two Faces of Cosmopolitanism: Culture and Politics*. Barcelona: Fundació CIDOB, 2006.

Harvey, David. *A Brief History of Neoliberalism*. Oxford: Oxford University Press, 2005.

Hay, Brian. "Missing Voices: Australian Children's Insights and Perceptions of Family Holidays." *Hospitality & Society* 7, no. 2 (2017): 133–55.

Hays, Sharon. *The Cultural Contradictions of Motherhood*. New Haven, CT and London: Yale University Press, 1998.

Heath, Sue. "Widening the Gap: Pre-university Gap Years and the 'Economy of Experience.'" *British Journal of Sociology of Education* 28, no. 1 (2007): 89–103.

Hess, Kendy. "Metaphors Matter: Ethics and the Meme of the Market." *Georgetown Journal of Law and Public Policy* 13 (2015): 321–36.

Hochschild, Arlie Russell. *The Managed Heart: Commercialization of Human Feeling*. Berkeley: University of California Press, 1983.

Hochschild, Arlie Russell. *The Outsourced Self: Intimate Life in Market Times*. New York: Henry Holt, 2012.

Hochschild, Arlie Russell. "Critique and the Sociology of Emotions: Fear, Neoliberalism and the Acid Rainproof Fish." Interview by Erik Mygind du Plessis and Pelle Korsbaek Sørenson. *Theory, Culture & Society* 34, nos. 7–8 (2017): 181–87.

Hoffman, Reid and Ben Casnocha. *The Start-Up of You: Adapt to the Future, Invest in Yourself, and Transform Your Career*. New York: Random House, 2012.

Holdsworth, Clare. *Family and Intimate Mobilities*. London: Palgrave Macmillan, 2013.

Holt, John. *How Children Fail*. New York: Dell, 1964.

Holt, John. *How Children Learn*. New York: Dell, 1967.

Holt, John. *Freedom and Beyond*. New York: Dutton, 1972.

Holt, John. *Escape from Childhood: The Needs and Rights of Children*. New York: Holt Associates, 1974.

Hookway, Nicholas. "'Entering the Blogosphere': Some Strategies for Using Blogs in Social Research." *Qualitative Research* 8, no. 1 (February 2008): 91–113. https://doi.org/10.1177/1468794107085298.

Howard, Adam and Gaztambide-Fernández, Rubén, eds. *Educating Elites: Class Privilege and Educational Advantage in the US*. Boulder, CO: Rowman & Littlefield, 2010.

Hunt, Alan. "Risk and Moralization in Everyday Life." In *Risk and Morality*, edited by Richard Victor Ericson and Aaron Doyle, 165–92. Toronto: University of Toronto Press, 2003.

Illich, Ivan. *Deschooling Society*. New York: Harper & Row, 1971.

Ince, Anthony and Helen Bryant. "Reading Hospitality Mutually." *Environment and Planning D: Society and Space* 37, no. 2 (2019): 216–35. https://doi.org/10.1177/0263775818774048.

Iyer, Pico. *The Global Soul*. New York: Random House, 2000.

Jakubiak, Cori. "Ambiguous Aims: English-language Voluntourism as Development." *Journal of Language, Identity & Education* 15, no. 4 (2016): 245–58. https://doi.org/10.1080/15348458.2016.1195270.

Jameson, Frederic. *Postmodernism or, the Cultural Logic of Late Capitalism*. Durham, NC: Duke University Press, 1999.

Jensen, Ole B., Mimi Sheller, and Simon Wind. "Together and Apart: Affective Ambiences and Negotiation in Families' Everyday Life and Mobility." *Mobilities* 10, no. 3 (2015): 363–82. http://dx.doi.org/10.1080/17450101.2013.868158.

Jones, Andrew. "Theorising International Youth Volunteering: Training for Global (Corporate) Work?" *Transactions of the Institute of British Geographers* 36 (2011): 530–44.

Kalčić, Špela. "Going Nomad: New Mobile Lifestyles Among Europeans." *Two Homelands* 38 (2013): 33–48.

Kang, Milliann. "Are Second-Generation Korean American Women Tiger Mothers? Strategic, Transnational, and Resistant Responses to Racialized Mothering." In *Second-Generation Korean Experiences in the United States and Canada*, edited by Pyong Gap Min and Samuel Noh, chapter 12. Lanham, MD: Lexington Books, 2014.

Kang, Milliann. "Up in the Air: Circuits of Transnational Asian and Asian American Mothering." In *Gendering the Trans-Pacific World*, edited by Catherine Ceniza Choy and Judy Tzu-Chun Wu, 246–55. Leiden: Brill, 2017.

Kannisto, Päivi. *Global Nomads and Extreme Mobilities*. London and New York: Routledge, 2017.

Kapitulik, Brian. "Resisting Schools, Reproducing Families: Gender and the Politics of Homeschooling." PhD diss., University of Massachusetts, 2011. https://scholarworks.umass.edu.

Kapitulik, Brian. "Homeschooling." In *Sociology of Education: An A-to-Z Guide*, edited by James Ainsworth, 358–60. London: Sage, 2013.

Kaplan, Caren. *Questions of Travel*. Durham, NC: Duke University Press, 1996.

Kendall, Lori. *Hanging Out in the Virtual Pub: Masculinities and Relationships Online*. Berkeley: University of California Press, 2002.

Kohn, Alfie. *Punished by Rewards: The Trouble with Gold Stars, Incentive Plans, A's, Praise, and Other Bribes*. Boston and New York: Houghton Mifflin, 1993.

Kohn, Alfie. *Unconditional Parenting: Moving from Rewards and Punishment to Love and Reason*. New York: Atria Books, 2005.

Korpela, Mari. *More Vibes in India: Westerners in Search of a Better Life in Varanasi*. Tampere: Tampere University Press, 2009.

Korpela Mari. "Lifestyle of Freedom? Individualism and Lifestyle Migration." In *Understanding Lifestyle Migration*, edited by Michaela Benson and Nick Osbaldiston, 27–46. London: Palgrave Macmillan, 2014.

Kunz, Sarah. "Privileged Mobilities: Locating the Expatriate in Migration Scholarship." *Geography Compass* 10, no. 3 (2016): 89–101.

Laoire, Caitriona, Fina Carpena-Méndez, Naomi Tyrrell, and Allen White. "Childhood and Migration: Mobilities, Homes and Belongings." *Childhood* 17, no. 2 (2010): 155–62.

LaPlante, Logan. "Hackschooling Makes Me Happy." Filmed, University of Nevada. TEDx Video, 11:13. www.youtube.com/watch?v=h11u3vtcpaY.

Lareau, Annette. *Unequal Childhoods: Class, Race and Family Life*. Berkeley: University of California Press, 2003.

Lash, Scott and John Urry. *Economies of Signs and Space*. London: Sage, 1994.

Lean, Garth. *Transformative Travel in a Mobile World*. Oxfordshire: CABI, 2016.

Lee, Ellie, Jennie Bristow, Charlotte Faircloth, and Jan Macvarish. *Parenting Culture Studies*. London and New York: Palgrave Macmillan, 2014.

Lee, Ellie. "Introduction." In *Parenting Culture Studies*, Ellie Lee, Jennie Bristow, Charlotte Faircloth, and Jan Macvarish, 1–22. London and New York: Palgrave Macmillan, 2014.

Lijadi, Anastasia and Gertina van Schalkwyk. "Narratives of Third Culture Kids: Commitment and Reticence in Social Relationships." *Qualitative Report* 19, no. 25 (2014): 1–18.

Locke, John. *Essay Concerning Human Understanding*. Oxford: Oxford University Press, 1689.

Lois, Jennifer. *Home Is Where the School Is: The Logic of Homeschooling and the Emotional Labor of Mothering*. New York and London: New York University Press, 2013.

Loker-Murphy, Laurie and Philip L. Pearce. "Young Budget Travelers: Backpackers in Australia." *Annals of Tourism Research* 22, no. 4 (1995): 819–43.

Lyng, Stephen. *Edgework: The Sociology of Risk-Taking*. New York and London: Routledge, 2005.

Lyons, Kevin, Joanne Hanley, Stephen Wearing, and John Neil. "Gap Year Volunteer Tourism: Myths of Global Citizenship?" *Annals of Tourism Research* 39, no. 1 (2012): 361–78. https://doi.org/10.1016/j.annals.2011.04.016.

Lythcott-Haims, Julie. *How to Raise an Adult: Break Free of the Overparenting Trap and Prepare Your Kid for Success*. New York: Henry Holt, 2015.

MacCannell, Dean. *The Tourist: A New Theory of the Leisure Class*. Berkeley: University of California Press, 1976.

Makimoto, Tsugio and David Manners. *Digital Nomad*. New York: Wiley, 1997.

Mancinelli, Fabiola. "A Practice of Togetherness: Freedom and Belonging in the Life of Location Independent Families." *International Journal of Tourism Anthropology* 6, no. 4 (2018): 307–322. https://doi.org/10.1504/IJTA.2018.096359.

Mascheroni, Giovanna. "Global Nomads' Mobile and Network Sociality: Exploring New Media Uses on the Move." *Information, Communication and Society* 10, no. 4 (2007): 527–46.

Massey, Doreen. "Power-Geometry and a Progressive Sense of Place." In *Mapping the Futures*, edited by Jon Bird, Barry Curtis, Tim Putnam, Gareth Robertson, and Lisa Tickner, 59–69. London: Routledge, 1993.

Matt, Susan J. *Homesickness: An American History*. Oxford: Oxford University Press, 2011.

Matthews, Amie. "Journeys into Authenticity and Adventure: Analysing Media Representations of Backpacker Travel in South America." *Literature & Aesthetics* 22, no. 1 (2012): 60–87.

Mclachlan, Debra A. "Global Nomads in an International School: Families in Transition." *Journal of Research in International Education* 6, no. 2 (August 2007): 233–49. https://doi.org/10.1177/1475240907078615.

McNay, Lois. "Self as Enterprise: Dilemmas of Control and Resistance in Foucault's *The Birth of Biopolitics*." *Theory, Culture & Society* 26, no. 6 (2009): 55–77.

Mikkelsen, Marie Vestergaard and Bodil Stilling Blichfeldt. 2015. "'We have not seen the kids for hours': The Case of Family Holidays and Free-Range Children." *Annals of Leisure Research* 18, no. 2 (2015): 252–71. https://doi.org/10.1080/11745398.2014.999342.

Miller, Peter and Nikolas Rose. "Governing Economic Life." *Economy and Society* 19, no. l (1990): 1–31.

Mills, C. Wright. *The Sociological Imagination*. Oxford: Oxford University Press, 1959.

Mohn, Tanya. "The Digital Nomad Life: Combining Work and Travel." *New York Times*, April 3, 2017. www.nytimes.com/.

Moravec, John W. "Knowmad Society: The 'New' Work and Education." *On the Horizon* 21, no. 2 (2013): 79–83.

Morgan, David H. J. *Family Connections*. Cambridge: Polity Press, 1996.

Mose, Tamara. *Raising Brooklyn: Nannies, Childcare, and Caribbeans Creating Community*. New York: NYU Press, 2011.

Mose, Tamara. *The Playdate: Parents, Children, and the New Expectations of Play*. New York and London: New York University Press, 2016.

Mostafanezhad, Mary. "The Geography of Compassion in Volunteer Tourism." *Tourism Geographies* 15, no. 2 (2013): 318–37. https://doi.org/10.1080/14616688.2012.675579.

Mostafanezhad, Mary. *Volunteer Tourism: Popular Humanitarianism in Neoliberal Times*. London and New York: Routledge, 2016.

Munt, Ian. "The 'Other' Postmodern Tourism: Culture, Travel and the New Middle Classes." *Theory Culture & Society* 11 (1994): 101–23.

Murphy, Laurie. "Exploring Social Interactions of Backpackers." *Annals of Tourism Research* 28, no. 1 (2001): 50–67.

Murray, Lesley and Susana Cortés-Morales. *Children's Mobilities: Interdependent, Imaged, Relational*. London: Palgrave Macmillan, 2019.

Naples, Nancy A. *Grassroots Warriors: Activist Mothering, Community Work, and the War on Poverty*. New York: Routledge, 1998.

Nelson, Margaret. *Parenting Out of Control: Anxious Parents in Uncertain Times*. New York and London: New York University Press, 2010.

Nette, John and Mary Hayden. "Globally Mobile Children: The Sense of Belonging." *Educational Studies* 33, no. 4 (2007): 435–44.

Noy, Chaim. "Sampling Knowledge: The Hermeneutics of Snowball Sampling in Qualitative Research." *International Journal of Social Research Methodology* 11 (2008): 327–44.

Obrador, Pau. "The Place of the Family in Tourism Research: Domesticity and Thick Sociality by the Pool." *Annals of Tourism Research* 39, no. 1 (2012): 401–20.

Oke, Nicole, Christopher C. Sonn, and Alison M. Baker, eds. *Places of Privilege: Interdisciplinary Perspectives on Identities, Change and Resistance*. Leiden and Boston: Brill Sense, 2018.

Oliver, Caroline and Karen O'Reilly. "A Bourdieusian Analysis of Class and Migration: Habitus and the Individualizing Process." *Sociology* 44, no. 1 (2010): 49–66.

Olwig, Karen Fog. "Privileged Travelers? Migration Narratives in Families of Middle-Class Caribbean Background." In *Going First Class? New Approaches to Privileged Travel and Movement*, edited by Vered Amit, 87–102. Oxford and New York: Berghahn, 2007.

Ong, Aihwa. *Neoliberalism as Exception: Mutations in Citizenship and Sovereignty*. Durham, NC: Duke University Press, 2006.

O'Reilly, Camille C. 2006. "From Drifter to Gap Year Tourist: Mainstreaming Backpacker Travel." *Annals of Tourism Research* 33, no. 4 (2006): 998–1017.

O'Reilly, Karen and Michaela Benson. "Lifestyle Migration: Escaping to the Good Life?" In *Lifestyle Migrations: Expectations, Aspirations and Experiences*, edited by Michaela Benson and Karen O'Reilly, 1–13. London: Routledge, 2009.

Pain, Rachel. "Paranoid Parenting? Rematerializing Risk and Fear for Children." *Social & Cultural Geography* 7, no. 2 (2006): 221–43.

Park, Nansook. "Military Children and Families: Strengths and Challenges During Peace and War." *American Psychologist* 66, no. 1 (2011): 65–72.

Parreñas, Rhacel. *Children of Global Migration: Transnational Families and Gendered Woes*. Stanford, CA: Stanford University Press, 2005.

Pollock, David C. and Ruth E. Van Reken. *Third Culture Kids, 3rd Edition: Growing Up Among Worlds*. Boston: Nicholas Brealey, 2010.

Puar, Jasbir K. "Writing My Way 'Home.'" *Socialist Review* 24, no. 4 (1994): 75–108.

Reay, Diane. *Class Work: Mothers' Involvement in Their Children's Primary Schooling*. London: UCL Press, 1998.

Reay, Diane, Sumi Hollingworth, Katya Williams, Gill Crozier, Fiona Jamieson, David James, and Phoebe Beedell. "'A Darker Shade of Pale?' Whiteness, the Middle Classes and Multi-Ethnic Inner City Schooling." *Sociology* 41, no. 6 (2007): 1041–60.

Reese, William J. *Power and the Promise of School Reform: Grassroots Movements During the Progressive Era*. New York and London: Teachers College Press, 2002.

Reese, William J. *America's Public Schools: From the Common School to No Child Left Behind*, 2nd edition. Baltimore, MD: Johns Hopkins University Press, 2011.

Reeves, Richard V. *Dream Hoarders*. Washington, DC: Brookings Institution Press, 2017.

Reichenberger, Ina. "Digital Nomads—A Quest for Holistic Freedom in Work and Leisure." *Annals of Leisure Research* 21, no. 3 (2018): 364–80. https://dx.doi.org/10.10 80/11745398.2017.1358098.

Riley, Gina. "Worldschooling: Homeschooling Away from Home." *International Journal of Education* 9, no. 1 (2017): 186–91.

Ritchie, Brent W., Neil Carr, and Christopher P. Cooper. *Managing Educational Tourism*. Clevedon: Channel View, 2003.

Robinson, Ken. "Do Schools Kill Creativity?" Filmed February 2006, Monterrey, California. TED Video, 19:14. www.ted.com/.

Robinson, Ken. "Changing Educational Paradigms." Filmed October 2010, RSA Animate. TED Video, 11:40. www.ted.com/.

Rose, Susan D. "Christian Fundamentalism and Education in the United States." In *Fundamentalisms and Society*, edited by Martin E. Marty and R. Scott Appleby, 452–89. Chicago: Chicago University Press, 1993.

Ross, E. Wayne and Rich Gibson, eds. *Neoliberalism and Education Reform*. Cresskill, NJ: Hampton Press, 2007.

Rousseau, Jean-Jacques. *Émile, or on Education*. Translated by Allan Bloom. New York: Basic Books, 1979 [1762].

Sandseter, Ellen and Lief Kennair. "Children's Risky Play from an Evolutionary Perspective: The Anti-phobic Effects of Thrilling Experiences." *Evolutionary Psychology* 9, no. 2 (2011): 257–84.

Schänzel, Heike and Paul Lynch. "Family Perspectives on Social Hospitality Dimensions While on Holiday." *Tourist Studies* 16, no. 2 (2016): 133–50.

Schänzel, Heike, Ian Yeoman, and Elisa Backer, eds. *Family Tourism: Multidisciplinary Perspectives*. Bristol: Channel View Publications, 2012.

Scharff, Christina. "The Psychic Life of Neoliberalism: Mapping the Contours of Entrepreneurial Subjectivity." *Theory, Culture & Society* 33, no. 6 (2016): 107–22. https://doi.org/10.1177/0263276415590164.

Schiffrin, Holly H. and Miriam Liss. "The Effects of Helicopter Parenting on Academic Motivation." *Journal of Child and Family Studies* 26, no. 5 (2017): 1472–80.

Schneider, Jack. "American Schools Are Modeled after Factories and Treat Students Like Widgets. Right? Wrong." *Washington Post*, October 10, 2015, www.washington-post.com/.

Schneider, Norbert F. and Ruth Limmer. "Job Mobility and Living Arrangements." In *Tracing Mobilities: Towards a Cosmopolitan Perspective*, edited by Weert Canzler, Vincent Kaufmann, and Sven Kesselring, 119–39. Aldershot: Ashgate, 2008.

Segrin, Chris, Michelle Givertz, Paulina Swaitkowski, and Neil Montgomery. "Overparenting Is Associated with Child Problems and a Critical Family Environment." *Journal of Child and Family Studies* 24, no. 2 (2015): 470–79.

Senior, Jennifer. *All Joy and No Fun: The Paradox of Modern Parenting*. New York: Harper Collins, 2014.

Sheller, Mimi. *Mobility Justice: The Politics of Movement in an Age of Extremes*. London: Verso, 2018.

Sheller, Mimi and John Urry. "The New Mobilities Paradigm." *Environment and Planning A* 38 (2006): 207–26.

Shih, Yi-Ping Eva. "Redefining Cosmopolitanism: The Inter-Generational Transmission of Global Cultural Capital in Taiwan." In *Aesthetic Cosmopolitanism and Global Culture*, edited by Vincenzo Cichelli, Sylvie Octobre, and Viviane Riegal, 385–414. Leiden: Brill, 2019.

Simpson, Kate. "'Doing Development': The Gap Year, Volunteer-Tourists and a Popular Practice of Development." *Journal of International Development* 16, no. 5 (2004): 681–92.

Simpson, Kate. "Dropping Out or Signing Up? The Professionalisation of Youth Travel." *Antipode* 37 (2005): 447–69.

Sin, Harng Luh. "Who Are We Responsible To? Locals' Tales of Volunteer Tourism." *Geoforum* 41 (2010): 983–92.

Skelton, Tracey. "Children's Geographies / Geographies of Children: Play, Work, Mobilities and Migration." *Geography Compass* 4 (2009): 1430–48.

Skenazy, Lenore. *Free-Range Kids: Giving Our Children the Freedom We Had without Going Nuts with Worry*. New York: Wiley, 2009.

Smith, Vernon, Robert Barr, and Daniel Burke. *Alternatives in Education*. Bloomington, IN: Phi Delta Kappa Educational Foundation, 1976.

Snee, Helen. *A Cosmopolitan Journey? Difference, Distinction and Identity Work in Gap Year Travel*. Oxon and New York: Ashgate, 2014.

Sørensen, Anders. "Backpacker Ethnography." *Annals of Tourism Research* 30, no. 4 (2003): 847–67.

Stainton, Hayley and Elitza Iordanova. "An Ethical Perspective for Researchers Using Travel Blog Analysis as a Method of Data Collection." *Methodological Innovations* 10, no. 3 (2017): 1–7.

Standing, Guy. *Work after Globalization: Building Occupational Citizenship*. Cheltenham, UK: Edward Elgar, 2009.

Standing, Guy. *The Precariat: The New Dangerous Class*. New York: Bloomsbury Academic, 2011.

Stevens, Mitchell L. *Kingdom of Children: Culture and Controversy in the Homeschooling Movement*. Princeton, NJ: Princeton University Press, 2003.

Suter, Brigitte. "European Corporate Migrants in Chinese Metropolises and the Pacing of Family Mobility." In *Pacing Mobilities: Timing, Intensity, Tempo and Duration of Human Movements*, edited by Vered Amit and Noel B. Salazar, 120–41. Oxford and New York: Berghahn, 2020.

Tanz, Jason. "The Techies Who Are Hacking Education by Homeschooling Their Kids." *Wired Magazine*, February 4, 2015. www.wired.com/.

Tarozzi, Massimiliano and Carlos Alberto Torres. *Global Citizenship Education and the Crises of Multiculturalism: Comparative Perspectives*. London: Bloomsbury, 2016.

The Foreigner's Home: Toni Morrison at the Louvre. Directed by Rian Brown and Geoff Pingree. Oberlin, OH: Ice Lens Pictures. 2018.

Thompson, Beverly Yuen. "The Digital Nomad Lifestyle: (Remote) Work / Leisure Balance, Privilege, and Constructed Community." *International Journal of the Sociology of Leisure* 2, nos. 1–2 (2019a): 27–42. https://doi.org/10.1007/s41978-018-00030-y.

Thompson, Beverly Yuen. "'I Get My Lovin' on the Run': Digital Nomads, Constant Travel, and Nurturing Romantic Relationships." In *The Geographies of Digital Sexualities*, edited by Catherine J. Nash and Andre Gorman-Murray, 69–90. Singapore: Palgrave Macmillan, 2019b.

Torres, Carlos A. and Daniel Schugurensky. "The Political Economy of Higher Education in the Era of Neoliberal Globalization: Latin America in Comparative Perspective." *Higher Education* 43, no. 4 (2002): 429–55.

Towner, John. *An Historical Geography of Recreation and Tourism in the Western World 1540–1940.* Chichester: Wiley, 1996.

Tullis, Tracey. "7 Entrepreneurial Skills Kids Can Learn to Lead a Successful Life." *lifehack* (blog). www.lifehack.org/.

Urry, John. *The Tourist Gaze.* London: Sage, 1990.

Urry, John. "Globalization and Citizenship." *Journal of World–Systems Research* 5, no. 2 (1999): 311–24.

Urry, John. *Sociology beyond Societies.* London: Routledge, 2000.

Urry, John. *Mobilities.* Cambridge: Polity Press, 2007.

Valentine, Gill. *Public Space and the Culture of Childhood.* Aldershot: Ashgate, 2004.

Van Galen, Jane A. "Ideology, Curriculum, and Pedagogy in Home Education." *Education and Urban Society* 21, no. 1 (1988): 52–68.

Veijola, Soile and Eeva Jokinen. "Towards a Hostessing Society? Mobile Arrangements of Gender and Labour." *NORA* 16, no. 3 (2008): 166–81.

Veijola, Soile, Jennie Germann Molz, Olli Pyyhtinen, Emily Höckert, and Alexander Grit. *Disruptive Tourism and its Untidy Guests: Alternative Ontologies for Future Hospitalities.* New York: Palgrave Macmillan, 2014.

Villalobos, Ana. *Motherload: Making It All Better in Uncertain Times.* Berkeley: University of California Press, 2014.

Vogt, Jay W. "Wandering: Youth and Travel Behavior." *Annals of Tourism Research* 4, no. 1 (1976): 25–41.

Vrasti, Wanda. *Volunteer Tourism in the Global South: Giving Back in Neoliberal Times.* New York: Routledge, 2013.

Wajcman, Judy. *Pressed for Time: The Acceleration of Life in Digital Capitalism.* Chicago: University of Chicago Press, 2016.

Weinstein, Emily. "The Social Media See-Saw: Positive and Negative Influences on Adolescents' Affective Wellbeing." *New Media & Society* 20, no. 10 (2018): 3597–3623.

White, Naomi Rosh and Peter B. White. "Home and Away: Tourists in a Connected World." *Annals of Tourism Research* 34, no. 1 (2007): 88–104.

Williams, Bianca C. *The Pursuit of Happiness: Black Women, Diasporic Dreams, and the Politics of Emotional Transnationalism.* Durham, NC: Duke University Press, 2018.

Williams, Daniel R. and Norman McIntyre. "Place Affinities, Lifestyle Mobilities, and Quality-of-Life." In *Handbook of Tourism and Quality-of-Life Research*, edited by Muzzafer Uysal, Richard Perdue, and M. Joseph Sirgy, 209–32. London: Springer, 2012.

Wittel, Andreas. 2001. Towards a Network Sociality. *Theory, Culture and Society* 18: 31–50.

Yar, Majid and Rodanthi Tzanelli. "Kidnapping for Fun and Profit: Voluntary Abduction, Extreme Consumption and Self-Making in a Risk Society." *Hospitality & Society* 9, no. 2 (June 2019): 105–124. https://doi.org/10.1386/hosp.9.2.105_1.

Young, Iris Marion. "The Ideal of Community and the Politics of Difference." *Social Theory and Practice* 12, no. 1 (Spring 1986): 1–26.

Young, Iris Marion. *Justice and the Politics of Difference*. Princeton, NJ: Princeton University Press, 1990.

Zahra, Anne and Alison J. McIntosh. "Volunteer Tourism: Evidence of Cathartic Tourist Experiences." *Tourism Recreation Research* 32, no. 1 (2007): 115–19.

Zaske, Sara. *Achtung Baby! The German Art of Raising Self-Reliant Children*. New York: Picador, 2018.

Zeddies, Margaret and Zsuzsa Millei. "'It Takes a Global Village': Troubling Discourses of Global Citizenship in United Planet's Voluntourism." *Global Studies of Childhood* 5, no. 1 (2015): 100–11. https://doi.org/10.1177/2043610615573383.

Zelizer, Viviana A. *Pricing the Priceless Child: The Changing Social Value of Children*. Princeton, NJ: Princeton University Press, 1985.

Zuelow, Eric. *A History of Modern Tourism*. London: Palgrave Macmillan, 2016.

ABOUT THE AUTHOR

Jennie Germann Molz is Professor of Sociology at College of the Holy Cross in Worcester, Massachusetts. She is the co-editor of *Mobilizing Hospitality: The Ethics of Social Relations in a Mobile World*, author of *Travel Connections: Tourism, Technology, and Togetherness in a Mobile World*, co-author of *Disruptive Tourism and Its Untidy Guests: Alternative Ontologies for Future Hospitalities*, and co-editor of the journal *Hospitality & Society*.